Brexit and the Political Economy of Fragmentation

Brexit means Brexit and other meaningless mantras have simply confirmed that confusion and uncertainty have dominated the early stages of this era-defining event. Though there has been a lack of coherent and substantive policy from the UK government, this does not prevent analysis of the various causes of Brexit and the likely constraints on and consequences of the various forms Brexit might take. Is Brexit a last gasp of neoliberalism in decline? Is it a signal of the demise of the EU? Is it possible that the UK electorate will get what they thought they voted for (and what was that)? Will a populist agenda run foul of economic and political reality? What chance for the UK of a brave new world of bespoke trade treaties straddling a post-geography world? Is the UK set to become a Singapore-lite tax haven? What is the difference between a UK-centric and a UK-centred point of view on Brexit? Will Brexit augment disintegrative tendencies in the European and world economy? These are some of the questions explored in this timely set of essays penned by some of the best-known names in political economy and international political economy.

The chapters in this book were originally published in multiple issues of *Globalizations*.

Jamie Morgan is Professor of Economic Sociology at Leeds Beckett University, UK, and is the former co-ordinator of the Association for Heterodox Economics. He co-edits the *Real World Economics Review* with Edward Fullbrook. He has published widely in the fields of economics, political economy, philosophy, sociology and international politics. His recent books include *Trumponomics: Causes and Consequences* (edited with E. Fullbrook, 2017) and *What Is Neoclassical Economics? Debating the Origins, Meaning and Significance* (Routledge, 2016).

Heikki Patomäki is Professor of World Politics at the University of Helsinki, Finland. He has also been a professor in the UK and Australia, and a visiting professor in Japan. Patomäki's research interests comprise of philosophy and methodology of social sciences, peace research, futures studies, economic theory, global political economy and global political theory. His most recent book is *Disintegrative Tendencies in Global Political Economy*.

T0347829

Rethinking Globalizations

Edited by
Barry K. Gills, University of Helsinki, Finland and Kevin Gray, University of Sussex, UK.

This series is designed to break new ground in the literature on globalization and its academic and popular understanding. Rather than perpetuating or simply reacting to the economic understanding of globalization, this series seeks to capture the term and broaden its meaning to encompass a wide range of issues and disciplines and convey a sense of alternative possibilities for the future.

For more information, please visit https://www.routledge.com/Rethinking-Globalizations/book-series/RG

Recent titles include the following:

Brexit and the Political Economy of Fragmentation

Things Fall Apart

Edited by
Jamie Morgan and Heikki Patomäki

LONDON AND NEW YORK

First published 2018
by Routledge

2 Park Square, Milton Park, Abingdon, Oxfordshire OX14 4RN
52 Vanderbilt Avenue, New York, NY 10017

Routledge is an imprint of the Taylor & Francis Group, an informa business

First issued in paperback 2019

British Library Cataloguing in Publication Data
A catalogue record for this book is available from the British Library

ISBN 13: 978-1-138-57604-9 (hbk)
ISBN 13: 978-0-367-89261-6 (pbk)

Typeset in Times
by diacriTech, Chennai

Publisher's Note
The publisher accepts responsibility for any inconsistencies that may have arisen
during the conversion of this book from journal articles to book chapters, namely
the possible inclusion of journal terminology.

Disclaimer
Every effort has been made to contact copyright holders for their permission to
reprint material in this book. The publishers would be grateful to hear from any
copyright holder who is not here acknowledged and will undertake to rectify any
errors or omissions in future editions of this book.

Contents

CONTENTS

Citation Information

The following chapters were originally published in multiple issues of *Globalizations*. When citing this material, please use the original page numbering for each article, as follows:

Chapter 1
Introduction: Special Forum on Brexit
Jamie Morgan and Heikki Patomäki
Globalizations, volume 14, issue 1 (January 2017) pp. 99–103

Chapter 2
Reviving Hayek's Dream
Owen Worth
Globalizations, volume 14, issue 1 (January 2017) pp. 104–109

Chapter 3
Brexit and the Future of the Left
Boris Kagarlitsky
Globalizations, volume 14, issue 1 (January 2017) pp. 110–117

Chapter 4
Brexit: Be Careful What You Wish For?
Jamie Morgan
Globalizations, volume 14, issue 1 (January 2017) pp. 118–126

Chapter 5
Brexit and its Consequences
Ann Pettifor
Globalizations, volume 14, issue 1 (January 2017) pp. 127–132

Chapter 6
The Organic Crisis of the British State: Putting Brexit in its Place
Bob Jessop
Globalizations, volume 14, issue 1 (January 2017) pp. 133–141

CITATION INFORMATION

Chapter 16
Brexit and the Economics of Political Change in Developed Countries
Jayati Ghosh
Globalizations, volume 14, issue 6 (October 2017) pp. 830–839

Chapter 17
In the Yugoslav Mirror: The EU Disintegration Crisis
Joachim Becker
Globalizations, volume 14, issue 6 (October 2017) pp. 840–850

For any permission-related enquiries please visit:
http://www.tandfonline.com/page/help/permissions

Notes on Contributors

Joachim Becker is Associate Professor at the Institute for International Economics and Development of the Vienna University of Economics and Business, Austria. His research focus is on theory of regulation, development models and crises, integration and disintegration.

James Galbraith is Professor at the Lyndon B. Johnson School of Public Affairs and at the Department of Government, University of Texas, USA. He is also a Senior Scholar with the Levy Economics Institute of Bard College, USA, and part of the executive committee of the World Economics Association.

Jayati Ghosh is Professor of Economics at Jawaharlal Nehru University, India. She is also executive secretary of International Development Economics Associates. She is the co-author of *Demonetisation Decoded: A Critique of India's Currency Experiment* (Rouledge 2017) and co-editor of *Handbook of Alternative Theories of Economic Development* (2016) among many other works.

Jo Guldi is Assistant Professor of History at Brown University, USA, and a member of the Society of Fellows, Harvard University, USA. She teaches the course History of Britain and its Empire at Southern Methodist University, USA. Among many other publications, she is the co-author with David Armitage of *The History Manifesto* (2014) and author of *Roads to Power: Britain Invents the Infrastructure State* (2012).

Bob Jessop is Distinguished Professor of Sociology at Lancaster University, UK. He is best known for his contributions to state theory, critical governance studies, radical political economy and social theory. He is the author of numerous books and articles since the early 1980s, and his latest book is *The State: Past, Present, Future* (2015).

Boris Kagarlitsky is a Russian Marxist theoretician and sociologist who has been a political dissident in the Soviet Union and in post-Soviet Russia. He is co-ordinator of the Transnational Institute Global Crisis project, director of the Institute of Globalization and Social Movements (IGSO) and editor in chief of *Levaya Politika* (Left Politics) quarterly in Moscow.

Steve Keen is Professor of Economics at Kingston University, UK. He is a prominent critic of conventional economics, one of the few to anticipate the 2008 financial crisis and a recipient of the Revere Award in Economics. His bestselling book *Debunking Economics* explains the many logical and empirical flaws in mainstream (and Marxian) economics without using mathematics.

NOTES ON CONTRIBUTORS

Jamie Morgan is Professor of Economic Sociology at Leeds Beckett University, UK, and is the former co-ordinator of the Association for Heterodox Economics. He co-edits the *Real World Economics Review* with Edward Fullbrook. He has published widely in the fields of economics, political economy, philosophy, sociology and international politics. His recent books include *Trumponomics: Causes and Consequences* (edited with E. Fullbrook, 2017) and *What Is Neoclassical Economics? Debating the Origins, Meaning and Significance* (Routledge, 2016).

Heikki Patomäki is Professor of World Politics at the University of Helsinki, Finland. He has also been a professor in the UK and Australia, and a visiting professor in Japan. Patomäki's research interests comprise philosophy and methodology of social sciences, peace research, futures studies, economic theory, global political economy and global political theory. His most recent book is *Disintegrative Tendencies in Global Political Economy*.

Ann Pettifor is a director of the think-tank Policy Research in Macroeconomics (PRIME), UK. Her background is in sovereign debt—particularly those of low-income countries. More recently, she has analyzed and written extensively on both the private and public debts of Anglo-American economies. She is an honorary research fellow at City Political Economy Research Centre, City, University of London, UK: and is chair of the Advisory Board at Goldsmiths College's Political Economy Research Centre, London, UK.

Leonard Seabrooke is Professor of International Political Economy and Economic Sociology at the Copenhagen Business School, Denmark. He is currently working on networks of influence in economic policy design, especially on taxation, finance and demographic change issues.

Noah Toly is Senior Fellow for Global Cities at the Chicago Council on Global Affairs and Professor of Politics and International Relations at Wheaton College, USA. He also directs the Center for Urban Engagement. He edits the Routledge series *Cities and Global Governance* and teaches on global cities at the Free University of Berlin's Center for Global Politics, Berlin, Germany.

Silke Trommer is Lecturer in Politics at the University of Manchester, UK. She is author of *Transformations in Trade Politics: Participatory Trade Politics in West Africa* (Routledge, 2014) and co-editor of *Expert Knowledge in Global Trade* (with Erin Hannah and James Scott, Routledge, 2016).

Peter Wahl is chairman of the Berlin-based think tank World Economy, Ecology and Development (WEED). The focus of his work is on European economic governance, in particular with regard to finance. He is author of numerous publications on the EU financial and economic crises and their political effects.

Duncan Wigan is Associate Professor of International Political Economy at Copenhagen Business School, Denmark. He is co-editor (with Leonard Seabrooke) of *Global Wealth Chains: Asset Strategies in the World Economy* (2018). His research focuses on issues of international taxation and finance.

Owen Worth is Senior Lecturer in International Relations at the University of Limerick, Ireland. His research interests focus on the nature of power, class and in particular the role of hegemony in the global political economy and in global political society. He is the author of *Rethinking Hegemony* (2015) and *Resistance in the Age of Austerity: Nationalism, the Failure of the Left and the Return of God* (2013).

INTRODUCTION

Special Forum on Brexit

JAMIE MORGAN & HEIKKI PATOMÄKI

As part of initial campaigning in January 2013, Prime Minister David Cameron pledged to hold an in/out referendum if the Conservatives won a majority in the general election of 2015.[1] Received wisdom before the 2015 general election was that there would be another coalition government, and that a Liberal Democrat Party partner to such a coalition would reject a referendum; so centrist Conservatives could make the pledge, benefit from it, and likely never have to implement it. Thereafter, the intent was to both undercut the growing popularity of the UK Independence Party (UKIP) and silence Cameron's own Conservative sceptics. European integration had been a source of division within the Party, particularly from the 1990s, based on issues that had never been resolved. These focused mainly on the sharing of sovereignty within the European Union (EU) through the Maastricht Treaty in 1992 and then the Lisbon Treaty in 2007.

The immediate effect of a referendum pledge was to focus debate on immigration, and provide a degree of legitimacy to UKIP and a point of convergence for Conservative sceptics. In reality, immigration and EU membership are largely separate issues. It has been typical ever since the UK joined the European Economic Community in 1973 for annual net migration to the UK from outside the region to exceed that from within. What matters in UK politics is that UKIP increased their vote from less than 1 million to 3.8 million in the 2015 general election. In essence, in attempting to confront the problem of the Euro-sceptic right, Cameron put short-term strategy for his own party before long-term collective interests. He thus contributed to shifting the 'Overton window'—the range of ideas that can assume the centre stage in political discourse by being acceptable to the public—to accommodate the sceptics and UKIP's way of positioning a much broader set of issues. Obviously, this shift also affected the outcome of the referendum in June 2016.

It is important, however, to take a longer term and wider view to Brexit and its consequences. Events and episodes occur within processes. A number of processes may not only occur simultaneously but also coalesce and interact in various ways. Already Thucydides, in his

Peloponnesian wars, understood the difference between events and underlying structures and processes. Thus, Thucydides distinguished between two types of causes, between *aitia* and *prophasis*. *Aitia* refers to the rationalization of action, and *prophasis* to the underlying causes, to the causes which are 'behind' or 'under' the level of rationalizations and concrete events (see, for instance, Edmunds, 1975, pp. 172–173). The 'going beyond' of rationalization can be done in at least three directions. The first direction is to move deeper into the discursive formations and meanings, for instance, by explicating the meaning structures underpinning a particular political stand, for example, in relation to the EU.

The second direction is to explain the concrete contextual and relational possibilities open to a positioned actor. A telling example is Cameron's apparent opportunity to increase his party's popularity by calling for a referendum. This opportunity was made possible by the underlying institutions (such as parliamentary democracy, voting system, laws concerning referendum, article 50 of the Lisbon Treaty) and the specific constellation of forces and developments preceding the call (such as continuous disputes about financial taxes and regulation as well as over the future of the City of London, and the rise of UKIP and related ideas across parties).

The third direction of going beyond mere rationalization is to analyse causal or existential, often unintended consequences of action, involving effects of power. Actors do not always know what they are doing does in terms of underlying structures and processes. Moreover, systemic intra- and inter-dependence may give rise to emergent powers and properties, which are (re)produced in the context of at least some unintended consequences of action. Brexit may, for instance, constitute a turning point in the European integration process and, beyond that, in the processes of global political economy and security. To use Alexander Wendt's (1999) categories, the prevailing culture of anarchy may further shift from Kantian and Lockean understandings towards Hobbesian understandings.[2]

This special forum consists of 10 contributions that shed light on the *aitia* and *prophasis* of Brexit. Owen Worth starts by delving deeper into the discursive formations and meanings of neoliberalism. He argues that the roots of the successful Brexit vote can be found in the free market purity that was implicit within the ideals behind Thatcherism. While the libertarian right can lay claim to have been the ideological victors of Brexit, the reality within British society has been that of increasing cleavages, stimulating right-wing reactionary forces (but also Jeremy Corbyn's precarious rise within the Labour Party). Worth concurs with Karl Polanyi that free market liberalism tends to generate the forces of its own demise. This seems to indicate a new Polanyian double movement (cf. Patomäki, 2014).

Boris Kagarlitsky agrees with Worth's analysis of the structural developments of British society, but takes a different viewpoint on Brexit. He points out that statistics show that the division of the Brexit vote does not coincide with racial or gender differences, but to a large extent reflects the difference in class. It was mainly the working class and the lower classes of society who voted for an exit from the EU. Kagarlitsky criticizes not only the neoliberal elites but also the Left intellectuals and cultural critics of capitalism for failing to address the concerns of ordinary citizens and for misrepresenting the 'Leave' vote. 'The very idea that masses of common people make their choice rationally, according to their real interests, is totally unacceptable for them.' He argues further that the role of intellectuals in popular movements should be to help people overcome these prejudices, to move from an intuitive sense of their interest to a conscious understanding. Supportive of Lexit (Left exit from the EU), Kagarlitsky declares that 'the English voters expressed new pan-European trends and needs (in their best and worst manifestations)'.

Jamie Morgan warns, however, 'to be careful what you wish for'. He stresses the relative openness of the immediate future. The British future from Brexit is not yet determined because its institutional form remains undecided. However, if dominant conceptual frameworks continue to apply, then it seems unlikely that Brexit will address the underlying causes of grievances, since these transcend EU membership. Morgan argues that they are a product of a common political economy, understood as an ideational framework within globalizing processes. A significant commonality in globalization is that labour is treated as just one more factor of production, a unit cost, measured and rewarded in terms of its marginal productivity, and where the labour market is ultimately no different from any other. The prevailing economic policy suppresses social and organized elements in labour markets and work organizations. This has contributed to the decline of trust among citizenry. At the end of his piece, Morgan raises the question whether all this could be understood also in terms of the nowadays unfashionable concept of alienation. Alienation expresses itself as a deep sense of inauthenticity, a lack of self-worth or existential meaninglessness, where the actual potentials of the human are somehow being harmed by the system we live in.

Ann Pettifor also takes up the theme of the role of economics in creating context for Brexit. Pettifor's focus is the role financialisation has played in creating the dissatisfactions that motivated much of the leave vote. Following Polanyi she describes this as 'a form of social self-protection from self-regulating markets in money, trade and labour'. As she concludes, the underlying processes involved are not new and are not restricted to the UK. Noah Toly provides an additional perspective focusing on the concept of the global city and the considerable 'leadership' challenges this creates for London to transform itself in response to Brexit.

Bob Jessop analyses the organic crisis of the British state, explicitly making a distinction between events and processes. His point of departure is that the Brexit vote was a singular event that is one symptom of a continuing organic crisis of the British state.

> The Brexit conjuncture reflected a long-running split in the establishment, a worsening representational crisis in the party system, a growing crisis of authority for political elites, a legitimacy crisis of the state, and a crisis of national-popular hegemony over the population.

These crises cannot be traced back to a single process or level of causation, yet political economy can provide a key to understanding many aspects of the relevant complex. Jessop underlines that finance-led neoliberal policies 'privilege opportunities for monetary profit over the provision of substantive use-values'. In the process, wealth and income have become polarized and social cohesion degraded. These policies fuel de-industrialization and generate financial crises in the worldwide context characterized by the Euro crisis, economic migration and refugee crises, and, beyond Europe, the shift of the global centre of economic gravity to East Asia. Jessop concurs that 'a choice for entry or exit would not affect the overall dominance of neoliberalism—only its specific form and mediations'. But he also argues for 'pursuing an offensive strategy for fundamental reform of the European Union and its place within a world society'.

Jo Guldi uses her knowledge of history to seek guidance for the future. She asks: 'How likely are utopian futures of the kind that Jeremy Corbyn has recently envisioned for the future of post-Brexit Britain?' In contrast to Morgan and Jessop, who anticipate neoliberal business-as-usual in the post-Brexit UK (without implying that there are no alternatives to it), Guldi explores the chances of implementing a 10-point plan for restoring the National Health Service (NHS), building homes, and reducing income inequality. 'A deeper history of state, democracy, and expert rule in Brexit can highlight the underlying tensions and point to some sources of possible outcomes.' Resonating with Morgan's analysis of ideational commonalities, Guldi is particularly interested in the role of expert power in government since the eighteenth century, and in democratic alternatives to the dominant modes of expert knowledge such as neoclassical economics. Manifold utopian ideas have emerged at times in British history. Although only a limited number of these ideas were ever actually put into effect, history provides a rich source of knowledge about democratic and participatory ideas and experiments. Although dystopian futures are also possible, Guldi stresses the positive potentials of still partly unrealized possibilities.

Peter Wahl looks at Brexit from the point of view of the future of the European integration process. 'The Brexit has put the question of the final goal of integration on the agenda.' The logic of thinking has been mostly binary: either Eurotopia or nationalism. Wahl maintains that the 'more Europe'-approach is unrealistic for the foreseeable future. In addition, he is also sceptical of its normative desirability, at least in its current neoliberal form. On the other hand, Wahl emphasizes that nationalism is an illusion that is potentially dangerous. The full disintegration of the Union would also be very costly. This can be generalized to globalization. 'It is not possible any more to disconnect from globalisation and the attempt to return back to the old style of nation-state is doomed to fail.' Thus, Wahl proposes a third way for the future of the EU. 'Differentiated integration' is characterized by two principles: flexibilization within the EU and opening towards the outside world. It would mean selective integration in certain areas and disintegration in certain others, both with variable participation. He takes up the example of the financial transaction tax to show what this could mean in practice—and not necessarily in Europe only, but globally.

James Galbraith alerts us to the dangers of prediction.

> In the immediate morning-after of the Brexit vote, the wide expectation was for economic chaos, a government of Leavers in Britain and a quick filing of Article 50, encouraged by the French, leading inexorably to Britain's exit from the EU under harsh conditions and to Scotland's exit from the UK.

In fact, the British exit from the EU is postponed, a mixed government of Conservatives has emerged and the London stock exchange recovered rapidly. 'The main economic consequence was a drop in Sterling, good for the FTSE 100 Index and potentially for the trade balance.' Hence, Galbraith's main point is about the EU as a whole. Can the Euro or the EU itself survive? 'Clearly under present policies [the Euro] will not survive indefinitely.' The current fragile hope for Europe lies in an effort to construct a pan-European democratic and social-democratic alliance. In the absence of progressive European transformations, also the prospects for global peace and security are going to diminish.

In the last piece of the Forum, Heikki Patomäki asks whether it is indeed true that either the EU will be democratized or it will disintegrate? Furthermore, if the current policies, principles and institutions of the EU generate counterproductive politico-economic effects and suffer from problems of legitimation, why is it that the European discontent is channelled, for such a large part, into nationalist politics of othering and scapegoating rather than into building a leftist-democratic movement for transforming the Union? Collective learning points towards the gradual spread of democratic and cosmopolitan sentiments, but the difficulties of learning and a two-phase causal mechanism from economic trouble, via existential insecurities and anxieties in everyday lives, to securitization and enemy-construction, explain why contrary tendencies may dominate. Trust in the EU has declined, in part due to a prolonged economic downturn and crisis (with deep roots in the global financialization process), but in part because of what is perceived to be the undemocratic or unchangeable nature of the EU. Problems of identity politics, securitization and enemy-construction are not confined to Europe. They give rise to tendencies towards disintegration and conflicts, also worldwide. Patomäki concludes by pointing out that modest policy proposals and tentative steps within the existing EU Treaty framework may be too little too late. The question is whether there is enough time for deeper transformations in Europe—and also globally.

Disclosure Statement

No potential conflict of interest was reported by the authors.

Notes

1   Initial reference by the Conservatives to a variety of referendum predates 2013 and can be found in the 2010 general election manifesto (as a commitment to do nothing to augment EU powers without a referendum). In the 2010 election, UKIP received just 3% of the vote, but by 2013, polls indicated that they had around 15% support, and could thus contest Conservative marginal seats. This then gave Conservative MPs a reason to support a referendum pledge, since it provided a campaign focus – 'vote Conservative and we will deliver on the EU, a vote for UKIP cannot do this' (as such the pledge broadened the appeal of an EU referendum beyond actual Euro-sceptics). Cameron's actual speech is a nuanced account of the need to make the EU more democratically accountable and to give its members/citizens a sense of commitment and voice in the wake of growing scepticism in a period of austerity politics, and so on. However, the media reports focus almost exclusively on the significance of the pledge as a response to Conservative Euro-sceptics.
2   According to Wendt (1999), the cultures of inter-state anarchy (meaning there is no world state) are shared ideas, which help shape state interests and capabilities, and generate tendencies in the international system. A Hobbesian culture is premised on unrestrained egoism and consequent war of all against all. In a Lockean culture, egoism is restrained, law and others are recognized, and cooperation and common institutions are more likely. In a Kantian culture, ethics and law matter even more, security can be collective and institutions of cooperation extensive and intensive. In Hobbesian cultures, the main subject position is 'enemy', in Lockean 'rival', and in Kantian 'friend'.

References

Edmunds, L. (1975). *Chance and intelligence in Thucydides*. Cambridge, MA: Harvard University Press.
Patomäki, H. (2014). On the dialectics of global governance in the 21st century: A Polanyian double movement? *Globalizations, 11*(5), 751–768.
Wendt, A. (1999). *Social theory of international politics*. Cambridge: Cambridge University Press.

Reviving Hayek's Dream

OWEN WORTH

ABSTRACT   *This short piece suggests that the roots of the successful Brexit vote can be found in the free market purity that was implicit within the ideals behind Thatcherism. Whilst the rhetoric of populist and British (or in many parts English) nationalism were utilised in order to win support, the ideological driving force implicit within many Brexit figureheads rested in the belief that the EU watered down their visions of a harder neoliberal reality. Yet, by stimulating right-wing reactionary forces, they may have created more than they bargained for. I concur with Karl Polanyi that free market liberalism tends to generate the forces of its own demise.*

Introduction

If there was ever a watershed moment in British/EU relations it was Margaret Thatcher's Bruges Speech to the College of Europe in 1988 when she stated that she had not 'rolled back the frontiers of the state in Britain, only to see them re-imposed at a European level'. Here was the first clear message that far from appearing as a body that looked to provide impetus to her neoliberal revolution in Britain it appeared as a threat to it. A sea of change was imminent within British political society. Until this point, the large bulk of opposition to the 'Common Market' came from the left. Eloquently argued by Tony Benn, the 'lexit' arguments of the 1970s and 1980s centred upon an alternative that pitched industrial democracy, technological collectivism, and socialism against the capitalism espoused by the then EC. This reached its prominence at the 1983 general election campaign, when the Labour Party, led by Michael Foot and heavily influenced by its recent 'Bennite turn', endorsed a complete withdrawal in its manifesto. By the turn of the 1990s however, the Labour Party, spurred on by Delor's vision of a 'Social Europe' were now fully signed up to the European project. Instead it was the Thatcherite wing of the Conservative Party that took the role of the chief Euro-sceptic, driven by the conviction that the EU was over-regulating in the economies of member states and diluting free market principles which reduce productivity.

The growth of the Euro-sceptic position within the neoliberal right in Britain is even more paradoxical considering the 'neoliberal' turn within the EU itself. Here, it appears that the pro-market forces that Thatcher along with Reagan heralded in the 1980s succeeded against any continental or social adaptation of capitalism (van Apeldoorn, 2002; Cafruny & Ryner, 2003). The rise of the influential political populist Euro-sceptic Party UKIP whose (wrongly) perceived threat to the Tories saw Cameron call for a referendum in the first place, also had their economic grounding in the free market dogmatism of Thatcherism. Their 2010 General Election Manifesto argued that less regulation, rather than more regulation was key to economic recovery and owed more to the libertarian rhetoric that was emerging across the Atlantic from the Tea Party than to any form of British nationalism (UKIP, 2010). Whilst the economic arguments were played down as Nigel Farage returned as leader after the election, in order to focus on the more familiar far-right concerns such as immigration and multiculturalism, the Party nevertheless grew from the Euro-scepticism of the Bruges Speech rather than from one of British exceptionalism. I suggest here that the major driving force behind Brexit was ideological, rather than the result of any 'anti-establishment' backlash and was drawn from economic neo-liberal ideals and these will play a significant role in attempting to shape the post-Brexit arena.

Brexit: The Return of Market Idealism?

One of the features of the leave campaign was the prominence of individuals, central to the political economy of the 1980s who reappeared to contribute to debate. Patrick Minford, one of Thatcher's main economic advisors, whose endorsement of supply-side economics was heavily influenced by Milton Friedman, headed the 'Economists for Brexit' unit that was heavily influential to UKIP and Conservative 'Leave' leaders alike.[1] Nigel Lawson, former Chancellor of the Exchequer to Thatcher and now residing in the House of Lords was provided with a rare platform to remind us in the immediate aftermath of the Brexit result that Mrs Thatcher could now 'finish what she had started'. Those prominent in the inception of think tanks such as 'The Adam Smith Institute' and 'Institute of Economic Affairs' joined those whose political careers were weaned on the ideas that they had articulated. In each case, whilst soundbites were given to the importance of parliamentary democracy, sovereignty and for the need to control immigration, their ideological underpinnings that they shared were never too far away.

In order to understand the form of market idealism that the Brexiters will try and pursue in the aftermath of their victory it is first interesting to note their wider context. Here, there are more parallels with the libertarian tradition in the US. This is hardly surprising. The Thatcher–Reagan doctrine unleashed a whole succession of ideals on the role of the state vis-à-vis the market. Both also lay claim to a strong liberal tradition which can be utilised as a form of 'national tradition' for popular support. The popular mobilisation around the idealism of the Tea Party and campaigns against the US Federal Bank with which men like Ron Paul became synonymous have been greeted in Britain with fondness (Hannon, 2010). In Britain, the target was not central banks but the EU. For them, the memories of their intellectual Godfather Hayek visiting their political Godmother in Downing Street in the early 1980s to build upon this free market utopia were halted by concessions to the EU at Maastricht, Amsterdam, and Lisbon. Whilst Hayek himself had an extremely ambiguous understanding of European Unity (Höpner & Schäfer, 2013), their reading of him was quite clear. The European Union, along with other forms of regional governance are regulatory bodies that seek to contain market forces (Borne, 2016; Congdon, 2016; Wapshott, 2012)

The Brexit solution for these 'hyper-liberals'[2] appears to be one which favours the full withdrawal from both the EU and the single-market (European Economic Area). Here, the much talked about 'WTO' option is presented. Rather than join any alternative regional organisations which had previously been talked about by Euro-Sceptics (such as North American Free Trade Agreement; see Redwood, 2001), Minford has argued that they should merely endorse a unilateral 'free trade' position by trading under WTO rules (Minford, 2016). This, he and colleagues have argued, would integrate the UK fully into the global market, free from regulatory mechanisms or protectionism (Minford, Gupta, Lee, Madambare, & Xu, 2015). The assumption goes that this will serve as a basis for the UK to embed itself within the confines of a market structure and provide the much anticipated revolutionary increase in economic production. The post-Brexit cabinet saw two key positions go to such free market Euro-sceptics. Liam Fox as the new Trade Minister was quick to state that regional trade blocs were a dated concept and that greater competitiveness, openness, and flexibility would provide Britain with a unique comparative advantage for the forthcoming century. Similarly, David Davis has been appointed to the new ministerial post for 'Brexit', and he is perhaps the closest politician the British have to Ron Paul. Steeped in Hayekian virtue, Davis stood against Cameron for leadership in 2006 with a distinct libertarian and Euro-sceptic mandate and has followed a similar strategy in setting out his ideas on the Brexit negotiations (Davis, 2016).

Proposals that have included domestic tax cuts, the attraction of foreign direct investment and the dramatic reduction or abolition of corporation tax have been frequently aired across the various associated free market think tanks. When (and perhaps for some if) article 50 is activated, these proposals will certainly be pushed. Just how far these forces of market idealism succeed in obtaining these advantages within policy is unknown, but they will appear as a significant presence within the process itself. Therefore, any hope that Brexit would lead to some form of wider structural attack on the forces of neoliberal capitalism will also have to account for the fact that it is a more concentrated 'hyper' form of market capitalism that has been the driving force behind it (Worth, forthcoming). In addition, as many media commentators have noted, the labour movement has become more and more on the defensive in response to capital and appears unable at present to forge a successful post-Brexit strategy (Mason, 2016 see also Hall, 2011). The failure of the lexit argument to produce anything more substantial than either just soundbites towards internationalism or conversely to the protection of sovereignty around 'left nationalism' was testament to this.

Brexiters should Fear Karl Polanyi

If the libertarian right can lay claim to have been the ideological victors of Brexit, the reality within British society has been somewhat different. Polarisation was seen not just across social class, but through age, race, geography, and urbanisation. The reality of the vote saw middle Englanders voting in tandem with the northern working classes to leave and financial workers voting alongside inner-city community workers to remain. The two factors that were strongly noticeable about the vote was the generational and ethnic divide. In the case of the first, the consistent correlation between the increase of the leave vote with age is something that, due to the closeness of the result, cannot merely be dismissed, especially as time develops and questions about its legitimacy increase.[3] The ethnic split however provides us with a more worrying trend. Both the Black/Afro-Caribbean vote (77% remain) and the Indian/Asian vote

(66% remain) far out-weighted the White vote in a campaign that was marked by its racial and xenophobic undertones.

The nationalist fervour that was unleashed by not just UKIP but also key leave figures such as Michael Gove presented a case for withdrawal that gave the overwhelming impression that the vote was merely about immigration. The subsequent increase in racist attacks after the vote resulted in a deeply divided nation and brought in a feeling of tension, not really witnessed within British society before. The eagerness of the libertarian right to mobilise forms of national-populism is not new. The Pinochet regime which was commended by both Hayek and Friedman used this to violently marginalise opposition, whilst both Thatcher and Reagan looked to nationalist sentiment to shore up support for their wider economic reforms. Yet, the move here represents a new phenomenon. The emergence of a form of English Nationalism, based upon the reaction of multiculturalism in traditionally labour industrial areas provides a different problem. The anti-EU/anti-immigration vote in these areas has been one that has grown out from socio-economic deterioration and neglect brought about by de-industrialisation and the effects of neoliberal globalisation. Any move towards a more de-regulated, more market-centric economy, devoid of EU cohesion funds would see a change from a soft-EU style of neo-liberal governance to a more hard-line one and signal an intensification of such nationalism. UKIP seem already eager to exploit such deprivation to further enhance their anti-immigration message and more organic far-right movements such as Britain First and the various groups that emerged from the implosion of the BNP are also gaining support. This in a country which prior to 2002, the far right had only gained one solitary local council victory in its history.[4]

As has been noted in a number of recent studies, far-right parties have managed to locate themselves within the wider framework of neoliberalism, which has appeared as a compatible terrain for the expression of reactionary politics (Saull, 2015; Worth, 2014). However, we should also look at the classic account of Karl Polanyi which indicates that this co-existence is not permanent. Nor, as Hayekians might suggest, do reactionary ideas disappear as society adjusts as the market economy flourishes. In *The great transformation* Polanyi shows how the ideals of the self-regulated market produced a set of 'double-movements' in the nineteenth century as the state or civil society looked to re-regulate to protect itself from the anarchism of the market. Yet, the persistence in pursuing an international society based upon the principles of liberal economics led to its final destruction and to the rise of fascism after the First World War. Both Hayek and Polanyi left their home city of Vienna to move to London and both wrote their respective testaments on liberalism at the same time during the war. But whilst Hayek's *Road to serfdom* argued that only a market economy can provide economic prosperity and enshrine individual liberties, Polanyi suggested that it was the persistence of market economic mentality that eventually led to crisis, breakdown, fall and collapse (1944).

Polanyi suggests a very different reality to the longevity of market economics and one that neither the libertarian idealists nor the political establishment can aptly respond to. It is also one that appears universal in its observations of post-crisis neoliberalism. Brexit was a unique British experience in the fact that the EU took the role of a 'scapegoat'; a position that it has fulfilled within British political culture since its entry in 1973. As has been stated many times since the vote, the levels of disillusionment with the political establishment combined with the negative results from nearly a decade of austerity went a long way to set the culture for Brexit. The populist factors such as immigration and British exceptionalism were then factored into this. Yet, despite this, trends seen in the Brexit referendum have appeared across other parts of international society in the post-crisis era. The growth of the far right across Europe, the rise of Trump in the US, the rise of religious extremism and the influx of national and ethnic

9

revivalism are all indicative of such double-movements against the process of the market-driven society that the forces and international institutions of neoliberalism have produced. Many are keen to point to the more progressive forms of 'counter-movement' that have looked to democratise or socialise these developments (Worth, 2013), but Polanyi's tale of the self-regulated market reveals more than that. It serves to remind us of the ultimate folly of the libertarian dream.

By consistently striving to uphold and indeed develop the workings and ideals of market economic liberalism (or in this case neoliberalism), a number of reactionary forces emerge which as time develops becomes impossible to contain. For Polanyi, the final result of this was destruction of the liberal system and a decade and a half of catastrophe. The many market puritans that have driven for a Brexit since the end of the 1980s should perhaps take this more seriously.

Disclosure Statement

No potential conflict of interest was reported by the author.

Notes

1   It should be noted that 'Economists for Brexit' might have provided the ideological framing for such Brexiters, but were largely insignificant within the media during the campaign. The majority of Economists dismissed their arguments as 'reckless' or 'misleading'.
2   This was a term used by Robert Cox to describe those who shared the ideological radicalism of concentrated market reform during the Thatcher–Reagan era and subsequently maintained these ideals in their aftermath (1987; 1997).
3   The age split of the vote was: 18–24: 26–74% (leave-remain), 25–34: 38–62%, 35–44: 48–52%, 45–54: 56–44%, 55–54: 57–43%, 55–64: 57–43%, 65+: 61–39%
4   By way of a contrast, the BNP peaked at 55 local councillors in 2008 and had representation in the European Parliament and London Assembly. UKIP had reached just under 500 local councillors by 2015, 1 MP (in 2015), 22 MEPs (from 2014), and 7 Welsh Assembly members (2016).

References

van Apeldoorn, B. (2002). *Transnational capital and the struggle over European integration*. London: Routledge.
Borne, R. (2016). *Hayek would have been a Brexiter*. Institute of Economic Affairs. Retrieved from www.iea.org.uk/blog/hayek-would-have-been-a-brexiteer
Cafruny, A., & Ryner, M. (Eds.). (2003). *A ruined fortress? Neoliberal hegemony and transformation in Europe*. Lanham, MD: Rowman and Littlefield.
Congdon, T. (2016). 'Too much regulation', in Economists for Brexit. In *The Economy after Brexit*. Retrieved from http://www.economistsforbrexit.co.uk/
Davis, D. (2016). *Trade deals, tax cuts and taking time before triggering article 50: A Brexit economic strategy for Britain*. Conservative Home. Retrieved from http://www.conservativehome.com/platform/2016/07/david-davis-trade-deals-tax-cuts-and-taking-time-before-triggering-article-50-a-brexit-economic-strategy-for-britain.html
Hall, S. (2011). The neoliberal revolution. *Cultural Studies*, 25(6), 705–728.
Hannon, D. (2010). *Tea party comes to the UK*. Retrieved from http://www.tfa.net/daniel-hannan/
Höpner, M., & Schäfer, A. (2013). Embeddedness and regional integration: Waiting for Polanyi in a Hayekian setting. *International Organizations*, 66(3), 429–455.
Mason, P. (2016, May 16). The left-wing case for Brexit (one day). *The Guardian*.
Minford, P. (2016). *No need to queue: The benefits of free trade without trade agreements*. Institute of Economic Affairs. IEA: Current Controversies 51.
Minford, P., Gupta, S., Lee, P. M., Madambare, V., & Xu, Y. (2015). *Should Britain leave the EU?* London: Edward Elgar.
Polanyi, K. (1944). *The great transformation*. Boston, MA: Beacon Press.

Redwood, J. (2001). *Stars and strife: The coming conflict between the USA and the European Union*. Basingstoke: Palgrave.

Saull, R. (2015). Capitalism, crisis and the far-right in the neo-liberal era. *Journal of International Relations and Development*, *18*(1), 25–51.

UKIP. (2010). *UKIP Manifesto 2010: Empowering the people*. Lexdrum House: Newtown Abbot.

Wapshott, N. (2012). *Keynes Hayek: The clash that defined modern economies*. London: W.W. Norton.

Worth, O. (2013). *Resistance in the age of austerity*. London: Zed Books.

Worth, O. (2014). The far right and neoliberalism: Willing partner or hegemonic opponent? In R. Saull & A. Anievas (Eds.), *The Longue Durée of the far-right: An international historical sociology*. London: Routledge.

Worth, O. (forthcoming). The battle for hegemony: Resistance and neoliberal structuring in post-crisis Europe. *Comparative European Politics*, *15*(1).

Brexit and the Future of the Left

BORIS KAGARLITSKY

ABSTRACT *The referendum on British membership in the European Union divided not only the society in the UK but also the left both in Britain and all over the continent. This division however is produced not so much by this specific debate but by a deeper problem of the left capitulating ideologically and accepting neoliberalism as something objectively inevitable (even without publically recognizing it), replacing class struggle by 'progressive' cultural values that themselves form an essential part of the new capitalist hegemony. Leftist intelligentsia with its cultural critique of capitalism is no alternative to the current system, rather it is one of its pillars. While class division was very visible in the Brexit vote, with the working class and poor massively voting for 'Leave', most of the left either sided with the establishment or was wavering. Thus the success of the 'Leave' vote can be claimed by nationalists. Even after this political disaster instead criticizing itself leftist intelligentsia is blaming the people for being provincial and not accepting their progressive European values. However it was exactly the mass of common people in England who by voting for 'Leave' contributed to the formation of the new European agenda. Overcoming and unmaking bureaucratic, authoritarian, and neoliberal EU institutions is the only way to progress towards the making of a new democratic Europe.*

Introduction

The British vote in favour of a break with the European Union, not only caused panic in the financial markets, but also resulted in a surge of indignation among liberal intellectuals around the world. Amazingly, the comments that we read in left-liberal European publications, almost word for word repeat the ones published by right-wing liberals in the Russian press. As political scientist Bickerton (2016) ironically put it, from the point of view of these intellectuals 'around 50% of Britons are foreigner-hating hooligans'.

These commentators attribute the choice solely to British provincialism, backwardness, xenophobia, homophobia, the fear of immigration, and even racism. The same way they interpret the rising popularity of Donald Trump in the presidential race in the US. The very idea that masses of common people make their choice rationally, according to their real interests, is totally unacceptable for them.

However the statistics showed that the division of the Brexit vote does not coincide with racial or gender differences, but to a large extent reflects the difference in class (*The Economist* 2016; Kirk 2016; McGill 2016). As Harris (2016) of *The Guardian* formulated: 'If you've got money, you vote in … If you haven't got money, you vote out'.

The Failure of the Left Intelligentsia

It was mainly the working class and the lower classes of society who voted for an exit from the EU. These social layers, as a rule, are not very well educated, often prejudiced and certainly not familiar with fashionable post-modern philosophy. But it is precisely this willingness of the left to withdraw into cultural ghettos, and their preference for communicating with foreign colleagues rather than educating their own 'immature' citizens that largely predetermines or, in any case, exacerbates this state of affairs.

It is very easy to love an imaginary and virtual working class depicted in romantic books or movies, it is much harder to understand the needs and requirements of actually existing men on the street. It is too dangerous to discuss the meaning and content of events, which can elicit unpleasant questions. This is why no one wants to discuss the developing crisis of the European Union, which is nothing but the embodiment of neoliberalism. Or how mass sentiment in Britain won over the elite consensus in a context in which all the major parties appealed to voters to accept the status quo. All the leading publications and official representatives of the expert community unanimously called upon the people to leave everything as it is, threatening all sorts of misfortunes in case of the wrong decision: the people still decided to vote for change.

As London based *Socialist Review* noted, majority of Britons did not only vote against the EU.

> They did so in the face of opposition from three quarters of MPs, the leadership of the biggest parliamentary parties—the Conservatives, Labour and the Scottish National Party—the overwhelming bulk of British industry and almost every major capitalist institution, from the Bank of England to the International Monetary Fund. (Choonara 2016)

This means that the Brexit vote was not only a rebellion against the neoliberal European project but also no less a popular uprising against Britain's own ruling elites, including both intellectual and political classes, business and media.

To represent Brexit voting as a manifestation of English (well, a little Welsh) nationalism is convenient and profitable for the elite both in Russia and in Western Europe, not only because it leads us away from the systemic nature of the crisis and from class divisions in today's European and British societies. It also shadows the fact that an important section of the left as well as most of the liberal intelligentsia were decisively on the side of the bourgeoisie and against the workers. The discussion is placed on the 'wrong track' to block a discussion of practical policies that will transform a single act of protest voting into the beginning of far-reaching changes of potentially revolutionary character.

Similar trends emerged among the Western left back when the anti-capitalist rhetoric of Antonio Negri and his fans became the justification for a campaign to accept the official Brussels project during the French referendum on European constitution. At that time, the vote against the

EU was in fact a victory not only for the left, but also for the supporters of 'French identity', but back then the left dominated the 'No' movement, and could ignore this fact.

From that time on, regardless of radical pronouncements, in every practical choice, respectable Left intellectuals took the side of neoliberal elites, against the 'uneducated' and 'backward' people. The betrayal of intellectuals became a pan-European phenomenon after class criteria were substituted by cultural, replacing class theory with all sorts of graceful 'discourses' whose reproduction became the main criterion that allows 'us' to be distinguished from 'them'.

On the Susceptibility to Nationalism

Betrayed and forgotten masses were not only left to themselves to maintain and cultivate their prejudices and political superstitions, they also proved to be more than ever susceptible to nationalist ideology. If the practical embodiment of 'internationalism' is the activity of bankers and 'corporations without borders', and democratic rights are being cut in favour of unelected officials answering to no one (except for the bankers), it is not surprising that ordinary people begin to associate their hopes for salvation with a nation-state.

It is interesting that European intellectuals were ready to justify such feelings among people in Latin America, but not in Russia. And even less so when a similar protest began to unfold in the countries of the 'centre' which can actually lead to changes of global significance. The ideologists of the liberal left stood united in the defence of the existing political order and the dominant ideology.

The European lower classes were declared 'backward' 'inadequate' and 'uncivilized' in the same way as 150 years before, when 'natives' were called uncivilized and backward and in need of being colonized or ruled by 'civilized' elites. The very fact that these days 'barbarians' and savages are discovered among Europeans based not on the colour of their skin simply proves the fact that racism is nothing but an ideological construct used for social and class domination.

It is significant that in this respect the Russian liberal public was once again a pioneer of anti-democratic ideological reaction. Their diatribes against their own 'irresponsible' people miraculously anticipated the images, ideas and stereotypes that later spread among the intellectuals in the West.

The fact that regardless of the level of culture and education among the 'natives' they still have interests and rights, is discovered only when the ignored and 'uncivilized' masses no longer remain silent. Yes, their speech is often tongue-tied or even backward. But this speech contains the truth and the will of those who were not heard for a long time.

Meanwhile, people's willingness to repeat inadequate, old-fashioned formulae does not mean the neglect of their *immediate* and *real interests*. They will begin to act according to their own needs, but will have to formulate their demands in an *inadequate form*. The left is to blame for this situation. In Britain and on the continent, they missed or failed to win the opportunity to dominate the mass protest movement.

A delightful self-poisoning of the left intelligentsia by fashionable liberal ideas has played a fateful role—not only for mass protests, but mainly for the intelligentsia, which cannot recover from the shock: it is being rejected by the population of England as well as Russia.

Not surprisingly, the split of the left on the continent (and in Britain itself) over Brexit is similar to what is going on in Russia and Ukraine in relation to the events in Novorossia. Both here and there we saw an uprising of the lower classes supported by a part of the radical left-wing movement who remain committed to class ideology. And here and there, we saw that the demand for social rights, the protest against the neoliberal policies of the EU and their own governments are often expressed in inadequate slogans: 'Russian world' or 'British identity' And here as there, refined liberal intellectuals use the politically incorrect 'discourse' of the people as an excuse to refuse solidarity to those who are really fighting for social change. The Russian intelligentsia, with its contempt for its own people and tendency to constantly rebuke them for their lack of understanding of 'European values', has finally found consistent supporters on both sides of the Channel. And if three or four years ago events in Ukraine and Novorossia[1] appeared as amusing and scary exoticisms to Western intellectuals, we can now see that they were a general model for pan-European, and perhaps global process.

The Future of the Left

Unfortunately, it is impossible to produce historic changes by a one-time expression of will at the ballot box. What we observe in Britain is just the beginning. The ruling circles of the island do not hide their desire to sabotage the will of the citizens, even while they recognize it in words. Only the coming to power of a left Labour government headed by Jeremy Corbyn would enable the referendum decision to be properly implemented. But Labour Left represented by Corbyn proved itself not ready for the task. When the results of voting were summed up, Lexit (2016), a coalition of left-wing groups opposed to the European Union published a statement which said: 'This could have been a great Labour crusade if it had put itself at the head of this working class revolt but the Blairites forced Jeremy Corbyn to abandon his long held opposition to the EU.'

However, the issue is not who on the left advocated Brexit, and who remained hostage to the establishment. Much more important is that the man in the street, not guided by left ideology, showed class consciousness mostly alien to intellectuals. As strange as it may seem, most Brexit supporters turned out to be remarkably similar to the supporters of Novorossia. Both here and there we see a bizarre mix of patriotism, local interests and a perceived need for the revival of the welfare state, which must be protected from local elites and external threats. In both cases, people would rather feel than understand: they do not always find the right words, and are often the victims of absurd prejudices. However, the role of intellectuals in popular movements is to help people overcome these prejudices, to move from an intuitive sense of their interest to a conscious understanding. Meanwhile, in England, as is the case with Novorossia, much of the Left chose to turn away in disgust from the 'wrong' people, rather than revolt with them. The bourgeoisie and the liberal elites are well spoken, much more educated and much better versed in the intricacies of politically correct discourse, than are workers, farmers and small entrepreneurs who are fighting to survive market reforms. Sooner or later everyone must choose.

Movement toward a way out of the EU will have to overcome not only the resistance of the conservative elites, but also the vacillations of the Labour leadership and even of its leader, who, at the time of the decisive choice, did not have the courage to publicly support his own backers.

In the course of this struggle there undoubtedly will be forces that will try to punish Britain by dismantling the state. The local left should rethink their attitude towards the nationalism of 'small nations' the same way as the Bolsheviks had to do after 1917. If they had not managed to maintain territorial unity, they would not have had the chance to carry out such large-scale transformations. And if Lenin and his associates did not have a strong defense industry and a rich military tradition, it is unlikely that 'reds' would have been able to win the civil war.

Today we see the same geopolitical logic in Britain. As soon as the majority spoke in favour of secession from the European Union, the demand for Scottish independence was repeated as a desire for a 'European and progressive' Scotland to separate from the 'backward and provincial' England. But just one glance at what is happening on the continent is enough to understand that the English voters expressed new pan-European trends and needs (in their best and worst manifestations).

While Scottish nationalists, despite their modernist and progressivist rhetoric, have shown themselves to be what they really are—the heirs of the reactionaries, the Jacobits, who fought against the English Revolution and resisted pan-European progress in the XVII–XVIII centuries. It was then that the issue of Scottish independence, which proved to be an obstacle to the pressing social changes not only in England, but in the first place in Scotland itself, was resolved.

The rise to power of Margaret Thatcher in 1979 marked the beginning of the neoliberal era, first in Europe and then in the whole world. These events, originally perceived as a manifestation of British exceptionalism, gradually acquired a global dimension. The reactionary offensive against 'socialism' proclaimed by Margaret Thatcher, ended in the defeat of the welfare state on the entire European continent, including the republics of the Soviet Union.

It was the Maastricht Treaty that secured the victory for the forces of reaction and transformed the European Union into a new prison of nations, where any attempt to overcome neoliberalism is an attack on the constitutional order. By that time the fate of the former Soviet republics was completely settled. Even without being officially included in the European integration process (allowed only for the 'clean' Baltic States), they would all in one way or another accept the logic of privatization and anti-social reforms. EU institutions were built precisely in order to make sure that the principles of neoliberalism formed the constitutional basis of the Union. If one were to encroach on these principles, the Union would fall apart. EU structures were created within the framework of this logic, the fundamental Maastricht and Lisbon treaties are based on it. At a time when the slogan of 'A United Europe' has become synonymous with the implementation of measures dictated by multinationals, financial capital and an authoritarian bureaucracy, it was not Voltaire, Diderot, Garibaldi, or even de Gaulle, but the functionaries of the European Central Bank who incarnated European values.

Now we are witnessing the beginning of a new historical stage, during which there is a chance to eradicate neoliberalism, changing the social order in our country as well as throughout Europe. The people, whose democratic sovereignty has been stolen by the liberal elites, finally have an opportunity for revenge.

The struggle of the peoples of Europe against the neoliberal regime of the European Union is the main political thrust of the era. The outcome of this struggle depends on the level of solidarity between grassroots movements, and on their ability to unite on the basis of common goals and objectives, overcoming prejudices and illusions, freed from obsolete language and labels. The British vote was a watershed event that marked the collapse of the cultural and psychological barriers that guaranteed the immutability of the neoliberal order. This is the beginning of change, not only for Britain but for the entire continent. Now it is impossible to dismiss the critique of the existing order suggesting that alternatives are marginal and frivolous. Conversely, it was discovered that what for many years was considered 'mainstream', in fact is rejected by society.

Contrary to being a vote 'against Europe', Brexit became a turning point marking the possibility of pan-continental change which is now replicated in demands to follow the British example which are now rising all over Europe. The left clearly faces a choice: stay with the

EU elites defending the status quo to be defeated together with these elites and to let popular mobilization be led by different kinds of nationalists-populists or participate in the movement exploring, developing and maximizing its progressive potential.

> Internationalism is not an expression of tender support for the integration policies pursued in the interests of global capital, it is rather providing leadership to resist these policies jointly and in a coordinated manner.

But is this traditional understanding of internationalism acceptable for the really existing Left of today? Experiences of Syriza government in Greece, of Bernie Sanders campaign in the US and even of the left Labour leadership of Jeremy Corbyn in Britain tell us that the Left is not ready to do what it has to do—to fight and face risks.

These risk are quite real. And long-term divorce between intellectual/political Left and the masses does not make them less. On the contrary, it increases the chances for a negative scenario. But this is not the question. The question is which side are we on. One cannot make an omelette without breaking eggs. And if concern for eggs is uppermost, the omelette cannot be made. The trouble is that all the efforts of the politically correct egg protectors are worthless. In the course of the story, eggs will be broken one way or another, however omelette will not be made.

Conclusions: Recalling the Principles of the Left Movement

Capitulations of the left are not accidental. There is one reason behind all of them: rejection of the simple principles that define the left movement. Half a century ago, these principles were self-evident, but today it is time to recall them. *The first is class interests.* Not the abstract demagoguery of sympathy towards the weak, inclusiveness, and minority rights, but the specific interests of real working class people, including the 'white males' so despised by liberals. *In fact, 'white males' is a notion invented by liberals specifically to undermine class solidarity and discredit the labour movement.* In reality, about half of the 'white males' are women, and no less than a third are representatives of non-white races. But it does not matter to the liberal discourse. The logic of unity in order to solve joint problems and achieve common goals is portrayed in this discourse as an attempt by 'white males' to discriminate against minorities with their special interests. It does not matter that the defence of special interests leads not only to discrimination against majorities, but also generates a 'war of all against all', in which minorities are the first to suffer. The goal of this politics is not to protect minorities, but to fragment society, while allowing the liberal elite to re-distribute resources among the minorities.

The second historic principle of the left was the notion of historic perspective and building a strategy based on it. In the 1930's, politicians as different as Roosevelt, Trotsky, and Stalin shared this definition, based on the urgent problems of development, whose resolution is the essence of progress. It is telling that the liberal left in the US continues to identify itself as 'progressive', although currently they do not even discuss the essence of historical progress, aside from organizing a few humanistic events.

Meanwhile, the issue is more than clear. Overcoming neoliberalism is the urgent historic task of today—not because we do not like this system, or because it does not correspond to our values, but because it has *exhausted its potential for development* and can only survive by devouring the resources needed for the basic reproduction of society. In other words, the longer this system remains, the more it will self-destruct, and undermine our livelihoods.

17

The historic perspective is connected to class interests by the answers to simple pressing questions: will jobs be created that not only allow survival, but also the cultural, professional, and moral development of workers? Will unions and other worker organizations be strengthened? In the course of the last two and a half decades, the left in unison criticized neoliberalism, the World Trade Organization that weakens and de-solidarizes the working class. However, it is reluctant to admit that the opposite principle is also true: *Under conditions of capitalism only protectionism strengthens workers' positions in the labour market, labour unions and political organizations based on them.* Western European protectionism gave birth to a powerful social-democratic movement, while support of domestic industry by the Russian governments of Vitte and Stolypin created the conditions for the revolution of 1917.

Without the old industrial countries transitioning to protectionism, consolidation of the labour movement in the countries of the global South, which also need to protect their own markets and their own industry, is impossible. That process will lead to local production becoming oriented towards domestic rather than global Northern markets which means that increasing wages rather than suppressing them would become necessary to sustain growth.

Democratic control and a Welfare state are also impossible without protectionism. Neoliberal politics has to be dismantled; the societal model has to be changed. If protectionism becomes a fact, the preconditions for a new social state will be created, a basis for a new popular movement will arise.

The third principle, which was always fundamental for left politics is the *struggle for power.* Precisely for power, not representation, influence or presence in the dominant discourse. It is telling that it was precisely Sanders' attempt to start a real struggle for power that caused the indignation of many left radicals, who perceive this as completely obscene. On the contrary, when the Vermont senator abandoned his positions, he consoled himself and his supporters with the fact that the Democratic Party adopted the most progressive platform in its history, although anyone who knows how the American state really works knows that this programme is not worth the paper it is written on.

The struggle for power requires an organization and much more rigid mechanisms of mobilization than network structures. But most of all, it requires a strong will and political independence. The political transformation, which is currently under way in the US and Western Europe, is changing the conditions under which people in the entire world live and struggle, opening new opportunities for them. The opposite is also true: Syriza's betrayal, Sanders' capitulation, Corbyn's wavering are not just issues of Greek, American, or British politics .... These are failures for which not only the left but all humanity will pay the price.

The neoliberal system, which the likes of Hillary Clinton and Francois Hollande are trying to preserve, is already so dysfunctional, so decayed that every day it survives undermines the basic means of societal reproduction. If we are not ready to fight for its deconstruction, it will break down naturally. But the alternative will not be a new nice social order imagined by anti-globalists, but rather chaos and barbarism growing spontaneously.

A paralysis of will, which struck the left movement during the epoch of neoliberalism, must be overcome. A global drama, in which everyone will have a role, is about to start. We must accept responsibility for risky decisions, understand that we cannot be nice to everybody, and that we cannot win without struggle and sacrifice.

Disclosure Statement

No potential conflict of interest was reported by the author.

Note

1   Novorossia (New Russia) is the self-definition of South Eastern Ukraine.

References

Bickerton, C. (2016, June 22). Brexit is not the property of the political right. The left is disenchanted too. *The Guardian.* Retrieved from https://www.theguardian.com/commentisfree/2016/jun/22/brexit-property-right-left-eu-expert

Choonara, J. (2016, July/August). *After the leave vote: We can beat back racism and austerity.* Socialist Review, 415. Retrieved from http://socialistreview.org.uk/415/after-leave-vote-we-can-beat-back-racism-and-austerity

The Economist. (2016, June 24). The Brexit vote reveals a country split down the middle. *The Economist.* Retrieved from http://www.economist.com/news/britain/21701257-results-paint-picture-angry-country-divided-class-age-and-region-country-divided

Harris, J. (2016, June 24). If you've got the money, you vote in . . . If you haven't got the money, you vote out. *The Guardian.* Retrieved from http://www.theguardian.com/politics/commentisfree/2016/jun/24/divided-britain-brexit-money-class-inequality-westminster

Kirk, M. (2016, July 1). EU referendum results and maps: Full breakdown and find out how your area voted. *The Telegraph.* Retrieved from http://www.telegraph.co.uk/news/2016/06/23/leave-or-remain-eu-referendum-results-and-live-maps/

Lexit. (2016, June 24). *End austerity—general election now! Lexit statement on leave vote.* Counterfire. Retrieved from http://www.counterfire.org/articles/opinion/18396-end-austerity-general-election-now-lexit-statement-on-the-leave-vote

McGill, A. (2016, June 25). Who voted for Brexit. *The Atlantic.* Retrieved from http://www.theatlantic.com/international/archive/2016/06/brexit-vote-statistics-united-kingdom-european-union/488780/

Brexit: Be Careful What You Wish For?

JAMIE MORGAN

ABSTRACT   *In this paper, I focus on the British future from Brexit. The institutional form this will take is not yet fixed. However, one can consider likely outcomes based on dominant economic frameworks. From this perspective, it seems unlikely that Brexit will address the actual grievances that resulted in Brexit. These transcend European Union membership.*

Introduction

Britain has asserted a new political geography.[1] Taken together the vote 23 June 2016 represents a sum of differently positioned disaffections, shared by an electorate drawn from the traditional left *and* right. These disaffections concern the quality and pressure on public services. They also concern wages and income levels, population growth and cultural change. There is a deep sense in the UK that a political elite cannot be trusted, and do not represent the electorate. Many voters also feel strongly that corporations are increasingly remote and lacking in accountability for their actions. There is a cumulative, though not cohesive, sense that, whatever its economic position in the world, Britain is also a divided system. This sense has created the grounds for misinformation, manipulation, easy targets for blame, and quick-fix solutions. The British future from Brexit is not yet determined because its institutional form remains undecided. However, if dominant conceptual frameworks continue to apply, then it seems unlikely that Brexit will address the underlying causes of grievances, since these transcend European Union (EU) membership. They are a product of a common political economy, understood as an ideational framework within globalising processes. In the rest of this paper, I focus on some of the common ideational issues arising from economics and the possible consequences; other papers in this issue provide additional context.

The Political Economy of a Divisive System

Leave and Remain as One-choice-as-no-choice?

Whilst it may be true to say that proper consideration of EU membership was hampered by a failure to make the case effectively regarding benefits, one cannot neglect that the grievances expressed through the Referendum arose in the context of that EU membership (for context, see Duroy, 2014; Longo & Murray, 2011; Sloam, 2016). However, there is more to this issue.[2] The worker within the modern corporation is weaker and poorer than she was 20 years ago. Much of the contemporary analysis of capitalism conceptualises it as a globalising system of processes (Brenner, Peck, & Theodore, 2010; Peck, 2013). Differences occur within commonalities expressed as core characteristics, which create scope for, but limit the degree of, variation.[3] The core is expressed through governance operative within the state, the region and more broadly. Governance is more than government, it involves regulatory systems and practices, which shape a socio-political economy. From this perspective, membership of the EU is a specification of more general processes. As such, the grievances that underlie Brexit may not be reducible to membership of the EU and whether one is inside or outside may not actually be the major issue. Rather, the major issue may be oppositional in a different way: grievances concerning a divisive past and present versus the potential for a more inclusive-as-fair and hence collectively legitimate future. Put another way, Brexit might be thought of as a kind of displacement activity: a way to express grievances, but where ultimately being inside or outside of the EU is not the fundamental problem, that problem is the exclusionary nature of dominant commonalities that transcend membership of the EU (Wrenn, 2014).

One can analyse dominant commonalities from various perspectives. For example, one can focus down on mainstream economics as a form of knowledge (see Lawson, 2015). One can argue that it is integral to the current forms of global, European and local governance. To focus in this way does not imply that only economics is of significance. But the nature of economics does have consequences for the social reality from which grievances can emerge (and in which xenophobia can be encouraged). A significant commonality is that in contemporary economics, labour is treated as just one more factor of production, a unit cost, measured and rewarded in terms of its marginal productivity, and where the labour market is ultimately no different from any other. One makes the market efficient through augmenting the factor (labour) and by reducing 'distortions' in its 'free' interactions. Anything that intercedes between the 'market' and the interacting individual becomes an impediment to 'efficiency'. As such, the collective is immediately positioned as antithetical to this efficiency and trade unions become a systemic problem (rather than integral solution), which must be suppressed through legislation.

A tension then arises since efficiency essentially means being more (maximally) productive, enabling falling costs through time, but also triggering rewards to labour in terms of higher wages to reflect an *individual's* contribution. Yet, for this to actually function then the individual must be the genuine and identifiable source of production, whereas one might argue that production involves an organised set of relations and co-operations. The individual in the labour market must also be able to do what collective representation previously did, and now is hampered in doing. That is, be aware of and adequately represent their own interests in the context of inscribed employment rights, and in the context of assumed competition of each and every worker against all other potential workers. This is in a context that assumes that any worker may undercut the individual, and technology creates a permanent threat to employment security. In practical terms, all labour is disempowered. A weakened institutional position is expressed through 'flexicurity'. Economic policy reduces the role of trade unions, focuses on supply-side economics for labour (improving skills and mobility, facilitating matching, etc.) and places the greater responsibility for systemically constrained outcomes on the individual (you are unproductive, you are insufficiently skilled, mobile, appropriate, valuable, etc.).

So, from a dominant conceptual point of view, policy translates the social human, as a locus of concern that an economy ought to serve, into an economic unit, servile within the needs of a particular kind of economy (though the justification remains that your interests are served by that system). Notably, the claim is that wages are more or less determined by the characteristics of workers in market contexts: what they are prepared to do. This is just or fair and the system will ensure that wages grow fairly, within a just-as-competitive system. This is a central component of a dominant ideational framework, which forms a common sense where markets are the idealised arbiters of all economic activity. This common sense transcends the EU. At its broadest, it is built into the dominant neoliberal discourse of globalisation (every component must conform to precepts of a particular construct of competition or fall behind).

Of course, globalisation as an outcome is not a cause of anything, it is something to be explained, and this includes the positioning of the very idea of globalisation as a necessary reason *why* states must conform to policy types. What is omitted here is the role of corporations as market actors able to affect what can be done, and the role of the state, and regional and global organisations in creating policy regimes that underpin the scope for activity of different actors, favouring some over others. That is, political power that spreads beyond the polity (as the formal institutions of the state) and which can then facilitate different institutional ways in which wage growth and income growth are reduced over time and more of wealth is captured or concentrated.

There are many further significant aspects to ideational positioning. Most importantly, the centrality of derived demand from labour (the centrality of wages and incomes to growth) is suppressed and the issue of the level of effective demand is neglected. This marginalises Keynes' central insight regarding the importance of equitable wages and income for the reproduction of a capitalist economy (see Grieve, 2014). Within Keynes' framework, institutions are required to ensure limits to inequality. Within the current dominant framework, the problem of inequality becomes incoherent. Furthermore, unemployment appears essentially voluntary. There is a 'natural rate'. The possibility of active expansionary fiscal policy and different investment multipliers are marginalised. Socialised investment and orienting and shaping investment for the social good, including along ecological lines where one might emphasise qualitative transformation rather than quantitative destruction becomes conceptually problematic. Fundamental fiscal and investment issues are subsumed and confused, becoming minor temporary or localised singular policy foci rather than system issues. They are translated and limited via the dominant ideational frame, which acts as a kind of obfuscation: that is, self-equilibrating, efficient-as-just, technologically dynamic free markets, imbued with indispensable corporate leadership by pioneering entrepreneurs.

The point to emphasise here is that this common sense is uncommon, but also misleading. It is recognised as unrealistic but is held also as an ideal (a rough 'how things can be and should be'). Its characteristics and timelines vary between states. For example, there are differences between the UK's experience beginning in the late 1970s, and Germany's, whose shift has been more gradual. The Hartz labour market reforms came as late as 2003–2005. However, the common sense has become integral to global, regional and state institutions, expressed in different ways to different degrees, and with different levels of resistance and critique (for example through DiEM25).[4] It is the mismatch between this common sense and actually experienced reality, which gives rise to the kinds of grievances expressed through Brexit. This is not simply an issue of left or right politics, though it can carry their traces. Both the Left Exit or Lexit position and the more inchoate combining of migration with moral panic have economic constituents.

The loss of trust expressed by citizens is caused rather than arbitrary (Morgan & Sheehan, 2015a, 2015b). The deep sense that there is one rule for the few and another for the many is created by experience. Intrinsic to this situation is a democratic deficit: where interests that have gradually developed this common sense have captured institutions, including the state. One finds recognisable versions of the common sense within the Washington and post-Washington consensus, including the particular policies of the World Bank and International Monetary Fund (IMF), and the coordinating activity of the World Trade Organisation (WTO), as well as the 'Anglo-Saxon' liberal economic model. And one finds it within the Single Market framework of the EU and increasingly within the practices of EU members who are also collectively and individually members and participants in these other institutions. The common sense forms the basis of shared tendencies and these have been variously stated (e.g. Streeck, 2011, 2014).

Hence, being inside or outside of the EU may not in itself be the main issue in terms of Brexit. The nature of globalisation is more broadly what is at issue (see Palley & Horn, 2013). It is in many respects a measure of the success of the common sense that critique of globalisation and use of terms such as the Washington consensus are loaded, carrying connotations of the political-as-pejorative, as though the common sense were simply the technical template of progress, and to question it was to be anti-progress. It is in many ways ironic that the political power that spreads beyond the polity has achieved this, and that to question the rules is somehow against the rules. It remains possible to provide marginal critiques from within the system but it is extremely difficult to get a hearing for critiques of the system (we have Fight Club economics).[5] Critique becomes a social movement problem typically externalised from policy. This too has become a source of grievance where externalisation has become synonymous with extreme, as though the many were not representative of a significant constituency.

The externalising of fundamental critique needs to be resisted in the name of reasoned argument. It is not anti-progress to question the nature of progress: to ask for whom, on what basis, and with what costs? If one considers the problem of growing inequality over recent decades, Thomas Piketty's work has done much to publicise the increasing concentration of wealth and income among a top 10%, 5% and 1%. The very fact that it has become meaningful to empirically differentiate a 1% (and 5% and 10%) from the rest indicates that the kinds of grievances expressed in Brexit are not just issues for localised left-behind minority interests—there is something more systemically pervasive to consider. Moreover, there is more to inequality than simple mechanisms (see Lopez-Bernardo, Lopez-Martinez, & Stockhammer, 2016; Morgan, 2015). Rather, there are multiple and developing relations: a complex and varied system of finance, production and trade, a positioning of corporations across many states, and flows of capital and goods. This cannot simply be deemed beneficial by virtue of existence; one must also consider its pathologies: financialisation, debt-dependence, exploitation of people and environments, wealth capture as well as wealth creation.

Inequality has manifested to its greatest degree in the USA, but has also occurred within all major economies. The UK has a greater income and wealth differential between the top 10% and bottom 10% than the EU average, and this is far higher for the top 1%. One cannot, therefore, attribute the actual level of inequality in the UK to EU membership in some simple way. Inequality varies within the EU, and beyond it. The extent within the UK will owe something to common factors that transcend the EU and then also some combination of factors related to membership (either positive or negative). Voting Leave because of economic grievances arising from inequality, as many apparently did, seems intuitively misconceived. At the same time, being a member of the EU did not prevent inequality and other socio-economic problems that have manifested in Brexit. Though it may be possible to distinguish between what being a member of the EU has been responsible for and what it has not prevented, if one considers the underlying dominant ideational framework, then the two start to converge. The real issues are: what are the consequences of the framework and what are the alternatives that might address the grievances otherwise expressed through Brexit?

Be Careful What You Wish For?

In the UK, the Leave Campaign theme focused on regaining control. However, this confuses formal separation with autonomy. It is unlikely that the UK will become more independent. It is far more likely that the terms of its dependencies will become more complex. The UK must now decide on its future institutional arrangements. These may range from becoming a member of the European Economic Area (EEA), to pursuing a range of bilateral agreements. There is an immediate problem here since membership of the EEA will likely result in acceptance of free movement preventing effective limits on European migration (a central commitment of Leave). Relatedly, limiting migration from outside of Europe may also be difficult and counterproductive. The UK already has a population that is diverse by ethnicity and country of origin. This legitimately draws in family members. Moreover, the UK has a perpetual need for both specialised high-skilled and unskilled labour, and this is situated to an ageing demographic and low replacement rate by birth. Various references made by politicians to an Australian style 'points-based' model seem unlikely to be workable in the UK context. Furthermore, one should not neglect that Australia actually has very high levels of immigration. The conflation of economic migration with the issue of asylum in Europe also requires one to remember that Australia's current refugee policy involves offshore isolation and indefinite detention of a kind that contravenes international law and has resulted in widespread vilification.

The main focus of concern stated for the UK's future institutional arrangements is trade relations. Policy discussion is currently about different emphases regarding *whom* to trade with, rather than more fundamentally, *what kind of* economy would address the range of problems that gave rise to Brexit. The UK must now negotiate in order to have institutional arrangements in place that can become active no later than two years after Article 50 of the Lisbon Treaty is activated (notification of withdrawal). Time is short, resources knowledge and skills to be used in negotiation are limited. This is not a position of power. Moreover, the point of negotiation is not just access to different countries' markets for goods and capital flows, it is relations with corporations as sources of production and finance. The logic of negotiation is not about level playing fields, but rather about competition to attract corporations, whilst articulating the common sense of 'free markets'.

The temptation will be to pursue policies advantageous to rising profit shares: that is, allowing more wealth capture from wealth creation. Typical means to these ends include: lowering corporation tax, providing investment subsidies, emphasising light touch regulation and the flexibility of labour (ability to rapidly hire and fire and suppress wage growth). Various think tanks have already begun to advocate policies along these lines as ways to transform the UK into the 'new Singapore'. They are, however, simultaneously all policy tendencies, which are liable to exacerbate problems such as inequality, whilst transferring greater power to corporations, enabling more capture and reducing accountability. In any case, many modern corporations operate long supply chains with complex production processes in different locales.

Being outside of a trading bloc disrupts one's capacity to be part of the chain. This is likely to intensify the need for concessions to attract corporate investment, and also further a temptation to attract reporting of revenues rather than actual economic activity—a tax haven effect. Thereafter, claimed positive consequences of economic policy are articulated through the neoliberal common sense. Innovation, investment, and productivity effects are by definition left as unintended consequences of market interactions: freeing markets leads to entrepreneurial dynamism, and 'better' growth implies marginal productivity gains that are translated into increased real wages. This discourse is familiar: it suggests that the solution to current problems is more and intensified versions of the policy justifications that gave rise to the current situation.

Concomitantly, the core concerns of post-Brexit policy in the UK seem likely to be tightly focused on the economy because of the disruption created by Brexit. They are unlikely to be concerned directly with inequality, social mobility, democratic accountability and social cohesion as the problems that helped to trigger Brexit. The Referendum, of course, must now mean that any ruling party is more aware than ever that these are issues to address. Equally, actually addressing them within dominant ways of thought and policy has become more difficult. If current forecasts of lower economic growth (or recession) prove correct, then tax revenues will fall. Based on current dominant common sense for economic policy, the result will be further austerity, leading to reductions in welfare spending, and restrictions on state investment, in the context of concerns over budget deficits and long-term net debt. The UK already has recognised problems in terms of its dependency on financial services (perhaps a 'finance curse'; Christensen, Shaxson, & Wigan, 2016).[6] It also has problems regarding the structure of its economy, translated and restricted by a framework of 'balancing' (Berry & Hay, 2016). Dependency and economic structure problems seem likely to be exacerbated by the need to rely on financial services tax revenue, as well as likely new limits on investment funding, unless the state changes it position on sovereign debt. The UK budget deficit for 2015–2016 was £75 billion and this was higher than forecast, public sector net debt in 2016 stands at £1.6 trillion or just over 83% of GDP. Missing targets for reductions in deficits, and expectations that deficits will now grow, combined with a continued increase in net debt are all triggers for financial retrenchment within dominant frameworks. This is different than the Treasury merely delaying its commitment to meet deficit reduction targets (an austerity framework remains ideationally dominant).

Responding to immediate economic dislocations in the absence of a genuinely active fiscal policy will also likely perpetuate the dominance of monetary policy through the role of the Bank of England. Loose monetary policy based on zero-bound interest rates seems likely to continue to constrain the value of savings, and because of the actual technical measures used, the current value of all pensions schemes. Pension scheme liabilities create problems for corporations in terms of funding requirements. This provides further motivations to shed pension liabilities (reducing pension benefits). In the meantime, investment is often delayed—so this is one more factor in a situation of uncertainty liable to reduce business investment, despite historic low interest rates. Lower interest rates also affect long-term annuity rates via the discounting calculations applied to bond valuations. The retired, the just-about to retire and those most dependent on the state are set, therefore, to be most adversely affected by the aftermath of Brexit in the UK (and these were all groups who actually tended to vote Leave).

In the end, Brexit is a regional and global issue not just a UK issue. Problems for the UK are also problems for partners and those positioned as competitors. Interactions between separated entities, rather than within integrated ones, create additional grounds for complexity, breakpoints, confusion, distortion and subversion. Brexit may well create problems for current initiatives for collective progress, limited though many of them so far have been. It inserts a new complication into the Trans-Atlantic Trade and Investment Partnership (TTIP) creating a potential distraction from the core problem of corporate accountability.[7] It creates further complications for collective solutions to tax avoidance, such as unitary taxation (see Morgan, 2016b). It introduces additional problems into the development and monitoring of mechanisms within the new Paris COP 21 climate change agreement (see Morgan, 2016a; Spash, 2016).[8] It may even have knock-on effects in terms of financial stability that exacerbate current problems for the Eurozone.[9] This may call forth more of the same policies that have socialised costs and created extreme distributional harms in some countries (for background, see Patomäki, 2013; Stockhammer, 2016). Both Deutsche Bank and Unicredit are deeply embedded in a set of currently vulnerable relations. Brexit may then signal a lurch in neoliberalism, a further evolution and perhaps its death throes (rather than merely a 'failing forwards').

Conclusion

At the moment, nothing is certain. Often, talk of crises comes to nothing and in retrospect, problems can lose the sense of significance that immediacy gave them. Yet, there is a further danger here. It does not require worse cases to manifest for opportunities for something better to have been lost. We should not need Brexit to be disastrous to realise that it signals something important. Systems are fragile and they are fragile because they are constituted through people, but this fragility is also a strength because it is the potential for transformative change. One might perhaps argue that the current situation is one of increasing alienation and this alienation is a measure of the fragility of the contemporary world. The term, of course, is deeply unfashionable, but it is worth considering what Marx actually meant (see Wood, 1984). For Marx, alienation expressed itself as a deep sense of inauthenticity, a lack of self-worth or existential meaninglessness, where the actual potentials of the human were somehow being harmed by the system we live in (even as the scope of those potentials was broadening through material progress based on that system). There is something ultimately Aristotelian about this: a recognition that there is a person who can both suffer and flourish. Brexit seems to want to answer this question of suffering and flourishing in partial ways without ever having explicitly asked it.[10]

Disclosure Statement

No potential conflict of interest was reported by the author.

Notes

1   Thanks to Steve Fleetwood and Tony Lawson for comments.
2   There has in the UK, for example, been a breakdown of the social contract between capital and labour, but also a breakdown of intergenerational solidarity. If one looks through recent data and reports from the Institute for Fiscal Studies or the Rowntree Foundation, then various trends emerge. The UK economy has increased in size by 50% since 1995; yet, the real income of the average 40-year-old (allowing for inflation and housing costs) is approximately what it was in 1995. At the same time, actual household debt levels are about twice what they were in 1995. Those below 40 are now increasingly renters (80% of those 25 or younger rent or live with their parents), they lack access to final salary pension schemes (there were 5 million private sector scheme members in 1995 and less than 500,000 in 2014), they now carry tuition fee debt, are less likely to be a member of a union, and those unions are weaker than at any time in the last 100 years in terms of the legal scope for action.
3   This is not to suggest that the whole is simply reproducing itself without any prospect of fundamental change or transformation.

4   The Democracy in Europe Movement whose initial prime movers include Saskia Sassen, Yanis Varoufakis, Noam Chomsky, Susan George and Tony Negri, https://diem25.org.

5   A good example of limited acknowledgements of problems from within the common sense is Ostry, Prakash, and Furceri (2016) published in an *IMF* journal.

6   Christensen et al. (2016, pp. 4–5) argue that advanced economies can suffer a finance curse that is analogous to the recognised resource curse that afflicts some developing economies: cumulative over dependence on a single economic sector has adverse effects on the overall structure and subsequent evolution of a political economy. The UK has the third largest financial sector in the world and is the largest of these by proportion of the economy. It is a centre of financialisation; capital inflows to the financial sector maintain high exchange rates which reduce the capacity of other sectors such as manufacturing to expand via exports (encouraging an import dependency within globalisation); finance attracts a disproportionate number of skilled workers who might otherwise contribute to other sectors; the state becomes dependent on tax revenues from the sector (despite tax avoidance) and lobby groups for finance pursue political capture that cumulatively shapes and distorts policy, encouraging the dislocation of representative democracy from the broader citizenship; the net effect is also to contribute to asset bubbles, periodic financial crises through pro ('light') finance regulation, the socialisation of costs, and a loss of trust in the political system.

7   TTIP is not about reducing real trade barriers between states, since there are few between EU members and the USA; it is mainly about protections of corporate privilege in the name of free trade: strengthening and extending copyright and patents and the creation of extra-judicial mechanisms (Investor-State Dispute Settlements) to settle disputes between corporations and states in ways that reduce the capacity of states to intervene in corporate activity in their own jurisdiction since this becomes a barrier to trade. TTIP creates a space for corporations to avoid democratic accountability and augments their power to increase profitability (lobbying has been led by telecoms, finance, pharmaceuticals and the large software firms). Notably, TTIP provides a mechanism through which corporations can resist emissions reduction regulation, since interventions can be categorised as trade barriers.

8   The new Conservative government under Theresa May immediately scrapped the Department of Energy and Climate Change and created a Business Energy and Industrial Strategy Department. Department of Energy and Climate Change had three main foci: cheap and secure energy for consumers and businesses, supporting economic growth and reducing carbon emissions. The three are in tension. The new department signals a further transition (already begun under the previous regime) away from prioritising carbon emissions reduction (via the Climate Change Act 2008). Achievement is left to market and technology changes over time.

9   This has various channels. For example, Brexit will likely cause at least short-term reductions in trading activity in the EU. This in turn may place greater pressure on firms and thus on the banks carrying their debts. Also, some banks continue to carry large volumes of non-performing loan 'assets' and are recycling debt for 'zombie' firms in order not to manifest losses on their accounts (though this varies by country). Fear effects related to anything that might upset this vulnerable position create grounds for collapses in equity as well as withdrawal of corporate deposits. This creates bank funding problems (in REPO markets, etc.). Low interest rates also narrow the transformation range for banks, reducing margins/returns on current lending. The overall damage to capitalisation and Tier 1 capital is potentially progressive but also subject to sudden triggers (such as failing a stress test). It creates calls on the state for recapitalisation and socialisation of losses (however, there are new rules for bank equity and bailouts/ins which create new compliance problems with unintended consequences). Italy is a prime candidate for financial crisis, based on these channels. According to the IMF, approximately 18% of debt at Italian banks is suspect (€360 billion).

10 Strictly speaking, since Brexit involved many differently positioned reasons and arguments then any adequate use of the term alienation must also address the issue of the different degrees of awareness of fundamental issues these positions might involve. For example, the Left Exit or Lexit movement was quite different from the United Kingdom Independence Party (UKIP) or Leave inspired positions. Both articulated issues of sovereignty and democratic accountability but involve quite different concepts of what democracy is as an actual form and how it relates to an economy. The Lexit position grew from the 1970s' socialist opposition to the then European Economic Community and so might be self-consciously anti-alienation.

References

Berry, C., & Hay, C. (2016). The Great British Rebalancing Act: The construction and implementation of a economic imperative for exceptional times. *British Journal of Politics and International Relations, 18*(1), 3–25.

Brenner, N., Peck, J., & Theodore, N. (2010). After neoliberalization? *Globalizations, 7*(3), 327–345.

Christensen, J., Shaxson, N., & Wigan, D. (2016). The finance curse: Britain and the world economy. *British Journal of Politics and International Relations, 18*(1), 255–269.

Duroy, Q. (2014). Neoliberal Europe: Enabling ethno-cultural neutrality or fueling neo-nationalist sentiment? *Journal of Economic Issues, 48*(2), 469–476.

Grieve, R. (2014). Right back where we started from: From the classics to Keynes, and back again. *Real World Economics Review, 68*, 41–61.

Lawson, T. (2015). *Essays on the nature and state of modern economics*. London: Routledge.

Longo, M., and Murray, P. (2011). No ode to joy? Reflections on the European Union's legitimacy. *International Politics, 48*(6), 667–690.

Lopez-Bernardo, J., Lopez-Martinez, F., & Stockhammer, E. (2016). A post-Keynesian response to Piketty's 'fundamental contradiction of capitalism'. *Review of Political Economy, 28*(2), 190–204.

Morgan, J. (2015). Piketty's calibration economics: Inequality and the dissolution of solutions? *Globalizations, 12*(5), 803–823.

Morgan, J. (2016a). Paris COP 21: Power that speaks the truth? *Globalizations*, doi:10.1080/14747731.2016.1163863

Morgan, J. (2016b). Corporation tax as a problem of MNC organizational circuits: The case for unitary taxation. *British Journal of Politics and International Relations, 18*(2), 463–481.

Morgan, J., & Sheehan, B. (2015a). Has reform of global finance been misconceived? Policy documents, and the Volcker Rule. *Globalizations, 12*(5), 695–709.

Morgan, J., & Sheehan, B. (2015b). The concept of trust and the political economy of John Maynard Keynes, illustrated using central bank forward guidance and the democratic dilemma in Europe. *Review of Social Economy, 73*(1), 113–137.

Ostry, J., Prakash, L., & Furceri, D. (2016). Neoliberalism oversold? *Finance & Development, 53*(2), 38–41.

Palley, T., & Horn, G. (Eds.). (2013). *Restoring shared prosperity: A policy agenda from leading Keynesian economists*. Creative Space Independent Publishing Platform. Retrieved from https://www.amazon.co.uk/Restoring-Shared-Prosperity-Keynesian-Economists/dp/1493749420/ref=sr_1_1?s=books&ie=UTF8&qid=1472727685&sr=1-1&keywords=Restoring+shared+prosperity%3A+A+policy+agenda+from+leading+Keynesian+economists

Patomäki, H. (2013). *The great Eurozone disaster: From crisis to global new deal*. London: Zed Books.

Peck, J. (2013). Explaining (with) neoliberalism. *Territory, Politics, Governance, 1*(2), 132–157.

Sloam, J. (2016). Diversity and voice: The political participation of young people in the European Union. *British Journal of Politics and International Relations, 18*(3), 521–537.

Spash, C. (2016). This changes nothing: The Paris agreement to ignore reality. *Globalizations*, doi:10.1080/14747731.2016.1161119

Stockhammer, E. (2016). Neoliberal growth models, monetary union and the Euro crisis. A post-Keynesian perspective. *New Political Economy, 21*(4), 365–379.

Streeck, W. (2011). The crisis of democratic capitalism. *New Left Review, 71*, 5–29.

Streeck, W. (2014). How will capitalism end? *New Left Review, 87*, 35–64.

Wood, A. (1984). *Karl Marx*. London: Routledge, Kegan Paul.

Wrenn, M. (2014). Unveiling and deconstructing the enabling myths of neoliberalism through immanent critique. *Journal of Economic Issues, 48*(2), 477–484.

Brexit and its Consequences

ANN PETTIFOR

ABSTRACT   *In this brief essay, I argue that the 'Brexit' vote is but the latest manifestation of popular dissatisfaction with the utopian ideal of autonomous markets beyond the reach of regulatory democracy. Brexit represented the collective, if (to my mind) often misguided, efforts of those 'left behind' in Britain to protect themselves from the predatory nature of market fundamentalism. In a Polanyian sense, it is a form of social self-protection from self-regulating markets in money, trade and labour.*

Introduction

Globalization was, and remains, the utopian ambition of those many economists, financiers, politicians, and policy-makers that were once aptly defined by George Soros as 'market fundamentalists' (Soros & Woodruff, 2008). When more than 17 million British voters opted to end ties with the European Union on the 23 June 2016, they exposed the fragility and even futility of the ambition to build markets beyond the reach of regulatory democracy. By doing so, British voters rejected the advice of dozens of leading economists and several powerful financial institutions. The outcome threatens to undermine the pivotal role played by the City of London in 'globalizing' and financializing the world economy.

The background to this historic event can be traced to the economic theories and policies that led to the Great Financial Crisis. These underpinned the structures and operation of an increasingly globalized, autonomous, self-regulating market in finance, trade, and labour. A project that peaked just before the 'debtonation' of 9 August 2007.

Liberal finance prior to the crisis had led to unfettered credit (debt) creation, high *real* rates of interest for those active in the real economy and volatility in capital flows across borders. These in turn led to the rise of international imbalances and to fluctuations in exchange rates. Financial and trade imbalances were accompanied by policies for (i) the privatization of state assets (often acquired through the creation of debt, and at a loss to taxpayers), (ii) the 'flexibility' of labour, and (iii) for wage repression. The result? The build-up of vast mountains of private debt and repression of the incomes needed to repay those debts.

This financial house of cards began to collapse as early as 2006.

On 'debtonation' day, 9 August 2007, inter-bank lending around the world froze, and the Great Financial Crisis—still ongoing in both Europe and in emerging markets—began in earnest. Since then both the ideology of globalization and the economic reality of liberal finance have weakened. The former set off countervailing populist, nationalist, and protectionist movements in the US, Europe, and in many emerging markets. The latter is now subject to considerable contraction as financial flows are domesticated, and trade flows contract.

Unfettered Financial and Trade Flows—and Brexit

Unfettered global financial flows are intrinsic to the globalization ideal, but flows collapsed during 2007–2009 and nearly 10 years later remain well below pre-crisis levels. At their peak, the world's 100 largest banks had a market capitalization of around $4.9 trillion, according to the Bank of England. That was around 8.5% of annual global GDP. At its trough, this had fallen to $1.4 trillion—a destruction of financial capital of $3.5 trillion. The market capitalization of the world's 20 largest banks today remains around half its value in 2007 (Haldane, 2016). 'Cross-border financial flows ... are now as "globalized" as they were in the year 1983' according to Kristin Forbes, of the Bank of England's Monetary Policy Committee, in a speech made well before the Brexit vote (Forbes, 2014).

The decline in flows to and from the City of London has led a global decline in flows, according to Forbes.

> The contraction in UK international lending and borrowing is larger—on an absolute basis—than for any other country for which data is available. In other words, the decline in bank flows into and out of the UK has contributed more to the global decline in banking flows than any other country. (Forbes, 2014)

That decline is now likely to be aggravated by the Brexit vote. As the Financial Times of 18 August 2016 reports, 'the biggest fear for many City grandees is that financial services could face a "cliff-edge" moment if the UK leaves the EU without a trade agreement in place, cutting off (bankers') access to the single market overnight' (Arnold & Binham, 2016). Given the key roles played by Brexiteers in the newly formed Conservative government led by Theresa May, all of whom have an aversion to the unfettered migration that is central to the European project, and given that free movement is a condition of access to the single market, such a trade agreement seems increasingly unlikely to serve the interests of the City. British bankers have 'given up hope of universal access to the single market' (Arnold & Binham, 2016).

The financial crisis also dealt a blow to world trade, which has slowed markedly. The rate of growth of world merchandise trade (by volume) between 2010 and 2012 oscillated (according to United Nations Conference on Trade and Development [UNCTAD]) between 2% and 2.6%, significantly below the average annual rate of 7.2% recorded during the 2003–2007 period (UNCTAD, 2015, p. 6). And since 2008, the G20 economies have become increasingly protectionist. According to the World Trade Organisation, the advanced economies have, since then, introduced 1583 new trade restrictions and removed just 387. In a recent report, the WTO noted that between mid-October of 2015 and mid-May of 2016, G20 countries introduced 145 new protectionist measures, a monthly average of 21, the highest since the WTO began monitoring such measures in 2009 (WTO, 2016).

The destabilizing consequences of the crisis and the reversal of the globalization agenda triggered countervailing nationalist and protectionist movements. These should have come as no surprise. First, the financial crisis was a self-inflicted wound. Re-regulation (not de-regulation) of the global economy to favour, detach, and strengthen the rentier (title-holders of money) sector was achieved by deflationary policies. These imposed substantial costs on the real, productive economy where millions expect to be employed, and both enriched and protected the rentier sector from oversight, penalties, and punishment.

Re-regulation of Finance

In Britain in the early 1970s, the Treasury and the Bank of England made a series of regulatory changes that served the interests of financial markets at the expense of UK industry.

Based on the ideas of Adam Smith, Thomas Malthus, and David Ricardo, the liberal finance argument that fuelled these changes ran thus: only the price mechanism could effectively bring the supply and demand for money into balance and assure the optimal use of financial resources. These ideas ushered in the new regulatory framework, Competition and Credit Control in 1971. From then on, bank lending would be determined not on the basis of the viability of a project or borrower; not on the likely revenue to be generated by the borrowing, but on the basis of cost, that is through interest rates. Loans would be granted to those companies and individuals that could pay the highest rates rather than to those that fulfilled the authorities' qualitative criteria. As the financial historian Duncan Needham has definitively explained: 'credit based on cost replaced years of rationing based on "control"' (Needham, 2014).

There followed a series of *re*-regulatory measures that strengthened the hands of Finance and weakened the hands of Industry and Labour. These have been documented by Aeron Davis and Catherine Walsh in an article published in Political Studies in April 2015. They explain that:

> 1979 and 1980 brought the release of exchange and credit controls and thus initiated a new credit boom. Big UK-based institutional investors started switching far more of their funds abroad and away from UK industry. Stamp duty on the purchase of shares and bonds was cut in stages from 2 to 0.5 per cent. Dividend payment controls were abolished in 1982. In contrast, although corporation tax was cut for all businesses, this was paid for specifically by removing capital investment allowances for machinery and plants—measures which primarily hit manufacturing. There were steady value-added tax (VAT) rates rises on goods and services, but financial and insurance services were made VAT-exempt. This doubly disadvantaged industry next to finance as the former made much greater use of real world goods and services than the latter.

Although the UK has had a strong financial sector for centuries, it expanded significantly from the late 1970s, as Davies and Walsh evidence:

> From 1979 to 1989, investment in financial services grew 320.3 per cent next to investment in manufacturing, which rose only 12.8 per cent (Coates, 1995, p. 6). Until the 1970s, UK bank assets had been equal to roughly half the value of UK GDP for a century. Following changes, by the mid-2000s, they had risen to five times the value of GDP (Haldane, 2010). In 1979/80, the equity value of the stock market (£30.8 billion) was roughly 40 per cent of government income (£76.6 billion). By 2012, it was worth £1.76 trillion, or three times government income (£592 billion; HMSO, 1980–2014). From 1997 to 2013, the UK's debt rose from £34 billion in 1997 to £1.3 trillion, or 88 per cent of GDP in 2013. By the time of the financial crisis in 2007–8, the UK's financial sector relative to its economy was bigger than any other G7 nation.

> In contrast, UK industry has suffered a faster decline than all its economic rivals in that same period. In 1970, UK manufacturing accounted for 30 per cent of GDP, 16.3 per cent of total world exports

(Coates, 1995, p. 7) and had trade surpluses of 4–6 per cent annually. Furthermore, 35 per cent of UK employment was in this sector. By 2010, 13 per cent of GDP and 10 per cent of total employment was in manufacturing, and the UK was running a trade deficit in this sector of 2–4 per cent (Chang, 2010, p. 90). (Davis & Walsh, 2015, p. 2)

Re-regulating the British economy in favour of finance and enriching the 1% while shrinking labour's share of income resulted in rising inequality and lit a still smouldering fuse of popular resentment. Resentment made most explicit in the Brexit vote.

The Failure of Economics

Finally, the economic profession's deflationary, liberal finance bias, and the failure to include money, debt, and banks in economic analyses and modelling made it nigh impossible for the profession to correctly predict, prevent, or mitigate the ongoing crisis. Perhaps most symbolically, even the Queen suggested that they did not know what they were doing.

The economic model that fostered the crisis remained intact after 2009, with only some tinkering at the margins of the banking system. As a result, today's policy-makers struggle to stabilize an unbalanced global financial system, and doggedly oppose expansionary policies needed to ensure employment and recovery. The necessary restructuring and rebalancing of the global economy have been postponed.

With the historic Brexit vote, the British people rejected this flawed brand of economics—and in particular the dominant liberal finance narrative. And they did so because the hardship they are experiencing—repressed wages, diminished public services, rising housing costs and shortages, and insecure employment—is indirectly a consequence of the theories and policies of the mainstream economics profession. Economists led the way to the re-regulation and 'liberalization' of the finance sector over the past 40 years and to soaring levels of debt, crises, and financial ruin. Economists dictated the terms for austerity that has so harmed the British economy and society over the past ten years. On 14 February 2010, 20 of the most senior UK economists wrote to *The Sunday Times* castigating the Labour government for inadequate efforts on deficit reduction and setting the tone not only for the general election of that year but seemingly ever since (Chick, Pettifor, & Tily, 2016, p. 3). As the policies have failed, the vast majority of economists have refused to concede wrongdoing, nor have societies been offered alternatives. It is hardly surprising, therefore, that the British public did not find the opinion of the 'experts' backing the Remain campaign compelling.

The Remain campaign chose to focus on the economy—to the exclusion of almost all else. All the heavyweights of the economics profession—10 Nobel Prize-winning economists, the OECD, the IMF, the Federal Reserve, the Bank of England, the NIESR, the Institute of Fiscal Studies, the London School of Economics—were wheeled out to warn the British people of economic facts known, and understood apparently, only to 'experts'. *The Financial Times* amplified their voices and repeated their dire threats and warnings over and over.

But the 'experts' and the economic stories they tell have been well and truly walloped by the result of this referendum. And rightly so, because while there is truth in the story that international and in particular European cooperation and coordination are vital to economic activity and stability, there is no sound basis to the widely espoused economic 'religion' that markets—in money, trade, and labour—must be unfettered, detached from democratic regulatory oversight, and must be left to 'govern' whole countries, regions, and continents.

The British people by voting Brexit rejected this mainstream, orthodox economics, a strain of fundamentalism that they rightly judge has proved deleterious to their own economic interests.

Conclusion

I voted to Remain. I do not believe that Brexit is a wise decision. I fear its consequences in energizing the Far Right both in Britain but also across both Europe and the US. I fear the break-up of the UK, and the political dominance of a small tribe of conservative 'Little Englanders'. They will diminish this country's great social, economic, and political achievements.

But Britain's 'Brexit' vote is but the latest manifestation of popular dissatisfaction with the economists' globalized, marketized society. And if there should be any doubt that these movements are both nationalistic *and* protectionist, consider Donald Trump's campaign threat to build a wall between Mexico and the US, to deter migrants, 'gangs, drug traffickers and cartels' (Trump website). Trump's plan for financing the wall involves the introduction of controls over the movement of capital. If the Mexican government resisted, argued Trump, the US would cut off the billions of dollars that undocumented Mexican immigrants working in the US send to their families annually. 'It's an easy decision for Mexico', Trump wrote in a note to the *Washington Post* on 5 April 2016. 'Make a one-time payment of $5–10 billion to ensure that $24 billion continues to flow into their country every year' (Woodward & Costa, 2016).

Nationalism, protectionism, and populism are not confined to Western nations. In India, a BJP MP, Subramanian Swamy, fired a salvo at the Reserve Bank of India (RBI) governor Raghuram Rajan that led to his unexpected decision not to seek a second term when his three-year reign ended in September 2016. Swamy made clear that 'the governor should have known the inevitable consequence of rising and high interest rate and (that) his policy was wilful and thus *anti-national* in intent' (my emphasis). The RBI governor's post, Swamy added, 'is very high in the Warrant of Precedence and requires a patriotic and unconditional commitment to our nation'.

Karl Polanyi predicted in *The Great Transformation* that no sooner will today's utopians have institutionalized their ideal of a global economy, apparently detached from political, social, and cultural relations, than powerful counter-movements—from the right no less than the left—would be mobilized (Polanyi, 2001). The Brexit vote was, to my mind, just one manifestation of the expected resistance to market fundamentalism. The Brexit slogans 'Take Back Control', 'Take Back Our Country', and 'Britannia waives the rules' represented an inchoate and incoherent attempt to subordinate unfettered, globalized markets in money, trade, and labour to the interests of British society. Like the movement mobilized by Donald Trump in the US, the Five Star Alliance in Italy, Podemos in Spain, the Front National in France, the Corbyn phenomenon in the UK, the Law and Justice Party in Poland, Brexit represented the collective, if (to my mind) often misguided, efforts of those 'left behind' in Britain to protect themselves from the predatory nature of market fundamentalism.

By doing so, they confirmed Polanyi's firm prediction that

> the idea of a self-adjusting market implied a stark utopia. Such an institution could not exist for any length of time without annihilating the human and natural substance of society . . . . Inevitably, society took measures to protect itself, but whatever measures it took impaired the self-regulation of the market, disorganized industrial life, and thus endangered society in yet another way. (Polanyi, 2001, p. 3)

Brexit has endangered British society in yet another way, but the vote was, I contend, a form of social self-protection from self-regulating markets in money, trade, and labour.

Disclosure Statement

No potential conflict of interest was reported by the author.

References

Arnold, M., & Binham, C. (2016, August 18). UK financial sector targets Swiss-style deal for EU market access. *Financial Times*. Retrieved from https://www.ft.com/content/5cebe746-655a-11e6-8310-ecf0bddad227

Chick, V., Pettifor, A., & Tily, G. (2016). The economic consequences of Mr Osborne. *Prime Economics*.

Davis, A., & Walsh, C. (2015). The role of the state in the financialisation of the UK economy. *Political Studies*. doi:10.1111/1467-9248.12198

Forbes, K. (2014, November 18). *Financial "deglobalization"?: Capital flows, banks, and the Beatles*. Speech given at Queen Mary University, London.

Haldane, A. (2016, May 18). *The great divide*. Speech given at New City Agenda Annual dinner, London. Retrieved from http://www.bankofengland.co.uk/publications/Documents/speeches/2016/speech908.pdf

Needham, D. (2014). *UK monetary policy from devaluation to Thatcher, 1967–8*. Basingstoke: Palgrave Macmillan.

Polanyi, K. (2001). *The great transformation*. Boston, MA: Beacon Press.

Soros, G., & Woodruff, J. (2008, May 15). The financial crisis: An interview with George Soros. *The New York Review of Books*. Retrieved from http://www.nybooks.com/articles/2008/05/15/the-financial-crisis-an-interview-with-george-soro/

Trump/Pence website: *Make America Great Again*. Retrieved from https://www.donaldjtrump.com/positions/immigration-reform

UNCTAD. (2015). *Trade and development report*. Retrieved from http://unctad.org/en/PublicationsLibrary/tdr2015_en.pdf

Woodward, B., & Costa, R. (2016, April 5). Trump reveals how he would force Mexico to pay for border wall. *The Washington Post*. Retrieved from https://www.washingtonpost.com/politics/trump-would-seek-to-block-money-transfers-to-force-mexico-to-fund-border-wall/2016/04/05/c0196314-fa7c-11e5-80e4-c381214de1a3_story.html

WTO. (2016, June 2). *Report on G20 trade measure (mid-October 2015 to Mid-May 2016)*. Retrieved from https://www.wto.org/english/news_e/news16_e/g20_wto_report_june16_e.pdf

The Organic Crisis of the British State: Putting Brexit in its Place

BOB JESSOP

ABSTRACT   *The Brexit vote was a singular* event *that is one symptom of a* continuing organic crisis *of the British state and society and a stimulus for* further struggles *over the future of the United Kingdom and its place in Europe and the wider world. This crisis previously enabled the rise of Thatcherism as a neoliberal and neoconservative project (with New Labour as its left wing) with an authoritarian populist appeal and authoritarian statist tendencies that persisted under the Conservative–Liberal Democrat coalition (2010–2015). The 2015 election of a Conservative Government, which aimed to revive the Thatcherite project and entrench austerity, was the immediate context for the tragi-comedy of errors played out in the referendum. The ensuing politics and policy issues could promote the disintegration of the UK and, perhaps, the EU without delivering greater political sovereignty or a more secure and non-balkanized place for British economic space in the world market.*

Introduction

There is a key difference between the conjuncture that enabled the rise of Thatcherism and the Brexit conjuncture. The former was a *rassemblement* of the establishment, 'the fusion of an entire social class under a single leadership, which alone is held to be capable of solving an over-riding problem of its existence and fending off a mortal danger' (Gramsci, 1971, p. 211; Q13§23, p. 1604). This was supported by key sections of the middle and working classes (for a good recent analysis, see Gallas, 2015). Mrs Thatcher's Conservative party mobilized a new cross-class alliance against those identified with the post-war social democratic settlement and its alleged failures (cf. Hall, Jefferson, Critcher, Clarke, & Roberts, 1978; Jessop, Bonnett,

Bromley, & Ling, 1988). In contrast, the Brexit conjuncture reflected a long-running split in the establishment, a worsening representational crisis in the party system, a growing crisis of authority for political elites, a legitimacy crisis of the state, and a crisis of national-popular hegemony over the population. Specifically, we can note:

- Entry into and continued membership of the EU have proved a neuralgic point in British politics, dividing imperial nostalgists, nationalists, Atlanticists, Europeanists, and globalists from the 1950s onwards in different ways at different times;
- A growing disconnect between the natural governing parties in Westminster, their members and their voters was reflected most recently in support for Scottish Nationalism and the United Kingdom Independence Party (UKIP);
- The loss of respect for the ruling classes (e.g. for corruption, cronyism, sleaze) and a loss in confidence among the ruling classes, enabled the disgruntled masses to enter politics as an autonomous force, moving from passivity to making radical demands for change that were countered by populist appeals;
- A legitimacy crisis as successive neoliberal projects failed to deliver nationwide prosperity and, in addition, created conditions for fisco-financial crisis.

These and other factors led David Cameron, the Conservative party leader and Prime Minister, into errors of judgement in an attempt to defuse internal party dissent and undermine popular support for UKIP, exposing his party (and the country) to 'an uncertain future by demagogic promises' (Gramsci, 1971, p. 210; Q13§23, p. 1603). Cameron did not expect to have to fulfil them—initially because he did not anticipate winning a parliamentary majority and then because he thought the politics of fear would produce a victory like that in the Scottish referendum. The problem with this tactic was that the power bloc had lost control over public opinion, the hinge between political and civil society, regarding the European Union. This resulted from decades-long hostility from what became the pro-Brexit press, which accounted for 82% of hard copy and on-line readers and would normally support the Conservative party in elections even when positioning itself to the right at other times. Another crucial factor in swinging public opinion in these uncertain times was the alliance of those 'charismatic men of destiny', Nigel Farage (populist leader of UKIP) and Boris Johnson (the high-profile Conservative Mayor of London) (cf. Gramsci, 1971, p. 210; Q13§23, p. 1603).

Conjunctural Shifts

Before turning to its aftermath, we should look beyond the immediate political situation and particular political conjuncture in which the referendum occurred to the wider domestic and international contexts. The integral economic context domestically was a protracted crisis of Britain's flawed post-war Fordist economy and, relatedly, of its insertion into the circuits of Atlantic Fordism and the world market, evident from the mid-1960s onwards. Politically this was associated with a crisis in the state form and state strategies. This crisis occurred because the state lacked the capacities to engage in statist intervention, or effective corporatist coordination, or a consistently rigorous laissez-faire line and therefore oscillated uneasily among different strategies that all failed in their different ways in different conjunctures (see Jessop et al., 1988).

Two general exit strategies from the crisis in/of Atlantic Fordism have been advocated: the knowledge-based economy (KBE), which became the hegemonic economic imaginary from the mid-1990s in Europe and elsewhere; and financialization, which relies less on Fordist wage-led growth or post-Fordist innovation- and knowledge-driven growth than on a debt-fuelled dynamic that favours interest-bearing capital rather than, as with Fordism and the KBE, profit-producing capital (see further, Lavoie & Stockhammer, 2013; Sum & Jessop, 2013, pp. 235–295, 395–439). Despite the lip-service paid to the KBE in governing circles, financialization became dominant through the pursuit of neoliberalism from 1975 onwards. Successive governments stressed the inevitability, desirability, and overall benefits of neoliberal globalization and promoted the interests of capital over labour in an open economy.

As pursued in the UK, neoliberalism is a relatively coherent and mutually reinforcing set of policies—which is not as such a guarantee that they will succeed (for an analysis of their inherent contradictions and their effects, see Jessop, 2015). These policies privilege opportunities for monetary profit over the provision of substantive use-values that meet social needs, facilitate human flourishing, protect the environment, and safeguard planet earth. In particular, they privilege interest-bearing capital and transnational profit-producing capital over other fractions of capital and the interests of subaltern classes, marginal communities, and oppressed social categories. In the UK, such privileging goes well beyond support for the commercial and financial dominance of the City of London as it operated until its deregulation in the mid-1980s. They promote it as the leading international centre for international financial capital. Thanks to 'light touch regulation', these policies have made the City the home for many of the most egregious financial scandals in 2007–2015, regardless of the nationality or primary seat of the financial institutions involved. Together with growing inequalities of wealth and income, this is one factor in the loss of respect for financial elites.

More generally, financial claims on the 'real' economy have grown as industrial productivity and output have failed to keep pace with financialization—creating a spurious and unsustainable debt-fuelled boom based on fictitious credit. This has increased the mass and share of profits going to interest-bearing capital at the expense of profit-producing capital that creates internationally tradable commodities. The same profit-oriented logic tends to polarize wealth and income and degrade social cohesion as well as generate financial crises. The ever more visible polarization of wealth and income, noted increasingly even in neoliberal circles as a major economic, social, and political problem, is generating popular discontent and corresponding measures to monitor the population, insulate government from popular demands for economic and social justice, encourage divide-and-rule tactics to this end, and, where necessary, repress dissent.

The neoliberal policies pursued by the Thatcher government and its successors have also reinforced de-industrialization and, where core industries survived, contributed to their balkanization. Successive governments declared Britain to be 'open for business' (and takeover), leading to competing and uncoordinated ties to foreign capital, including, recently, Chinese, Indian, and Russian interests alongside 'the usual suspects'. Without the economic, political, and social bases for a concerted national economic strategy, Britain's economic fortunes came to depend heavily on the vagaries of finance-dominated accumulation and the wider world market and a low-skill, low-tech, low-wage, and even zero-hour service sector associated with a neoliberal race to the bottom. This economic configuration remains as a major structural constraint on efforts to take back control over the future of the British economy. Neoliberal policies and public investment decisions (including the regional allocation of infrastructure projects) also intensified uneven development to the benefit of London and the rest of the South-East—regions that, against the post-referendum received wisdom, cast more Brexit votes than the 'Labour heartlands' in northern England (Williams, 2016).

Overall, the combination of weak state capacities in the period of flawed post-war economic expansion and the subsequent pursuit of neoliberal strategies has produced a seriously weakened 'real economy' and hypertrophied rent-seeking financial sector. Thus, successive governments have failed to provide adequate technical and vocational training to address labour shortages, protect worker and union rights to limit the race to the bottom and spur productivity-boosting capital investment, encourage research and development to promote the KBE, overcome the housing crisis and reduce the unproductive 'housing sector borrowing requirement', fund the NHS rather than the military–industrial complex, moderate uneven regional development, and so on. This failure is partly intellectual as well as structural. It reflects the dominance of a 'money concept of capital' associated in ideal-typical terms with interest-bearing capital over a 'productivist concept of capital' that corresponds to the profit-producing capital (on 'concepts of capital', see Overbeek, 1990; on fractions of capital and their implication in industrial and financial crises, see Marx, 1894/1967).

This meant that the social bases of economic and political power have come to rest on the fragile foundations of popular capitalism, authoritarian populism, and a self-disciplinary entrepreneurial culture. The aspirational 'one nation' Keynesian Welfare National State based on jobs for all and social welfare was replaced by a more explicitly 'two nations' project. This promoted popular capitalism, especially home ownership, and 'privatized Keynesianism' (i.e. borrowing to support consumption despite declining real incomes) to curry electoral popularity at the expense of investing in long-term competitiveness based on export-oriented productive investment. It benefitted the 'have lots', produced a divided and ruled squeezed middle class of 'haves', and expanded the 'have not' population. And it has intensified 'north–south' and other regional and local inequalities (including inside major cities). Combined with representational and political crises, this conjuncture was both a threat and an opportunity for the neoliberal project. The measures taken by New Labour aimed to bail out the financial sector and, as a result, transformed a financial crisis into a fiscal crisis marked by rising public sector deficits that were ruthlessly exploited by the Conservative Party, the City of London, and right-wing press to discredit New Labour's hard-won reputation for economic competence. It also provided the excuse to move beyond the politics of austerity towards a 'state of enduring austerity' (on the austerity state, see Jessop, 2016; Seymour, 2014). Given her initial rhetorical critique of the economic and social injustices of past policies, it remains to be seen whether this state form will survive under Mrs May's premiership (see further below).

The Eurozone Crisis

The international context was an economic and financial crisis in the European Union, notably in the Eurozone, the intensifying democratic deficit in its political institutions, the hegemony of Germany in Northern Europe and its domination over Southern Europe, the economic migration and refugee crises, and, beyond Europe, the shift of the global centre of economic gravity to East Asia. These factors reinforced the view that British sovereignty was being sacrificed to European political institutions even though the real loss of sovereignty was more temporal than territorial and rooted in the space of flows and the power of transnational capital rather than formal juridico-political relations among national states.

The Eurozone crisis was triggered in part by contagion effects rooted in the transnational integration of credit relations; these effects were especially evident in the purchase by European financial institutions of toxic asset-backed securities. Contagion was mediated through a general liquidity crisis, the exacerbation of 'global imbalances', and decline in world trade.

There were also home-grown features, including a Ponzi-finance-induced recession linked to housing bubbles in Southern Europe and the Irish Republic as well as the crisis of competitiveness in several EU economies. The EU was increasingly organized along neoliberal lines, with its competitiveness, stability, growth, economic governance, and fiscal pacts (Stützle, 2013). There are established crisis-management responses for liquidity crises, speculative bubbles, and challenges of national competitiveness. More important in generating the Eurozone crisis is the 'incompossible dream' of a European Monetary Union without stronger fiscal and political integration. This could not address the strong national divergences among accumulation regimes, modes of regulation, social power constellations, and economic imaginaries in the EU. These problems were masked by a short-term boom as credit flowed from Northern to Southern Europe following adoption of the euro. But contagion effects of the North Atlantic Financial Crisis interacted with these basic structural flaws to destabilize the Southern European economies, which may not exit the Eurozone and cannot boost exports in a weakened world market.

The result has been a debt-default-deflation trap reinforced by capitalist market forces, home-grown as well as contagious austerity intended to bring about internal devaluation, and conditionalities and sanctions imposed by the Troika. The latter comprises the European Central Bank, European Commission, and International Monetary Fund (IMF), which are jointly tasked with imposing and monitoring the conditions for sovereign bailouts in the Eurozone. This has reinforced tendencies towards neoliberal authoritarianism that combines surveillance with pre-emptive policing to limit, stifle, or block popular resistance (Bruff, 2013; Oberndorfer, 2015; Seymour, 2014). Overall, the burden of adjustment is falling on subaltern groups everywhere, especially in Eurozone deficit countries. This benefits the dominant transnational profit-producing and interest-bearing capital fractions and the geopolitical interests of leading member states and their transatlantic allies. Recent research reports by IMF research staff (e.g. IMF, 2015; Ostry, Loungani, & Furceri, 2016) and its Office of Internal Evaluation (Independent Evaluation Office of the International Monetary Fund, 2016) now recognize the folly of this approach, especially for Greece, although such recurrent admissions clearly have limited impact on those who actually make and enforce policy (for a critique, see Varoufakis, 2016).

Implications for the Referendum

The dominance of neoliberalism indicates that the choice posed in the referendum was misleading: the real choice should have been in or out of neoliberalism rather than in or out of the European Union. As posed, the choice was ill-defined:

> ... the question to be voted on offers two choices 'Stay or Leave' without any clue whatsoever about how either choice would be implemented. 'Stay' might seem a simple default choice, but its consequences would depend on the future evolution of an EU already in crisis and heading for major changes with quite unpredictable effects. And 'leave', as we all now can see, has so many possible variants that no consensus either on which variant would be chosen or on its effects would be conceivable. (fosforos, 2016)

A choice for entry or exit would not affect the overall dominance of neoliberalism—only its specific form and mediations. A remain vote would have consolidated an authoritarian neoliberal Conservative regime committed to enduring austerity; the Brexit vote might produce a J-curve depression with eventual recovery below long-term trend-line growth, at best, with secular stagnation or long-term depression and more austerity as the more likely outcome. The crucial issue that remained largely unvoiced was that real or imagined crisis symptoms were not caused by membership of the European Union as such. Rather, they were rooted in its neoliberal form, the crisis of Eurozone crisis-management, and the long-run failure to address crucial domestic issues that undermined economic and extra-economic competitiveness.

Similar problems were evident in the conventional wisdom around the referendum. For, as Zoe Williams noted, there was no effective challenge to assumptions such as

> people who oppose free movement will always oppose it; that it is pointless explaining the lump of labour fallacy, because that is yet more elitist sneering; that public services are under pressure because of foreigners rather than underfunding; that housing is expensive because of demand rather than rent extraction by a capital class empowered by inequality; that the voters have spoken, and now our humanitarian duties to refugees must come second, to the point that we don't even mention them; that the metropolitan elite must simply accept that it let immigration get out of control and must pay the price of a mistrust of unknowable proportions and unguessable length. (Williams, 2016)

What Next?

There has been a measure of *political recovery* by the power bloc since the shock generated by the largely unexpected 51.9% vote in favour of Brexit. As Gramsci observed regarding earlier crisis conjunctures:

> The traditional ruling class, which has numerous trained cadres, changes men and programmes and, with greater speed than is achieved by the subordinate classes, reabsorbs the control that was slipping from its grasp. Perhaps it may make sacrifices … but it retains power, reinforces it for the time being, and uses it to crush its adversary. (1971, pp. 210–211; Q13§23)

This can be seen in the speed with which the Conservative Party selected its new leader to preside over a government now morally obliged to take Brexit forward. At issue now is how the ruling class and governing elites will use this power to defend the interests of dominant fractions of national and transnational capital while keeping a divided public content with the speed and outcome of Brexit negotiations. The UK's activation of Article 50 of the Lisbon Treaty, which is required to trigger formal exit negotiations, has been postponed—possibly beyond the French and German elections in 2017, with potential connivance from their current governments. This enables economic, financial, and political elites to concur with Mrs May that 'Brexit means Brexit' while buying time to establish the machinery of government and state capacities to negotiate and then implement new treaties and trade agreements (Rutter & McRae, 2016). The civil service count is at its lowest for decades, but the state needs to expand to deal with these complexities, prepare the necessary legislation, and expand its independent diplomatic service. The Secretary of State for Exiting the European Union (colloquially known as the Minister for Brexit), David Davis, has failed so far to mobilize resources from other Whitehall departments, each of which is setting up its own internal Brexit teams. This is likely to fragment pursuit of the Brexit project due to divergent departmental economic sponsorship interests and other commitments regarding Europe and the wider world.

It is also proving hard to recruit the treaty and trade experts needed to negotiate Brexit because trade negotiation was transferred to the EU. At the time of writing (August 2016), Whitehall has only 20 experienced trade negotiators compared with 600 in the European Commission. Other experts work for corporate consultancies and law firms, which can expect lucrative Brexit business on their own behalf. This could well reinforce the neoliberal imaginary—especially as the City of London is likely to seek special privileges to preserve the 'passporting' arrangements that enable firms registered in the UK to offer services throughout the European Economic Area. At least two devolved governments also have policies that conflict with those of central government. Scotland may hold another independence referendum and Northern Ireland, which shares a land border with the Irish Republic, may seek reunification. In short, the crisis of the state continues in the United Kingdom and this is compounded by the continuing crisis of multi-spatial metagovernance in Europe.

The representational crises that contribute to Britain's organic crisis have been exacerbated by the Brexit vote. This can be seen in the Conservative Party itself; the toxic split between the Blairite rump of the Parliamentary Labour Party and the wider party membership, which has several features of a social movement rather than a natural governing party; debates over the future of UKIP, which could reposition itself to capture northern working class votes, especially when it loses its place inside the European Parliament and wider European Union; and in elec-toral and other struggles between rival tendencies and parties in Scotland over its status in the UK and Europe.

The legitimacy crisis is also still present and could become worse if public opinion, spurred on by the pro-Brexit press, becomes dissatisfied with progress and suspects a deliberate policy of backsliding on the part of government. A different but related danger is that continued efforts to protect City interests, maintain the politics and policies of austerity, or, more generally, a slowing economy lead to reduced financial and political support for tackling uneven develop-ment, especially through the Northern Powerhouse and Midlands Engine. These rival regional imaginaries with their respective centres of economic gravity in Manchester and Birmingham are unlikely to attract sufficient funds without more intense industrial policy initiatives and increased budgets. Failure to deliver would be a further source of popular resentment. The legacy of a balkanized UK economy will also provide obstacles to take back control over the economic destiny and rebalance the conditions for sustainable recovery. In the increasingly unli-kely event of the adoption of the Transatlantic Trade and Investment Pact, it would become even clearer that sovereignty is disappearing.

Conclusions

The preceding remarks might seem to lend support to the approach to Brexit associated with Jeremy Corbyn, leader of the Labour Party during the referendum campaign, namely, 'remain and reform'. In general terms, not necessarily those of the remain currents in the Labour Party, this would have involved popular struggles to overcome the democratic deficit, to extend monetary union to a fiscal union, transfer union, and solidarity union that included the United Kingdom among its members, and a move beyond neoliberal strategies to a red–green approach to European and global problems. Such policies provide the ultimate horizon of action and valid and valuable aspirations for future mobilizations but they are not immediately feasible given the inherited structures within the United Kingdom, the European Union, and the broader transatlantic economic region linked to continued US political domination.

Brexit is so polyvalent a notion and so complex a process that its present meaning is hard to define and its future trajectory hard to discern. Over the next two to three years, we are likely to observe a process akin to a three-dimensional chess game with many participants and even more stakeholders playing according to uncertain rules open to contested renegotiation. While the pol-itical situation and political scene have clearly been changed by the Brexit referendum outcome, the political conjuncture is still shaped by the double helix formed by the inherited structural constraints and the organic crisis of the British state and society and analogous phenomena in the European Union. This remark does not justify defeatism, fatalism, or cynical opportunism over the next few years—although these reactions will certainly occur in some circles. It does call for a realistic conjunctural analysis oriented to moving from the search for tactical victories within a period where the left has long been on the strategic defensive in the face of a protean neoliberalism that, as Peck (2010) observed, tends to fail forward. This strategic reorientation requires shifting the balance of forces through popular mobilization combining social movements and party organization and conducted over different spatio-temporal horizons of action with a view to pursuing an offensive strategy for fundamental reform of the European Union and its place within a world society threatened by a triple crisis—economic, energy, and environmental—as well as the tensions and conflicts created by geopolitical rivalries and local oppression.

Acknowledgements

The author thanks Jamie Morgan for the invitation to contribute to this forum on Brexit and, with the usual and necessary disclaimers, for his excellent and well-informed comments on the first draft of this article. The influence of Antonio Gramsci and Nicos Poulantzas should also be evident to attentive readers.

Disclosure Statement

No potential conflict of interest was reported by the author.

Funding

This article was written while I was in receipt of Economic and Social Research Council funding in the context of the WISERD-Civil Society programme at Cardiff University [award: ES/L009099/1].

References

Bruff, I. (2013). The rise of authoritarian neoliberalism. *Rethinking Marxism, 26*, 113–129.
fosforos. (2016). Comment on *Naked Capitalism* website. Retrieved August 3, from http://www.nakedcapitalism.com/2016/08/brexit-realism-maybe-voters-were-not-dumb.html#comment-2647912
Gallas, A. (2015). *The Thatcherite offensive: A neo-Poulantzasian analysis*. Leiden: Brill.
Gramsci, A. (1971). *Selections from the prison notebooks*. London: Lawrence & Wishart.
Hall, S., Jefferson, T., Critcher, C., Clarke, J., & Roberts, B. (1978). *Policing the crisis: Mugging, the state and law and order*. London: Macmillan.
Independent Evaluation Office of the International Monetary Fund. (2016). *The IMF and the crises in Greece, Ireland, and Portugal*. Washington, DC: IMF.
International Monetary Fund. (2015). *Greece: Preliminary draft debt sustainability analysis* (IMF Country Report No. 15/165).
Jessop, B. (2015). Margaret Thatcher and Thatcherism: Dead but not buried. *British Politics, 10*, 16–30.
Jessop, B. (2016). The heartlands of neoliberalism and the rise of the austerity state. In S. Springer, K. Birch, & J. MacLeavy (Eds.), *The handbook of neoliberalism* (pp. 410–421). London: Routledge.
Jessop, B., Bonnett, K., Bromley, S., & Ling, T. (1988). *Thatcherism: A tale of two nations*. Cambridge: Polity.

Lavoie, M., & Stockhammer, E. (2013). Wage-led growth: Concept, theories and policies. In M. Lavoie & E. Stockhammer (Eds.), *Wage-led growth: An equitable strategy for economic recovery* (pp. 13–49). Basingstoke: Palgrave-Macmillan.

Marx, K. (1894/1967). *Capital, vol. 3: The process of capitalist production as a whole*. London: Lawrence & Wishart.

Oberndorfer, L. (2015). From new constitutionalism to authoritarian constitutionalism. In J. Jäger & E. Springler (Eds.), *Asymmetric crisis in Europe and possible futures* (pp. 184–205). London: Routledge.

Ostry, J. D., Loungani, P., & Furceri, D. (2016). Neoliberalism oversold? *Finance & Development, 53*(2), 38–41.

Overbeek, H. (1990). *Global capitalism and Britain's decline: The Thatcher decade in perspective*. London: Unwin & Hyman.

Peck, J. A. (2010). *Constructions of neoliberal reason*. New York, NY: Oxford University Press.

Rutter, J., & McRae, J. (2016). *Brexit: Organising Whitehall to deliver. Briefing paper*. London: Institute for Government.

Seymour, R. (2014). *Against austerity: How we can fix the crisis they made*. London: Pluto.

Stützle, I. (2013). *Austerität als politisches Projekt* [Austerity as a political project]. Münster: Westfälisches Dampfboot.

Sum, N.-L., & Jessop, B. (2013). *Cultural political economy: Putting culture in its place in political economy*. Cheltenham: Edward Elgar.

Varoufakis, Y. (2016). *IMF confesses it immolated Greece on behalf of the Eurogroup*. Retrieved July 7, from https://yanisvaroufakis.eu/2016/07/29/the-imf-confesses-it-immolated-greece-on-behalf-of-the-eurogroup/

Williams, Z. (2016). Think the north and the poor caused Brexit? Think again. *The Guardian*. Retrieved from https://www.theguardian.com/commentisfree/2016/aug/07/north-poor-brexit-myths

Brexit, Global Cities, and the Future of World Order

NOAH TOLY

ABSTRACT *The emergence and role of global cities provide a rubric by which we can understand Brexit and illuminate the present tensions between those who favor open economic policies and those who favor closed economic policies. Economic inequality, political disenfranchisement, and social exclusion at the regional level are now driving a fresh interrogation of the relatively open world order that requires global cities—sites densely populated with institutions necessary for orchestrating global economic activity. While questions about the legitimacy of economic openness may undermine the economic output, political power, and cultural influence of global cities, those same cities may, if they harness economic output for broader regional benefits, demonstrate the potential of an alternative and newly legitimate open world order.*

The Brexit Map

By now it is a familiar map of the United Kingdom—the one showing the geographic distribution of the June 2016 vote to 'Leave' or to 'Remain' in the European Union. Along with the majority in Scotland and a few mid-sized English cities, Londoners voted in large numbers to continue the UK's membership in the EU. Twenty-nine of the city's 33 boroughs voted to 'Remain'. All told, roughly 60% of the total London vote favored staying in the EU. Notwithstanding the votes of its most populous and urbanized areas, the UK, as a whole, voted narrowly to leave.

This relationship between London, one of the world's quintessential global cities, and the less densely populated, less wealthy parts of the UK, is one key to understanding Brexit. More broadly, the emergence and role of global cities, and specifically the fortunes of those cities and the misfortunes of their hinterlands, are an important lens for understanding both the post-Brexit landscape and the future of world order.

Whether or not Brexit foreshadows an even more dramatic turn in global political economy, it does suggest what some have described as 'the new political divide', the growing gap between those who favor open societies and those who favor closed societies (The New Political Divide, 2016). The emergence and role of global cities can illuminate this new division. An increasingly open economy has required global cities as platforms for orchestrating global commerce. Those cities have become the focus of economic activity, concentrating large numbers of 'winners' in the open economy and attaining new levels of political influence. At the same time, global cities are icons of inequity. The inequality between global cities and their regions—like that between London and the rest of England—threatens to undermine the political consensus surrounding open economies and global engagement, in favor of closed economies and isolationist disengagement. However, if cities can live up to their own claims of growing global political influence, they may be able to bridge this emerging divide. Specifically, bridging the gap between those who favor open economies and those who favor closed economies will require global cities to address regional economic disparities and to enfranchise and advance the interests of those beyond their borders. If they are up to this task, global cities may be the key to saving the open economy from itself.

Global Cities and Their Discontents

Over the past half-century, global cities, like London, have emerged as increasingly strategic sites and influential actors in global affairs. Global cities are not synonymous with large cities or multi-cultural cities. While many global cities are large and multi-cultural, some are not (see, for example, Zurich and Tokyo, respectively). Nor is 'global city' simply another term for a locale with a disproportionately externally oriented economy. Rather, global cities represent a novel form of urban settlement organized around meeting the need to orchestrate economic activities that span borders and continents. Global cities are an artefact of a neoliberal economic order, a necessity of an open global economic system.

For all their concentration of people and institutions, global cities are the paradoxical result of forces of diffusion. Technological advances—such as transportation and information technologies that allow people to be anywhere, either physically or virtually—coupled with increasingly permeable boundaries and open trade, have been surprising forces of urbanization. While these technologies and policies undergird the opportunity for global dispersal of people and goods, they simultaneously demand institutions and organizations that coordinate geographically dispersed, but still socially concentrated, capital. Where it was once the case that a Chicago-based firm might own and operate a factory in Chicago, it is now the case that a Chicago-based firm might just as well own and operate a factory in Chennai or Chengdu. Such global operations often require the support of advanced producer and financial services firms—global management consultants, accountants, import/export specialists, and the like. To take advantage of propinquity—the density of people and institutions in cities—firms that orchestrate global business activity have, over time, clustered in a select number of urban areas. These urban areas become hubs for efforts to coordinate global economic activity. As that activity becomes more global, these cities become more strategic (Sassen, 1991).

By concentrating powerful institutions, global cities have reached new heights of economic prosperity accompanied by bifurcated labor markets and rising local inequality. As Sassen (1991) points out, global cities are home to the 'global mobile', a class of global elites who steer and profit from global political economic changes, and the 'global immobile', who toil in obscurity, perhaps cleaning hotel rooms, offices, and airplanes for the jet-setting class, but are no less important to the day-to-day operations of the global economy. Global cities have what Abu-Lughod (1999) has described, writing of Chicago, as 'an elegant façade and a deeply shadowed backstage' (p. 100).[1]

At the same time, global cities are often both surrounded by and separated from economically distressed communities in their regions. Connected by telecommunication systems, transportation infrastructures and information technologies, and characterized by a certain division of labor—Hong Kong, London, New York, and Tokyo concentrate global financial institutions, while Shanghai and Chicago are leading centers for companies directing manufacturing—global cities have formed a global urban system that often eclipses national urban systems, disembedding them, to a certain extent, from their national context. While global cities follow idiosyncratic development paths—Paris and Seoul remain very different places despite their similar status in global affairs—their fates are often more intertwined with each other than they are with other cities in their home countries.

The regional inequalities that accompany this disembeddedness are often as stark as global cities' internal inequalities between elites and the dispossessed—and sometimes more hopeless. While global cities themselves concentrate both deprivation and opportunity, often in equal measure, their hinterlands often watch opportunities relocate to metropolitan hubs. As Florida (2005) has noted, the global economy is 'spiky', with a disproportionate amount of prosperity and opportunity concentrated in select metropolitan areas. Because of this dynamic, Chicago may advance, economically, while the Midwest as a whole lags (see Longworth, 2009). Beijing, Hong Kong, and Shanghai can prosper while rural China, still home to almost half the country's population, suffers. London may flourish while Leicester flags. While global cities *have* an elegant façade and a deeply shadowed backstage, they have in some ways *become* the elegant façades of their national contexts, accompanied by deeply shadowed regional backstages. This regional dynamic can lead to resentment of and alienation from global cities and the open global economic system that has fueled their rise.

Strangling the Golden Geese

Though the growth of global cities has sometimes come at the expense of adjacent regions, and though their sometimes languishing hinterlands may resent the increasing divide between regional haves and have-nots, global cities are still often assumed to be engines of regional economic prosperity and channels by which those regions connect to their new economic lifeblood, global consumers and supply chains. Nowhere has this relationship been more complicated than it has been in England, where benefits of global connectedness have accrued to the southeast while other parts of the country have languished. Yet, attenuating London's economic boom has often been seen as a surefire way to trigger the next phase of the cycle—an economic bust. As a center of steady economic productivity and conduit to the world economy, London has often been compared to the goose that laid the golden egg (Massey, 2007). It has simply been too valuable to kill.

Until June, when the majority of UK voters decided to strangle the goose.

Though London has been a magnet for global business, the majority of UK voters no longer believe that the benefits of global interconnection and regional openness actually make their way north of London or, even if some of those benefits do make their way north, they do not outweigh inequality or any of the perceived downsides that come with the free movement of people and goods. The Brexit movement mobilized distressed voters on the margins of the global economy. As Habmermas (2016) notes:

> This goes with the other finding that poorer, socially disadvantaged and less educated strata voted more often than not for Leave. So, not only contrary voting patterns in the country and in the cities but the geographical distribution of Leave votes, piling up in the Midlands and parts of Wales—including in the old industrial wastelands that have failed to regain their feet economically—these point to the social and economic reasons for Brexit.

One thing the 'Leave' voters realized: in an open global economy, in a world of global cities, like London, boom and bust are not only cycles, following one after the other, but adjacent places.

Among other things—and Brexit is clearly about *many* things, from nationalist sentiment, to cultural backlash, to political self-determination (see Inglehart & Norris, 2016)—Brexit is a vote of no-confidence in the very technological and political economic shifts that have propelled global cities from bit parts to leading roles in the drama of global politics. The Leave Campaign was a sustained interrogation of the legitimacy of an open economic order (see Darvas, 2016; Johnson, Jones, & Manley, 2016; Langella & Manning, 2016; Wren-Lewis, 2016).

What does this mean for London? On the one hand, the vote to Leave, the decision to swing the pendulum back toward a more closed economy, does not mean that London will somehow fall off the map. In one sense, London was a global city long before anyone knew the term, and borders and barriers are sometimes boons to urban development (Polese, 2011). For the immediate future, a number of initiatives—such as the effort to retain EU passporting and free movement of labor for the financial elite—seek to maintain London's status as a hub of European and global financial markets. On the other hand, Brexit would seem to herald London's greater embeddedness in the UK's own urban system, closer and more equal relationships with other English cities, and slightly diminished role in global affairs. In the long run, we might see ripple effects that further reshape the urban system of Europe. For example, Frankfurt and Paris are already positioning themselves as alternative sites for key financial institutions. Moreover, a possible Scottish vote for independence from the UK, in favor of continued membership in the EU, would likely further diminish London's role and propel Glasgow to new levels of significance in Great Britain and Europe. However, as long as Brexit is an outlier in an otherwise ongoing trend toward continued global connectivity, we should not expect dramatic changes in the fortunes of London or other global cities.

But what if Brexit is not a blip? What if our future holds more franken-words, portentous portmanteaux like Departugal, Italeave, Czechout? Haass (2016) has already suggested that several more countries are likely to leave the EU in the next five years. Some analysts consider that a conservative estimate.

If Brexit is the beginning of a trend toward more closed and modestly scaled economies, we will likely witness a winnowing of global cities. Absent an open global economy demanding the concentration of globally influential institutions that orchestrate business activity in far-flung corners of the world, some cities will lose their strategic importance in global affairs as they become increasingly re-embedded in their national systems. Liberal economic policies made global cities, and more restrictive policies will, to a certain extent, unmake some of them. More cities will matter—this will put pressure on once-proud and long-forgotten places as cities with decaying urban infrastructure regain population and clout—but fewer of them will be essential nodes in the global economy. We will see a leveling of the urban playing field within countries, but greater gaps between countries.

A movement toward greater regional equality by means of a more closed economy would come at least in part at the expense of global cities. In a sense, global cities have been the biggest mega development project of a globalizing economy, and curbing the economic forces that have led to their growth could leave the world dotted with the biggest white elephants in history—misfit cities bigger and more complex than closed national economies demand, better fits to the open global economy that drove their growth. For example, in a world of more restrictive trade and movement, Luanda is less likely to persist in its role connecting West Africa to the global economy, less likely to benefit from ties to other global cities, and less likely to continue its run as one of the most expensive cities in the world—West Africa's San Francisco or the Lusophone London—and more likely to develop closer connections with, affinities to, and resemblance of other Angloan cities.

Widespread withdrawal from global interconnectedness may lead to less 'spiky' national urban systems—with fewer and smaller differences between the prosperity of cities within a given country—but it will not reverse the multi-century trend of global urbanization. Some capabilities and characteristics of global cities are here to stay. Decades of free movement of goods and people have made global cities some of the most diverse places on the planet. Cities will still have to deal with the advantages and challenges that come with multiculturalism and political pluralism. While the global political economic system that has undergirded the growth of global cities is in some question right now, the technological infrastructure of telecommunications, transportation, and information that has built them is not going anywhere. Even in a more closed economy, technological infrastructure will support many of the opportunities and vulnerabilities of openness.

'A Politics of Place Beyond Place'

While global cities are shaped by forces beyond their control, they are not only passive artefacts of world order (Curtis, 2014, in press). While they once were merely results of an open world order constructed largely by nation states, global cities, along with other actors in that order, have cultivated capabilities and inherited influence in global governance—such that some now suggest cities are not only strategic sites, but are uniquely poised to take the lead in addressing the most pressing global challenges (see Barber, 2013; Bloomberg, 2015). If global cities are partly constitutive of world order and influential in it, and they may be poised to help bridge the gap between 'Open' and 'Closed' by stemming the tide of resentment that otherwise could, theoretically, lead to fundamental shifts in a political economic system that has undergirded their development.

To do so, they must assume an entirely new posture that rescales their interests and prioritizes the difference they can make beyond their municipal or metropolitan limits. For all the appearances of globalism, the rhetoric surrounding the emergence of global cities has shrouded a paradoxically localist posture, often favoring unhindered movement of people, goods, and services because that allows *those global cities* to concentrate wealth and amass influence. But to address the aggrieved, global cities must adopt what Massey (2007) has described as 'a politics of place beyond place', a politics that meets the needs of global cities but 'addresses head on the responsibilities of "powerful places"' (p. 15). This politics of place beyond place resonates with Lawrence Summers' (2016) recent call for a 'responsible nationalism' that acknowledges the obligations of a state to seek its citizens' economic well-being while circumscribing its ability to damage the interests of others.

Accepting this responsibility means developing strategies and platforms for global engagement that move beyond claims to cultural relevance, political influence, and economic importance to acknowledgments of responsibility to other places (Massey, 2007). Global cities must pursue their own interests without exacerbating inequality within, or undermining the economic well-being and political enfranchisement of, their regions. They must be capable of what we might describe as a 'benevolent devolution'. In response to Brexit, for example, London mayor Sadiq Khan has held a 'devolution summit' exploring possibilities for further devolution of authority to London—greater power over taxation, housing, immigration, planning, transportation, public health, and criminal justice policy. Khan has insisted that London is not seeking a 'bigger piece of the British pie', but is, instead, seeking to enhance the position of the whole UK economy. The future of global cities, and the future world order, depends upon the credibility of precisely this kind of claim. The devolution of authority must be used to bridge the gap between the haves and the have-nots of the open economy.

Cities Can Lead the Way

Given the present interrogation of and challenges to the legitimacy of the hitherto prevailing political economic pattern of global integration, global cities cannot count on structural forces alone to position them for influence in this ongoing debate. Present uncertainties put a premium on leadership. Contrary to assumptions that global cities simply emerge from the ether of global political economic changes, there is a legacy of city leadership positioning urban areas, sometimes well and sometimes poorly, for a role in global affairs. Some cities have failed in their bids to become global cities because of leadership shortcomings, and others have succeeded because of strong leadership. This leadership should be harnessed to reshape a still open and integrated, but more equal, global economy.

If they want to reshape openness and restore confidence in integration, global city leaders must develop strategies and platforms for global engagement that are rooted in a desire to drive regional prosperity. In other words, global cities should be centrifugal forces for flourishing, spinning out the benefits of economic interconnectedness and political influence to their regions. This might mean redirecting political attention and economic development resources away from, say, splashy mega events that draw attention to the city, and toward regional transportation and infrastructure initiatives that reflect and raise the stakes of less populous and wealthy areas in their hinterlands. It can cost as much as $50 billion to host the Olympics, an investment that returns chiefly ephemeral and highly localized benefits. That level of investment could furnish a region with between 900 and 2900 km of high-speed rail, a durable infrastructure the benefits of which accrue to an entire region (Ollivier, Sondhi, & Zhou, 2014).

While leaders who have become accustomed to cooperation with peers around the world will need to emphasize afresh cooperation with and accountability to other others in their regions, none of this means that mayors and others should abandon global collaborations and networks in favor of strictly local and regional interests. On the contrary, existing levels of economic interdependence dictate that the future of any given global city is not dependent only on their own region's or country's disposition toward an open or closed economy, but on the dispositions of those around the world. The relative openness of the global economy can only be sustained if a large number of nations and regions are behind it. Practically speaking, Chicago's status as a global city does not depend only on the dispositions of the Midwest and the United States, but on the dispositions of those around the world. If bridging the gap between 'open' and 'closed' economic visions is a worthwhile endeavor, then global city leaders should wield their hard-won national and global influence not to push back against calls to level the playing field, but to take the lead in that movement. So, global city leaders should commit to and collaborate on a systematic reduction of regional inequities, leveraging transnational municipal networks and clout with national governments in order to promote both interconnectedness and equality.

The importance of leadership assumes the contingent development of global cities and the global political economic order in which they endure. World order is not on auto-pilot. Indeed, it may be in a period of lurching change, the outcome of which will be determined by a handful influential institutions and individuals. If the Brexit vote proved anything—if the Leave and Remain campaigns shared any one assumption—it was that the economy has been shaped by, and can be reshaped by, people with real influence who know that there are, indeed, alternatives. If that is correct, then perhaps the leadership of global cities can also reshape global interconnectedness in a way that diminishes regional inequality and drives regional benefits. Whether they do or not will prove whether their leadership is merely technical—helping us to do the same old things more effectively and efficiently than before—or political—helping lead the way to a new, newly equitable, and newly legitimate, world order.

Disclosure Statement

No potential conflict of interest was reported by the author.

Note

1   While Abu-Lughod first uses this term with reference to the 1890s, her analysis suggests that this is an enduring characteristic of the city.

References

Abu-Lughod, J. (1999). *New York, Chicago, Los Angeles: America's global cities*. Minneapolis: University of Minnesota Press.

Barber, B. (2013). *If mayor's ruled the world: Dysfunctional nations, rising cities*. New Haven, CT: Yale University Press.

Bloomberg, M. (2015, September/October). City century: Why municipalities are the key to fighting climate change. *Foreign Affairs*. Retrieved from https://www.foreignaffairs.com/articles/2015-08-18/city-century

Curtis, S. (2014, September). Cities in a global order. *The World Financial Review*. Retrieved from http://www.worldfinancialreview.com/?p=2861

Curtis, S. (in press). *Global cities and global order*.

Darvas, Z. (2016, July 13). *Brexit vote boosts case for inclusive growth*. Retrieved from http://bruegel.org/2016/07/brexit-vote-boosts-case-for-inclusive-growth/

Florida, R. (2005, October). The world is spiky. *The Atlantic*, pp. 48–51.

Haass, R. (2016, June 24). Political losses from Brexit will be deep and enduring. *Financial Times*. Retrieved from http://www.ft.com/cms/s/0/63769fb6-3a03-11e6-a780-b48ed7b6126f.html#axzz4Ipw6xRzN

Habmermas, J. (2016, July 12). Core Europe to the rescue: A conversation with Jurgen Habermas about Brexit and the EU crisis. *Social Europe*. Retrieved from https://www.socialeurope.eu/2016/07/core-europe-to-the-rescue/

Inglehart, R. F., & Norris, P. (2016, July 25). *Trump, Brexit, and the rise of populism: Economic have-nots and cultural backlash*. Paper presented at the presidential plenary panel on legitimacy of political systems: System support from comparative perspective, 24th World Congress of the International Political Science Association, Poznan.

Johnson, R., Jones, K., & Manley, D. (2016, July 2). *Predicting the Brexit vote: Getting the geography right (more or less)*. Retrieved from http://blogs.lse.ac.uk/politicsandpolicy/the-brexit-vote-getting-the-geography-more-or-less-right/

Langella, M., & Manning, A. (2016, July 6). *Who voted Leave: The characteristics of individuals mattered, but so did those of local areas*. Retrieved from http://blogs.lse.ac.uk/politicsandpolicy/explaining-the-vote-for-brexit/

Longworth, R. C. (2009). *Caught in the middle: America's heartland in the age of globalism*. New York: Bloomsbury.

Massey, D. (2007). *World city*. London: Polity.

The New Political Divide. (2016, July 30). *The Economist*. Retrieved from http://www.economist.com/news/leaders/21702750-farewell-left-versus-right-contest-matters-now-open-against-closed-new

Ollivier, G. P., Sondhi, J., & Zhou, N. (2014). *High-speed railways in China: A look at construction costs, china transport topics, no. 9*. Washington, DC: World Bank Group.

Polese, M. (2011). *The wealth and poverty of regions: Why cities matter*. Chicago, IL: University of Chicago Press.

Sassen, S. (1991). *The global city: New York, London, Tokyo*. Princeton, NJ: Princeton University Press.

Summers, L. (2016, July 11). How to embrace nationalism responsibly. *Washington Post*. Retrieved from https://www.washingtonpost.com/opinions/global-opinions/how-to-embrace-nationalism-responsibly/2016/07/10/faf7a100-4507-11e6-8856-f26de2537a9d_story.html?utm_term=.cee97f4355c3

Wren-Lewis, S. (2016, August 8). *A divided nation*. Retrieved from https://mainlymacro.blogspot.com/2016/08/a-divided-nation.html

The Case for Utopia: History and the Possible Meanings of Brexit a Hundred Years On

JO GULDI

ABSTRACT *How likely are utopian futures of the kind that Jeremy Corbyn has recently envisioned for the future of post-Brexit Britain? Such utopian scheming to restore the welfare state at the cost of the state gibes with the forecast of austerity from the Chancellor's office, and pronouncements from canny observers that a post-EU Britain will need cash to support even its current programs, and therefore be forced to come to terms with the demands of banks and corporations. Corbyn's utopianism is ridiculous unless we take into account long-term forces like the rebellion against expert rule and advocacy of democratic accountability by participatory movements. A deeper history of state, democracy, and expert rule in Brexit can highlight the underlying tensions and point to some sources of possible outcomes.*

Introduction

We are not even two months on from Brexit, and Jeremy Corbyn has already announced a program that some would find brash, given the wavering courage of his party members. Indeed, he has now outlined a 10-point plan for restoring the NHS, building homes, and reducing income inequality. On its face, the chance of a return to the welfare state looks absurd. Such utopian scheming to restore the welfare state at the cost of the state gibes with the forecast of austerity from the Chancellor's office, and pronouncements from canny observers that a post-EU Britain will need cash to support even its current programs, and therefore be forced to come to terms with the demands of banks and corporations. As Lanchester (2016) quips, 'Nervous governments, desperate for revenue, are likely to bend even further backwards to give the City the policies it wants.' A great deal hangs in the balance between these two possible poles—the reestablishment of the welfare state and the further neoliberalisation of Britain.

The striking fact about any historical event worthy of inspection by historians is precisely that it creates a discontinuity where earlier rules of engagement do not apply. Much of what has been so fascinating to historians about recent events is precisely this discontinuation of the norms of politics—the vote itself; the subsequent silence and baffling disappearance of Boris Johnson; Cameron's abdication; the attempted coup in the Labour Party, followed by the locking-out of Labour Party members from Parliament by Corbyn. Together, they seem to signal the upheaval of political expectations, the kind of event that Robert Darnton spoke of, in reference to the episodes that led up to the French Revolution, as 'moments of suspended disbelief'.

Political topsy-turvies in Whitehall were not the only discontinuities around. There were also the surprises of the vote itself, demonstrated by the surprise and outrage vented by cosmopolitan intellectuals like Simon Schama and Zadie Smith in reaction to the vote. Referendums are common outside of Britain, but newer to British politics with its representational traditions and House of Lords that have historically functioned precisely to slow down popular disruptions of this kind. Such reversals of expectation as these are a clue that the normal stacking of actors and incentives is at risk of being reordered. When a moment of suspended disbelief happens, it generally suggests that longer-term forces are on the horizon.

Corbyn's utopianism is ridiculous unless we take into account long-term forces like the rebellion against expert rule and advocacy of democratic accountability by participatory movements. A deeper history of state, democracy, and expert rule in Brexit can highlight the underlying tensions and point to some sources of possible outcomes. This essay will survey the roots of Brexit in the 1970s, the roots of a deeper struggle between state-aided capitalism and democracy in the eighteenth century, and the seeds of possible models for that struggle's reconciliation in the history of twentieth-century Britain. These long-term historical forces determine the space in which utopian turns post-Brexit operate, and they may tell us a great deal about realistic utopian outcomes for Britain and the whole of Europe.

Brexit's Roots in the 1970s

Given the stagnation of working-class wages and failing opportunities for non-Londoners since the 1970s, Brexit has been assessed by both sociologist Will Davies (2016) and *Guardian* editor Gary Younge (2016) as the result of a 1970s turn towards neoliberalism that left the working class behind in a program of pit closures and denationalization. Princeton historian Harold James (2012) has underscored the way that the European Monetary System (EMS) grew out of proposals for an international money markets, replacing the state-issued currencies created by nation-states in the nineteenth century, but echoing proposals for an international currency as old as the 1867 World Monetary Conference and afterwards theorized by both Keynes and Hayek. This system promised to escape from national cycles of nations issuing currency to expand wages, only to be faced with inflation, which had recently wreaked havoc over Germany's finances. From 1977 onward, the EMS made available cheap credit, backed by European nations, to private banks. James's account suggests how this stability-focused monetary policy created a twenty-first-century economy that was unaccountable to the working-class individuals whose vote still mattered in national politics. The new system of a EMS created an issue of diminished national control.

The identity of the European Union is wrapped up in hopes for the peace of Europe. Importantly, it also stands for the rise of rule by financial experts and the discounting of class-based, representational politics in a nation's financial life. Effectively, the financial expertise that had once been beholden to local and national political considerations was now placed in the hands of an international body, where it was entrusted with the cause of creating monetary stability. It necessarily had to do this at the cost of accountability to the nations. Compounding this, national governments like Britain's were losing control (or simply divested themselves) of what levers they once had claimed for raising wages—for instance, through the nationalized industries disassembled under Thatcher, whose existence insured that the state was a player in bargaining between workers and employers. In short order, CEO pay ratcheted up and wages stagnated. Indeed, a landscape of ruins was left behind, detailed by leading architectural historians and cultural commenters; in place of factories and state housing: little manufacture, few jobs, but a growing number of prisons and detention centers for illegal immigrants.

Such an assessment is compelling, in part because it explains both the case of a reactionary electorate outside of London cut out of economic opportunity, and because it employs class consciousness to analyze the levers of history: in this version, the *lumpenproletariat* used their voting power on the Referendum to exact an uncertain 'revenge' upon the nation's ruling elite. The drama proposed here more or less parallels another narrative famous among historians, Marx (1852/1907) account of the drama of the dissatisfied petite bourgeoisie who rebelled against the nation in the 1851 French coup that made France a temporary despotism. The analysis in both cases is cunning, but in the case of Britain, we need more information. Understanding Brexit as the fruit of 1970s class resentment does not go far enough towards explaining what the possible fallout is.

Some political scientists have made a theoretical leap from class resentment to the cause of participation: Scottish political scientist Mark Blyth ('Mark Blyth', 2016) has argued that Brexit typifies a global moment of participatory rebellion against the structures of expert rule, and political historian Richard Tuck (2016a, 2016b) argues that the left must embrace Brexit if the EU's elite of economic arbiters is to be replaced by a participatory process. Commentators such as these contrast the idea of participatory democracy against the system of unelected appointment at the EU. In their reading, there is a historical and ongoing relationship between the EU and neoliberalism, and Brexit deserves to be understood as a rebellion against anti-participatory, expert-run, neoliberal regimes.

These materials are important for charting out the poles around national politics on an abstract level. But they risk leaving out the impediments to the goals they seek, the historical actors who stand against democracy. Accounts without a history of actors do little to orient us to the actual movements towards which voters and politicians might be organizing themselves. For that, we would need some combination of ideal political theory and histories of institutions and social movements.

In order to make sense of the possible directions that overall policies might turn, beyond the machinations of monetary policy, we need a longer history of the contestation between expert rule and participatory democracy—a dialectical understanding of the past that would put into perspective the notion of an underclass 'revenge' against the elite, what its origins and prospects are.

The Eighteenth-Century Roots of the Present Crisis

The history of this contestation has been studied carefully over the past three decades, probably motivated by historians' curiosity about the ultimate causes of the political tensions they saw around them. Much of that work, including my own (Guldi, 2012) has fixed upon characterizations of the role of expert power in government since the eighteenth century. Around that time, capitalists came to value professional knowledge about the economy of a kind possessed by only a few individuals, and their lobbying efforts succeeded in implanting a few of those expert individuals into the structures of power as permanent consultants in such a way that would be very difficult to reform later in the name of participatory democracy or transparency.

The eighteenth-century state was experimenting, by the 1780s, in forms of expert rule that would come to structure the later work of the state. In this model, experts employed by landlords became the advisors of the state, dispensing ideas about roads, coasts, bridges, and ports to develop, and coming to manage great portions of the state with relatively little oversight from above. The model of capitalism at stake was one dominated by large landholders, whose commercial interests were anchored to landed estates and their development. State funding of roads, bridges, and transportation helped to connect these large estates. In the model of state administration designed to service these estates, cadres of professional engineers and agrarian experts were established as bureaucrats working for the state. Their assigned task was essentially to make the economy more lucrative for the landlord; they had no accountability whatsoever to the electorate.

The model of landlord-managed development was not equally friendly to Britons of all classes. Indeed, it depended upon the eviction and clearance of large numbers of English, Scottish, and Irish peasants from the land, and their replacement, especially in eighteenth-century Scotland, by enormous sheep ranches, while landlords experimented with scientific agriculture marked by the importation of lime, clay, and marl to improve the soil.

Long-Term Contributions to Utopian Thinking

By the 1790s, British radicals paying attention to larger forces in the Atlantic World had come to propose a democratic alternative to this state–capitalism nexus, propounding first of all an expanded right to vote. In pamphlets and tracts, would-be reformers began to promote the cause of a democratic system of governance. Their vision was postponed in one political event after another: the Reform Act of 1832 enfranchised a sliver of the middle class, but not the masses; the Chartists and their petitions in the 1840s were shut down by anti-protestor violence; even after 1867, with the enfranchisement of the working masses, employer surveillance of the polls served to keep most working-class communities under the thumb of their employers.

In the twentieth century, new models for democratic participation appeared, many of them linked to the rethinking of expert rule and the bureaucracy itself. Patrick Geddes's many papers on urban planning contained a critique of the bureaucrat himself as well as the university-based book learning that formed a part of the professional economist's education (Stalley, 1972, p. 15). Through the 1960s, student and worker movements protested for greater inclusion of their agendas into politics, and British radicals like Colin Ward (Ward, Wilbert, & White, 2011) theorized what self-government on the local level might look like, drawing inspiration from worker-owned cooperatives and the self-built public housing schemes of Sweden.

A limited number of these ideas were ever actually put into effect. The Mass Observation movement of wartime Britain used mass participation, rather than expert bureaucracy, as a model of anti-spy surveillance. From the 1980s forward, Britons experimented with participatory mapping as a means of performing regional planning where everyone could participate. Their results were mostly limited and trivial.

Understanding the ongoing struggle between the expert-led state and the participatory one allows us to consider Brexit as another kind of flare-up: a showdown between the ideal of state and capitalism forged in the eighteenth century, and the ideas about a participatory democracy articulated in the early nineteenth century, fought for in the twentieth century, and left still incomplete at present.

Indeed, Brexit affords abundant opportunities to contemplate what a participatory economy, or a participatory EU, might look like. Consider the group 'Rethinking Economics,' an international union of economics students committed to a critical and participatory public discourse over economic policy. The group launched itself with a university roadshow in 2013, and subsequently launched a website, http://www.ecnmy.org/, dedicated to an open forum on economic policy. Around the time of Brexit, its members began to rail against 'econocracy' in the pages of the *Economist*. A movement to revise the bureaucratic structures of state rule for the twenty-first century is afoot. It stands to gain traction from Brexit to address the fundamental disequilibria— that is to say, the 200-year dialectic between expert rule and participation rather than merely the 30-year ejection of the working class from economic rewards.

Some utopians have been trying to respond to the gaping question of Britain's twentieth-century economy left in shambles by deindustrialization. While William Morris and John Ruskin dreamed of a craft-based economy as early in the 1860s, patronizing local lace-making activities and helping to turn the Lake District into a center for middle-class tourism, institutional answers to deindustrialization were also pioneered in Britain. From the 1920s forward, the Dartington Estate hosted experiments in organic agriculture were inspired by questions about locally sustainable economies. In the 1960s and 1970s, Britain became the source of the utopian visions of development followed E. F. Schumacher's 'small is beautiful' mantra of local economic development. In the 2000s, Britain saw the birth of the Transition Town movement for a sustainable adjustment of towns to locally based economies. In contrast to the grand vision of economic development with access to massive international credit characterized by the EU, these home-grown movements have long proposed a model for economic development that could be intentionally democratic and under local control.

There are international templates for utopia as well. The unfinished business of the twentieth century looms large in these conversations. We have experimented with international governance over 100 years (League of Nations, UN, Bretton Woods, NATO, EU, World Bank, WTO, etc.), but none of those experiments has been very democratic in nature. Richard Tuck (2016a, 2016b) has argued that the Left must regroup around demands that the EU become democratically accountable, a theme taken up by James Galbraith and Heikki Patomäki in this volume.

Since the 1930s, around the globe, student and worker movements have rallied for more democracy and more participation, experimenting with participatory budgeting, worker-built housing, etc., so there is a vast, unsatisfied hunger for more democratic models; then there is the much-maligned welfare state, bled dry by neoliberal reforms in the 1980s, centralized but not rebuilt in more recent decades; and finally, there are the questions about how well globalization will work. Some Brexit ads promised that the UK would reinvigorate the NHS; some conversations promised the return of good farm jobs; both underline the fantasy of a democratized UK reinvigorating the old welfare state in the service of the people, and indeed this is Corbyn's current vision.

A history of the structures of expert rule and the forces pressing for greater participation allows us to round up some of the possible materials for a utopian future: Britain could revisit 1945, and orchestrate a return to the welfare state, as inspired by the #rhodesmustfall/ #feesmustfall student movement with its calls for increased state provisions for academic participation. Britain could revisit 1815, sponsoring a new concert of Europe based in more carefully formulated (i.e. less Brussels-managed) responsibilities for member nations, driven by the rise of a new guard of British diplomats who will arise to manage the situation. Britain could revisit 2003, with Scottish independence and land reform as a model, increasing its commitment to the Transition Towns movement for economic devolution based in ecological sustainability.

There are darker futures too: consider the dystopian thriller *Children of Men* (Cuarón, 2007; James, 1993) with its concentration camps for migrant workers comes to mind (the seeds are already sown at Harmondsworth). A nationalist UK, especially one faced with economic hardship, might well start hunting migrant laborers and refugees, including ones who were legal under the EU, and questioning their right to NHS medics, Oxbridge places, or even British farm jobs. Whatever happens, it is unlikely that the future will be homogenous; some sample of dystopian and utopian strains is likely.

Conclusion: The Contribution of Long-Term Historical Analysis to Utopian Politics Today

In *The History Manifesto*, David Armitage and I argued (Guldi & Armitage, 2014) for the importance of doing counterfactual history of this kind that reckoned possible sources for the past against some of the possible sources of the future. We were not hoping to return to the counterfactual history of Harvard historian Niall Ferguson (1999) (which attempts to reconstruct the conference room and psychology of a handful of Etonians in order to better understand the contingency of a particular political decision—an effort at mind-reading that even most psychologists would hold too contingent to be useful); rather, we were imagining the kind of exercise demonstrated here, which can usefully be put to any moment in the present by examining the sources of the recent and long-term past that contributed to a particular political juncture, as well as the sources of the ancient and recent past that might provide happier and more miserable resolutions of the crisis.

History, in this mode, offers a tool for calculating the promise or failure of earlier generations of reform. It is a type of historical reasoning that we might trace back to J. S. Mill or Goldwin Smith's liberal anti-empire history theorizing about Ireland, slavery, and democracy in the colonies in the 1860s. Key to their thinking was the use of counterfactuals—how might this colony have evolved differently had it been given sovereignty earlier or had slavery been abolished?—as well as utopian reasoning, reckoning alternative futures that might have been played out *had* various political ideals been more in circulation at another time.

Indeed, one good reason to write and think more about the long history of utopian models (participatory democracy, land reform, transition towns, international governance, and democratic participation, for instance) is so that there will be clear models to follow for those seeking them. The interpretation of any particular event in the present is built out of the curation of a variety of events in the past according to a particular theory—anti-racist, imperial debt, or utopian. What happens after a discontinuity is nevertheless informed by the models of the past. In a vacuum of leadership like the one at present (Cameron's resignation, Corbyn's crisis, Johnson's blundering), new leaders will have to come up with positive ways forward.

Even as we innovate and dream, we inevitably recapitulate the work done by our forebears, whether we are radicals or experts. We all have only the available models of the past to work with. For this reason, historians' work can be instructive to anyone attempting to understand the present and the futures that may follow it. A synthesis of the past's work in the present is the nearest thing we have to a map of the future.

Disclosure Statement

No potential conflict of interest was reported by the author.

References

Cuarón, A. (2007). *Children of men* [Film]. Universal City, CA: Universal Pictures.

Davies, W. (2016, June 24). *Thoughts on the sociology of Brexit*. PERCblog. Political Economy Research Centre. Retrieved from http://www.perc.org.uk/project_posts/thoughts-on-the-sociology-of-brexit/

Ferguson, N. (1999). *Virtual history: Alternatives and counterfactuals*. New York, NY: Basic Books.

Guldi, J. (2012). *Roads to power: Britain invents the infrastructure state*. Cambridge, MA: Harvard University Press.

Guldi, J., & Armitage, D. (2014). *The history manifesto*. Cambridge: Cambridge University Press. Retrieved from http://historymanifesto.cambridge.org/

James, H. (2012). *Making the European Monetary Union*. Cambridge, MA: The Belknap Press of Harvard University Press.

James, P. D. (1993). *The children of men*. New York, NY: A.A. Knopf.

Lanchester, J. (2016, July 28). Brexit blues. *London Review of Books, 38*(15), 3–6. Retrieved from http://www.lrb.co.uk/v38/n15/john-lanchester/brexit-blues

"Mark Blyth discusses Brexit." (2016, June 20). Watson Institute, Brown University. Retrieved from http://watson.brown.edu/news/2016/mark-blyth-discusses-brexit

Marx, K. (1852/1907). *The eighteenth Brumaire of Louis Bonaparte*. Chicago, IL: Charles H. Kerr. Retrieved from http://archive.org/details/theeighteenthbru00marxuoft

Stalley, M. (Ed.). (1972). *Patrick Geddes: Spokesman for man and the environment*. New Brunswick, NJ: Rutgers University Press.

Tuck, R. (2016a, July 12). For the British left to succeed, the UK must leave the European Union. *Vox*. Retrieved from http://www.vox.com/2016/7/12/12159936/brexit-british-left

Tuck, R. (2016b). The left case for Brexit. *Dissent magazine*. Retrieved August 6, from https://www.dissentmagazine.org/online_articles/left-case-brexit

Ward, C., Wilbert, C., & White, D. F. (2011). *Autonomy, solidarity, possibility: The Colin Ward reader*. Oakland, CA: AK Press.

Younge, G. (2016, June 30). Brexit: A disaster decades in the making. *The Guardian*. Retrieved from http://www.theguardian.com/politics/2016/jun/30/brexit-disaster-decades-in-the-making

Between Eurotopia and Nationalism: A Third Way for the Future of the EU

PETER WAHL

ABSTRACT   *The Brexit has put the question of the final goal of integration on the agenda. The debate is characterised by a binary logic: either ever more deepening of integration or total disintegration with falling back into a system of nation states. While further integration is stopped by the heterogeneity of member states returning to the nation state is unrealistic, as European integration overlaps and is amalgamated with globalisation. There is a third way: flexibilisation through selective integration in certain areas and selective disintegration in others, based on variable coalitions of the willing.*

Introduction

For the first time in the history of the multiple EU crises, the Brexit raises for the broad public existential questions about the future of the EU. Former crises have always been seen as exceptional challenges, which can be kept under control in the given framework. And this framework was the continuous deepening of the integration process, the 'ever closer union' as stipulated in the preamble of the treaties. At the end this would lead to the political union, the *United States of Europe*. Crises were seen as obstacles on the way to this goal but the goal as such was not put in question. This is the essence of the 'European idea'. Although euro-scepticism both from the right and the left is on the rise, the followers of the European idea are still dominating among elites in many member countries, and in some key countries also among the people, for instance in Germany (PEW Research Centre, 2016).

But things might change now. The Brexit has another quality than the 2008 financial crash, the subsequent debt crisis of the Eurozone, economic stagnation, or the refugee problem. What makes the difference is the heavy blow for the self-confidence for the *European idea*. It is a tremendous narcissist hurt for all who believed that the EU would be the best of all possible worlds. Just like a husband who all of a sudden is abandoned by his wife, they could not imagine that a country could leave the EU. Now they see that the soft power, which they considered to be such an attractive asset, proved to be too weak for the UK. And now they realise that the British might not be the only ones, whose enthusiasm for the EU is rather limited.

Hence, in the statements of the top personnel in Brussels and in the capitals of the member states there is broad consensus that business as usual is impossible now. Basically, there are three options for a way out of the present situation, of course with sub-variants:

- the great leap forward, as it has been proposed for example by Martin Schulz, chair of the European parliament (Schulz, 2016) and supported by prominent personalities such as Jürgen Habermas (Habermas, 2016). They want to upgrade drastically supra-national governance, cover the democratic deficit, and establish an EU parliament with full-fledged rights;
- returning back to the system of the nation states from the nineteenth and the first half of the twentieth century, as advocated by right-wing and nationalist parties such as the French *Front National*;
- a type of cooperation, characterised by two principles: flexibilisation within and opening towards the outside world. This would mean selective integration in certain areas with variable participation and disintegration in certain others, and this also with variable participation. As a working title, we call it here 'differentiated integration'.

The option of muddling through can be considered as a sub-class of option 2, because it is an unstable mode of operating and will first lead to continuous erosion and earlier or later to explosive disruption.

Structural Barriers for Eurotopia

First of all the 'more Europe'-approach is unrealistic for the foreseeable future. All opinion polls confirm that even among the so-called pro-Europeans, many favour a moratorium in the integration process. Also important sectors of the elites in key countries such as France, Poland, and Italy do not want further transfers of sovereignty to Brussels. Donald Tusk, president of the EU Council, represents well this stream of thinking. Three weeks before the UK referendum he said:

> It is us who today are responsible for confronting reality with all kinds of utopias. A utopia of Europe without nation states, a utopia of Europe without conflicting interests and ambitions, a utopia of Europe imposing its own values on the external world. ... Obsessed with the idea of instant and total integration, we failed to notice that ordinary people, the citizens of Europe do not share our Euro-enthusiasm. ... The spectre of a break-up is haunting Europe and a vision of a federation doesn't seem to me like the best answer to it. (Tusk, 2016)

Tusk is right, for several reasons that I am outlining below.

The Nation State—No Phase-out Model

The first category of reasons has to do with the unbroken robustness of the nation state and of national identities. In spite of globalisation and European integration, the nation state remains the dominant form of organising society, both worldwide and in the EU—whether we like it or not. The Habermas assumption of the post-national constellation (Habermas, 1998), or

Hardt/Negri's concept of the Empire (see Hardt & Negri, 2001) proved to be theoretically exaggerated and empirically flawed. At the latest after the 2008 financial crash the nation state was the only actor which disposed of the financial, legal, and political instruments to cope at least in some degree with the challenges. The EU instead was marginalised in the crisis management. No wonder, its statehood is the peculiar mix between an alliance of nation states and supra-national components. This hybrid is structurally weak compared to nation states. Also major arrangements for stabilisation, such as the *European Stabilisation Facility*, were established outside the EU rules through intergovernmental agreements. The supra-national structures and procedures could not deliver what was needed to overcome the crisis.

Of course, the nation state is an ambiguous phenomenon. It creates a space of particular dense and intensive communication between its citizens, which leads to the establishment of a specific identity. This is normal, all human communities develop group specific identities. However, national identity can turn into nationalism and similar behaviours, such as xenophobia and racism—not automatically but under certain conditions.

Nationalism is not an essentialist category but an ideology, which is determined by other factors. Already in the nineteenth century, the German philosopher hit the point when he wrote: 'Every miserable fool who has nothing at all of which he can be proud adopts, as a last resource, pride in the nation to which he belongs' (Schopenhauer, 1861, pp. 342–343; German, transl. PW).

In other words, when people are marginalised and underprivileged, if respect and dignity is refused to them, if their social status is threatened, nationalism is one way to compensate for that, in particular, in the absence of an emancipatory alternative. Indeed, four decades of market fundamentalism, liberalisation, deregulation and privatisation have loosened social cohesion and created an ever-deeper social polarisation. The rich are getting richer, the middle class is frightened by social insecurity, while the poor are getting poorer and marginalised. The UK was since the Thatcher era a forerunner of these developments in the EU. In addition, the management of the 2008 financial crisis through austerity has further worsened the situation. Those who could not cope with the requirements of the new age take their revenge now, as we can see well in the social structure of the British referendum.

But here is also the key for a remedy: ending austerity and changing the economic paradigm towards social cohesion, public welfare, and solidarity would not solve all problems, but it would dry up at least by half the camp of the supporters of the Farages and LePens.

Too Much Heterogeneity

A second category of reasons, why supra-nationalism has not worked as expected, is the economic heterogeneity of the EU member states. In the name of solidarity the advocates of deeper integration suggest to bridge the gaps through transfers from the richer to the poorer countries, in particular under conditions of crises. However, the differences between the highly developed economies in Northern and Western Europe and the economies of the South and the East in economic and social terms are so wide, that only unrealistically high transfers could overcome them.

There are calculations according to which the richer countries would have to pay between 8% and 12% per annum of their GDP over at least a decade in order to bridge the gap (Artus, 2012; Sapir, 2012). In such a 'transfer union' the German share would be between 272 bn. and 408 bn. Euro. The concept of *solidarity* is a noble ideal. But when it comes to the real figures, no German, Dutch, or Finnish government would survive more than three weeks, if it would agree to such a solution.

Neo-liberal Constitutionalism Is Dividing the EU

In addition, the socio-economic heterogeneity of the EU is deepened by the basic rules of the Union. The centrepieces of integration are market integration and competition. Unlike social or environmental issues they are governed by hard law and can be enforced by the *European Court of Justice*. Critiques call this *neoliberal constitutionalism* (see Gill, 2002). As abundant experience shows, market competition leads to inequality if there is no corrective mechanism through political intervention. So, the rules by themselves constitute a barrier to harmonisation and real integration.

A strategy to overcome this problem would have to change the economic paradigm. But this requires a change of the treaties. Changing the treaties, in return, requires unanimity among all member states—in other words, another utopian project. Of course, an alternative would be that a major country—let us say Italy, France, or Germany—or a coalition of countries are simply ignoring the treaties, breaking the rules, or even threatening to leave the EU. The French *Parti de Gauche* (Left party) has proposed such an approach. Jean-Luc Mélenchon, the candidate for the left in the French presidential campaign, has launched the slogan: *The European Union, we change it, or we leave it!* (*L'Union européenne, on la change ou on la quitte!* (Mélenchon, 2016)).

Unanswered Questions of Supra-national Democracy

Finally, there is the democratic deficit of the EU, which has been described very often (Wahl, 2013, pp. 17–19). Even Euro-enthusiasts such as Schulz admit that there is a big problem, when he suggests 'to transform the European Commission into a real European government, a government which is liable to the control of the European Parliament and a second chamber representing the member states' (Schulz, 2016).

But, how to process such a proposal? There is no European public, no communication between EU citizens, which would be comparable to the public that exists at national level. However, such a communication would be the precondition for a functioning democracy. Only a community whose members are communicating with each other over common issues can constitute the 'demos', the sovereign of democracy.

Furthermore, the nation state and modern democracy are genetically and structurally amalgamated. The territorial principle and its borders are the precondition for the constitution of citizenship. But there is no equivalent for democracy at international or transnational democracy by now. All examples, from the UN, over the IMF to the EU show substantial democratic deficits and unresolved problems compared to democracy in nation states. As long as there are no answers to these questions, deepening integration is only possible without and against the citizens.

The Nationalist Illusion

The rising right-wing movements and parties promise that a return to the system of European nation states as it existed in the nineteenth and the first half of the twentieth century would bring the solution. To begin with, such a reversion is no longer possible. The economic, juridical, communications, cultural, and other interrelations have become so dense and intensive, that even Marine LePen would quickly come up against their limits if she tried to test them. Would she kick out the Mercedes plant in Lorraine, where some 1000 workers are producing the

SMART? What about the network of Deutsche Bank subsidies all over France? And what should happen to the Airbus Corporation, which is a French–German–British–Spanish joint venture?

Either there is a negotiated exit, then compromises would be required. Or it is a disruptive and confrontative separation, which would have such destabilising effects on the country, that LePen would rapidly lose the support of her electorate. Indeed a frequently voiced and cogent criticism of right-wing parties is that they would not make good on their promises if put to the test. Apart from the already-mentioned economic and political costs of an exit, there are two main reasons for that.

First, they all stick, although with nuances, to the neo-liberal paradigm. Hence, their economic receipts would not solve the social problems, which are behind popular dissatisfaction and protest. Second, a fundamentally new component has come into play, which was not present in the first decades of European integration: globalisation. Although this process is not the end of the nation state, as already mentioned above, it has affected the nation states and changed the relations between them. Since quite some problems today have taken on a transnational character, cooperation across borders has become imperative, even if the world's political power hierarchy makes the pressure to cooperate look different for Burkina Faso than it does for the US, and different for Switzerland than for China.

This means that integration within the EU overlaps and is modified and amalgamated by a similar but more embracing process. This has become a reality in many spheres. Accordingly German exports are increasingly shifting towards non-European markets. The financial industry of the EU has already since years expanded its terrain of activities to global markets, as the EU is not enough for them. And of course the Internet establishes a global interconnectedness, which cannot be restricted nor to national borders neither to a continent. It is not possible any more to disconnect from globalisation and the attempt to return back to the old style of nation state is doomed to fail.

The Third Way

If the 'ever closer union' is a utopia and the return to the system of the nation state an illusion there is nevertheless a third option: *differentiated integration*, based on the respect for diversity and plurality and the interest in international cooperation. For the internal development of the EU this would be a mix of selective integration and disintegration (Nölke, 2013, p. 7), organised along principles such as decentralisation, regionalisation, and subsidiarity. Of course, it would have to be a managed process.

Towards the outside world it would mean more openness, particularly to neighbouring regions such as Northern Africa, Middle East, Balkans and Russia and the Eurasian Economic Union. It could also include the transatlantic area, under the condition that it becomes not part of a new geo-political bloc, a kind of economic NATO.

Participation of member states would be based on the idea of variable geometry, that is, coalitions of the willing. To give an example: those who want to cooperate for ambitious targets in CO_2 reduction can do this, even if not all 27 member states participate. Vice versa can those who stick to their nuclear or coal-fired power plants do this without blocking the others. Unity at any price at the lowest common denominator, which leads too often to paralysis, would end.

The same procedure could be applied in all other areas such as refugee politics or the economy. If a country opts for austerity, it can do this for itself. But austerity cannot be imposed anymore to others, as it happened to Greece and others. If a country prefers a Keynesian approach to economy, let it do it. In that case the currency system would have to be adapted, too. Under the straight-jacket of the Euro regime such a flexibility would be impossible. So, if a country or a group of countries wants to leave the Euro, it can do it—in a managed way and concerted with the others who want to remain.

Of course, *differentiated integration* would not put an end to the dispute between the major political orientations and economic paradigms. But the decision is transferred inside the respective member states and hence within the established rules and institutions of democracy. Decisions thus get democratic legitimacy and avoid the unresolved problems of supra-national democracy. It would not be possible any more to impose decisions from democratically not legitimised gatherings, such as for instance the Euro-Group, the Troïka, etc.

Differentiated integration would also break with the path-dependency of neo-liberal constitutionalism. Essentially it would mean a reduction of the supranational components and their replacement by quasi-intergovernmental agreements. The agreements could be facilitated by common institutions, which means that the Brussels institutions could continue to exist but with a focus on servicing and supporting the member states. Of course, it is reducing the supra-national component of the EU. In particular the power of the ECB and the European Court of Justice would shrink.

Differentiated integration is less exotic, than it seems at first glance, because there exist already several cases where it happens de facto. The split of the EU-28 into the Euro zone and the non-Euro zone is an example, as well as the Schengen agreement. Not to talk about the informal differentiations between, centre and periphery, rich states north of the Alps and the crisis countries in the South, debtors and creditors, NATO members and non-NATO members, etc. Also the cooperation of Poland, the Czech Republic, Slovakia, and Hungary in the *Višegrad Group* is such a case. Recently it worked successfully in refusing the refugee policies as suggested by Germany and the EU Commission. One might dislike the content of their decision of the Group as nationalist and xenophobic, but trying to impose another attitude through supra-national pressure does not work—and if it would work it would probably be counterproductive.

Furthermore, already now the regulations of the EU foresee a procedure, which contains in embryonic form the idea of differentiated integration: the *Enhanced Cooperation Procedure* (*ECP*). Already now a group of at least nine countries, representing 60% of the EU population and 75% of votes in the Council, can establish projects without the others. At present, the financial transaction tax is negotiated in such a coalition of 10 willing member states. The rules of the ECP are still too restrictive and rigid, but the concept goes into the right direction and can be further developed.

Will *differentiated integration* not lead to a total disruption at the end? I do not think so, because the existing links, in particular in the economy and the respective interests are so strong, that cutting them would lead to economic suicide. Furthermore, neighbouring countries have common interests per se: in trade, in infrastructure, movement of people, etc. Of course, much would also depend from an appropriate set up of the remaining institutions. If they succeed to really serve as a facilitator in the new framework and prove to be beneficial for all, such a type of European Union would find more acceptance than the present model.

Of course, *differentiated integration* means to say farewell to the *ever closer union*, to the sacralisation of the EU and the nostalgia for a European super-power. But this is in any case preferable to an uncontrolled process of erosion or even confrontative disruption.

Disclosure Statement

No potential conflict of interest was reported by the author.

References

Artus, P. (2012). *La solidarité avec les autres pays de la zone euro est-elle incompatible avec la stratégie fondamentale de l'Allemagne : rester compétitive au niveau mondialLa réponse est oui.* Paris: NATIXIS, Flash-Économie, n°508, 17 juillet 2012. Retrieved from http://cib.natixis.com/flushdoc.aspx?id=65118

Gill, S. (2002). *Power and resistance in the new world order.* Basingstoke: Palgrave MacMillan.

Habermas, J. (1998). *Die postnationale Konstellation - Politische Essays.* Frankfurt/M: Suhrkamp.

Habermas, J. (2016). Die Spieler treten ab. Interview in: Die Zeit, n°29, 07.07.2016. Retrieved from http://www.zeit.de/2016/29/eu-krise-brexit-juergen-habermas-kerneuropa-kritik

Hardt, M. N., & Negri, A. (2001). *Empire.* Cambridge, MA: Harvard University Press.

Mélenchon, J.-L. (2016). Du Brexit et de Madrid, perplexe mais motivé. L'ère du Peuple. Le Blog de Jean-Luc Mélenchon. Retrieved from http://melenchon.fr/2016/06/28/du-Brexit-et-de-madrid-perplexe-mais-motive/

Nölke, A. (2013). Dampf ablassen! Plädoyer für einen selektiven Rückbau der europäischen Wirtschaftsintegration. *JPG-Journal 12.12.2013.* Retrieved from http://www.ipg-journal.de/schwerpunkt-des-monats/die-zukunft-der-europaeischen-union/artikel/detail/dampf-ablassen/.

Pew Research Center. (2016). Euroskepticism beyond Brexit. Significant opposition in key European countries to an ever closer EU JUNE 7, 2016. Retrieved from http://www.pewglobal.org/2016/06/07/methodology-23/

Sapir, J. (2012). Le coût du fédéralisme dans la zone Euro. RussEurope. Blog de Jacques Sapir sur la Russie et l'Europe. Retrieved from http://russeurope.hypotheses.org/453

Schopenhauer, A. (1861). *Parerga und Paralipomena, Kleine Philosophische Schriften.* Berlin: Hahn.

Schulz, M. (2016). Mit Herzblut und Leidenschaft. Essay in Frankfurter Allgemeine Zeitung. 11-07-2016. Retrieved from http://www.faz.net/aktuell/politik/die-gegenwart/zerfaellt-europa-11-mit-herzblut-und-leidenschaft-14322032.html?printPagedArticle=true&hash;pageIndex_2

Tusk, D. (2016). Speech by President Donald Tusk at the event marking the 40th anniversary of European People Party (EPP). 30.05.2016. Retrieved from http://www.consilium.europa.eu/en/press/press-releases/2016/05/30-pec-speech-epp/?utm_source=dsms-auto&utm_medium=email&utm_campaign=Speech+by+President+Donald+Tusk+at+the+event+marking+the+40th+anniversary+of+European+People+Party+%28EPP%29

Wahl, P. (2013). Welche Zukunft hat die EU? In T. Sauer & P. Wahl (Eds.), *Welche Zukunft hat die EU. Eine Kontroverse* (pp. 17–19). Hamburg: VSA.

Europe and the World after Brexit

JAMES GALBRAITH

ABSTRACT *The aftermath of Brexit has been contrary to prediction and even to the fears widely voiced on the morning the vote came in. What will happen next depends first on British politics, second on EU law, third on the rapidly evolving geometry of Europe, and finally, on the actions of external powers. The prospect is not good; reform through democratization of the European project remains one frail hope for a better outcome.*

In the immediate morning-after of the Brexit vote, the wide expectation was for economic chaos, a government of Leavers in Britain and a quick filing of Article 50, encouraged by the French, leading inexorably to Britain's exit from the EU under harsh conditions and to Scotland's exit from the UK.

Instead, David Cameron is gone, along with George Osborne and his never-ending politics of austerity, the moderate Remainer Theresa May is Prime Minister, Boris Johnson has been muzzled and kicked upstairs, interest rates have been cut and inequality is now a Tory issue, more or less. Nigel Farage has disappeared. The main economic consequence was a drop in Sterling, good for the FTSE and potentially for the trade balance. Following a deft meeting in Edinburgh, Nicola Sturgeon rides high, but Scotland has not called a second referendum. And the Article 50 filing has been deferred at least into next year. The future would appear to hinge on rabbits not yet pulled from hats. Prediction, in short, is dangerous.

On the assumption, though, that someday Article 50 will be filed, what will happen? A few facts appear clear from EU law and policy.

First, London-based international banks will have to move some operations to EU territory, as passporting is conditional on free movement of persons, which Brexit would end. Paris will gain, also likely to some degree, English-speaking Dublin. This will be bad for London and the pound, but again good for exports, industry, middle-class jobs, and stocks.

Second, British universities and scientific institutes enjoy a large share of present EU research funding, because researchers from all over the EU move to the UK to take advantage of facilities, colleagues, and the research climate. They also enjoy Erasmus funding for the same reason. They will be hit hard. This will be a loss to all Europe since there is no other EU country with comparable excellence in higher education and research. The principal gainer will be the United States.

Third, EU law contains no provision limiting departure of refugees from EU territory. Therefore, the present burden-sharing arrangements which are keeping people blocked up at Calais will no longer apply. Refugees on French or Belgian soil will be free to hire small boats for the Channel crossing, just as they presently do to get from Anatolia to Lesbos. Presumably, the market will provide.

Inside Britain, the arrival of a moderately non-austerity Tory government will either collapse Labour altogether or force it to seek a restored base among the Labour Leavers, now adrift. This will be difficult: a question of pitting a highly progressive economic program against the ethno-nationalist impulse behind the Leave vote. It may be the case that with the effective dissolution of UKIP (United Kingdom Independence Party)—its mission accomplished—English politics will now lose its ethno-nationalist organizing force, making Corbyn's task easier—on the now-credible assumption that he survives as Labour's leader.

Inside Europe, the big gainer in relative stature is Italy, as was immediately apparent in the wake of the vote. This is interesting because of all the crisis countries, Italy has done the most, if quietly and so far without great effect, to bend the fiscal rules to try to stanch the ongoing decline of its economy. More will come along these lines as the pressure from Five-Star grows. Portugal and Spain remain outside the austerity choke-hold that applies to Greece; Spain because the survival of the PP (Popular Party/Partido Popular) government is at stake and Portugal because one can hardly apply rigidly to Portugal measures from which one is conspicuously exempting Spain. So, for the moment in Southern Europe and except in demoralized Greece, strict austerity is in slight abeyance and a fragile peace prevails.

France is a different story. There, a state of emergency was recently extended. Thanks to the terrifying events in Paris, Nice, and also in nearby Brussels, the Right is in firm ascendance, whether or not the National Front can win the next election. Civil society knows the score and is fighting to preserve what it has won over the decades since the Popular Front. But there is no coherent political leadership on the Left, so the fate of France will depend on what the Right does with power. Perhaps it will blow up the EU. Perhaps it will blow up the welfare state. Perhaps it will not do either of those things, but merely blow up the refugees, the immigrants, and the Muslims. France is a smoldering volcano, an eruption is likely but the date, direction, and force cannot be predicted.

Enough. My crystal ball, such as it is, does not extend to Germany. Except to note that the pillar of European federalism and ordo-liberal enforcement, the Finance Minister Wolfgang Schäuble, is old. It seems unlikely that he will be around long enough to see the troika installed in Paris, as he told Yanis Varoufakis he was determined to do. He too sits on a volcano, and when it erupts, he will be gone. Who and what will follow, light or darkness, one cannot say.

The hope for Europe lies in a small movement just underway: the Democracy in Europe Movement 2025 (DiEM25),[1] an effort to construct a pan-European democratic and social-democratic alliance, building first robust institutions of popular democracy at the European level and then moving on to restore the European economy as a single, integrated, stable, and prosperous unit. Prospects for success are remote, but the consequences of failure make the effort worthwhile.

The substantive program for European economic stabilization and progress could follow the lines set forth in The Modest Proposal (Varoufakis, Holland, & Galbraith, 2013), which set out four major elements: a restructuring of crisis-country debts through the European Central Bank, case-by-case resolution of failed banks at the European level, an investment program through the European Investment Bank and European Investment Fund, and a program of direct assistance to the most vulnerable households for nutrition, unemployment insurance, and other critical purposes, funded by the Target2 surpluses. These measures would not require immediate changes in any European treaty or charter, and they could buy the time necessary to build consensus and effect changes that are more far-reaching still. There are many competing proposals and the evolution of events since 2013 needs to be taken into account.

Can the Euro survive? Clearly, under present policies, it will not survive indefinitely. Barring successful change of ideas and policy at the Eurozone level, Stiglitz (2016) argues that the best solution would be for Germany to exit and for the new Deutsche Mark to rise—a solution that places its faith in the ability of exchange rate appreciation in Germany to cure that country's now-chronic trade surplus. An alternative, favored by Skidelsky (2016), would be to rebuild the Eurosystem on Bretton Woods lines, with a core Euro held in the North, national currencies in the weaker economies, and the adjustments managed in part by the European Central Bank, playing the original role of the International Monetary Fund.

If a coherent democratic and progressive reform of Europe cannot be had, Europe's larger role in the world can only fade away. That will leave the geopolitical space to the resource-rich global and regional powers: the United States, Russia, China, and in the Middle East, Iran. While Europe thrashes and squabbles, they will reorganize the world, as indeed, they are presently doing, with a politics of pipelines, development banks, and naval patrols.

Dangers abound, with provocation and response in Ukraine, the horrific war in Syria alongside chaos in Libya and Yemen, the unresolved conflicts in Iraq and Afghanistan, the refugees flowing from the above, the failed coup in Turkey and now its possible realignment, and the dangerous although (so far) *opera bouffe* confrontation over sandbars in the South China Sea.

In these matters, all depends on what the United States, Russia, China, and Iran decide to do. Europe could play a role in tempering potential conflicts, especially between the United States and Russia. But the more divided, undemocratic and preoccupied with its internal failures Europe is, the more likely it will be a pawn rather than a player in the interactions of the large external states.

And if the project of sustaining peace between the outside powers cannot be made to work, at least one of the frontiers is on the borders of Europe, and there will be hell to pay.

Disclosure Statement

The author is a member of the Democracy in Europe Movement.

Note

1   See DiEM25's website at https://diem25.org/.

References

Skidelsky, R. (2016, April 15). *A British bridge for a divided Europe*. Project Syndicate. Retrieved from https://www. project-syndicate.org/commentary/british-bridge-for-divided-europe-by-robert-skidelsky-2016-04

Stiglitz, J. (2016). *The euro: How a common currency threatens the future of Europe*. New York, NY: Norton.

Varoufakis, Y., Holland, S., & Galbraith, J. (2013). *A modest proposal for resolving the Eurozone crisis—version 4.0*. Retrieved from https://yanisvaroufakis.eu/euro-crisis/modest-proposal/

Will the EU Disintegrate? What Does the Likely Possibility of Disintegration Tell About the Future of the World?

HEIKKI PATOMÄKI

ABSTRACT   *Is it true that either the EU will be democratised or it will disintegrate? I concur that the current policies, principles, and institutions of the EU both generate counterproductive politico-economic effects and suffer from problems of legitimation. These effects and problems, which are not confined to Europe, give rise to tendencies towards disintegration. My second point concerns the timing of the required learning and reforms. Modest policy proposals and tentative steps within the existing EU Treaty framework may be too little too late. The question is whether there is enough time for deeper transformations in Europe—and also globally.*

Introduction

Brexit provides an opportunity to consider the context and possible futures of the European project. The slogan of Democracy in Europe Movement 2025 (DiEM25), 'The EU will either be democratised or it will disintegrate!', associated with Yanis Varoufakis, was written more than half a year before the British referendum of 23 June 2016. It was written following the Greek debacle of summer 2015, but may seem even more relevant now (cf. Varoufakis, 2016).

In the DiEM25 Manifesto, read widely in the first half of 2016, the idea of there being only two main alternatives is explicated further: 'If we fail to democratise Europe within, at most, a decade [. . .], then the EU will crumble under its hubris, it will splinter.' In its current form the EU has alienated Europeans and is stirring up 'a dangerous anti-European backlash'. What is more, Europe seems to be returning to its barbarous past. 'Proud peoples are being turned against each other. Nationalism, extremism and racism are being re-awakened.'[1]

The UK Leave-campaign stressed the problems of EU democracy by proclaiming that 'we are going take back control of our sovereignty'. But the result of the UK referendum seems to confirm that the discontent among lower classes, peripheries, and at the margins of society has been channelled into a politics of othering and scapegoating. The Leave-campaign did not involve any plan for improving democracy. Rather its main narrative was that 'others' should not make decisions for 'us'.

In what follows I interrogate DiEM25 claims about potential for further disintegration by scrutinising their explanatory grounds. I concur that the current policies, principles, and institutions of the EU suffer from problems of legitimation and tend to have counterproductive politico-economic effects. A problem is, however, that the prevailing theories provide a framework that effectively preclude alternative interpretations and thus make learning difficult. Moreover, the dynamics of ethico-political positioning are ambiguous and complex. The second problem is that modest policy proposals and tentative steps towards democratisation of the EU may be too little too late. I conclude by outlining some of the wider implications of possible disintegrative developments in Europe. What is the true lesson of Brexit and similar developments in Europe—and elsewhere?

What Grounds Our Expectations about the Future of the EU?

Deep-seated theoretical assumptions and general models of thinking about politics and economics shape our anticipations about the future. Crucial to the EU's future are economic theories and theories of legitimation, the latter meaning moral, legal, and political acceptability (see Patomäki, 2013, pp. 108–114). Economic theories can be divided into two main groups: (i) variations of liberal economic theories, which usually rest on microeconomic models of optimal equilibrium and on hypotheses of efficient markets, and in part rely on new-classical macroeconomic doctrines; (ii) post-Keynesian (and more generally heterodox) theories, according to which the capitalist market economy is in many ways unstable, including in such ways that processes of uneven growth and growing inequalities tend to be self-reinforcing (see Table 1).

Theories of legitimation can be roughly separated into two groups. On one side are those according to which capitalist free markets and the resulting affluence suffice to ensure political legitimacy, provided liberal human rights (including property rights) are guaranteed and political leaders can be periodically chosen and changed in elections. This theory is often associated with Joseph Schumpeter. On the other side are more demanding theories of legitimation according to which the acceptability of political rule requires good and generalisable ethico-political ends that are significant to us and really mean something to our lives, such as generalisable human development, social justice, and citizens' active participation in democratic practices

Table 1. Prognoses for the EU.

	Legitimation theory: Schumpeter	Legitimation theory: Habermas
(Neo- or ordo)liberal economic theory	A. The EU basic treaties are firmly founded, the EMU is legitimate and functional.	B. The EMU may work, but EU's legitimacy is weak and unstable.
Post-Keynesian/ heterodox economic theory	C. The EU basic treaties are unstably founded. The EMU strangles Europe economically, and is prone to crises.	D. The current EU basic treaties are unjustified, and the likely economic crises will eventually destroy its legitimacy.

and processes. One important contributor to this line of thinking has been the German philosopher and social theorist Jürgen Habermas.

The whole EU, and particularly the Economic and Monetary Union (EMU), has been built on interpretation A. Interpretation B is critical of the EU basic treaties and of the EMU, but it is agnostic on economic theory. From this perspective, the legitimation of the EU lies on shaky foundations because of 'democratic deficit', lack of identity, and proper citizenship. Further, from the standpoint of interpretation C, the future of the EU looks uncertain and dubious. However, according to this view the reason is not problems of legitimation but the harmful economic effects of the EMU. Interpretation D combines the two critical viewpoints as outlooks for the EU. Economic troubles resonating with problems of legitimation are likely to result in a full-scale legitimation crisis.

None of these perspectives is categorically false. The euro seemed to work well for the first six years. The available evidence indicates that citizens' trust in the EU institutions tends to correlate with economic performance, perhaps implying interpretation A. Yet the early and brief success of the euro was ambiguous, as it was built on imbalances sustained by debt in a financialised world. Since the global financial crisis of 2008–2009 and the subsequent euro crisis, the appeal of the EU has declined both inside and outside the EU.

The fact that the proposed new EU constitutional treaty was rejected in the 2005 referendums in France and Netherlands speaks in favour of interpretation B. Throughout the early years of the euro, the EU was constantly under criticism (as it was in the 1990s), despite the fact that the economy appeared to be growing quite briskly in many countries. This makes it understandable why the official objective of the Lisbon negotiations was not only to strengthen the EU's identity and decision-making, but also to reduce its 'democratic deficit'. The small steps taken in the Lisbon treaty, however, did not remedy the situation (see Patomäki, 2014).

The crises of 2008–2009 and 2010– accord with post-Keynesian economic anticipations in interpretation C. And yet, the EU's official responses have so far remained broadly within the range of interpretation A. From studies in cognitive science, we know that causal and counterfactual reasoning about major historical events is largely theory-driven (i.e. it is predictable from our abstract preconceptions; Tetlock 1999). Also the liberal doctrine of efficient free markets and sound money comprises a circular chain of reasoning that is used to impose discipline on states and their policy-making. Within the reasoning, the doctrine itself cannot be at fault; the problem is always that it has not been properly implemented. Ad hoc explanations make it possible to continue with the same basic framing of problems. For instance, particular actors may be blamed for the problems, such as the 'lazy and corrupt Greeks'. The logic of the circular system is such that it tends to further sustain the orthodoxy as it is, rather than revising it, or even replacing it, in light of the unintended consequences of its implementation.

What makes this partly understandable is that in open systems with complex processes of causation, it is next to impossible to create decisive tests for theories. This applies to all theories, including those of Table 1. Plausibly, Varoufakis (2016, pp. 226–227) relies on interpretation D in making his prognosis about the future of the Union. He states that the on-going moves towards a political union and 'more Europe'[2] constitute a 'never-ending loop of frightful reinforcement, authoritarianism and economic malaise'. This 'will complete the business of delegitimizing Europe'. While actual legitimation is contingent on many events and processes, crucially it depends on the turns of the economy. With the partial fading away of the euro crisis since 2014 and fragile recovery of the EU economy in 2015–2016, the image of the EU among citizenry seems to have been improving somewhat, although in autumn 2015, after the Greek episode, trust in the EU stood at almost all times low.[3]

Explaining the Prevailing Tendency Towards Scapegoating and Othering

While recent macrohistoric experience seems to support interpretation D, also as the most likely future option, why is it that the European discontent is channelled, for such a large part, into nationalist politics of othering and scapegoating rather than into building a leftist-democratic movement (such as DiEM25) for a transformed EU? Why is it that Varoufakis (2016) and many others are evoking historical analogies to the First World War and its aftermath, and to the rise of fascism and Nazism in Europe in the 1920s and 1930s, to understand our current predicament? If post-Keynesian or heterodox economic and Habermasian legitimation theories are on the mark, surely a rational response to the crisis of the EU would be to make the EU institutions more functional and democratic?

Every question, whether practical-political or more theoretical, has a set of presuppositions. In formulating our questions, we need to consider critically our presuppositions. For instance, it is important to avoid making invalid assumptions about continuity and discontinuity. Both the EU itself and many specific EU treaties have been rejected in national referenda over the decades, even within the original EEC6 (in France and Holland). Norway has rejected EU membership twice. If the order of the 1994 referenda in the Nordic countries had been different, at least Sweden would have stayed out and perhaps Finland, too. The number of UK voters supporting staying in the EU was roughly the same in 2016 as it was in 1975 (16,141,241 and 17,378,581, respectively). Population growth and higher turnout enabled the 'leave' side to get two times more votes in 2016 than it did in 1975. It is also significant that many nationalist right-wing parties in Europe have relatively long historical roots. The Austrian Freedom Party was founded in 1956 and the French National Front in 1972. Most of these parties with a substantial number of seats in parliament in 2016 emerged between the late 1980s and early 2000s.

The dynamics of the shifts we are observing are complex. Consider the four possibilities presented in Table 2. Support for the EU, or criticism of it, does not stem self-evidently from any of the four options. In terms of the left–right division, the EU is typically perceived to be mainly a right-wing (neo-liberal) project, yet many on the left and right anticipate that this can change. The prevailing perceptions and anticipations have themselves been changing over time (Harmes, 2012).

For instance in the UK, Margaret Thatcher's conservative party at times supported, rejected/resisted and sought to shape the European integration process. It has been acceptable in so far as

Table 2. Ethico-political alternatives in European politics.

	Left-orientation (cooperation, solidarity; freedom and efficiency require socio-economic equality)	Right-orientation (competition, private markets; freedom and efficiency require socio-economic differences)
National orientation ('we' = ethnic nation or citizens of a sovereign state)	National welfare-state and democracy	National determination of policies and inclusion/exclusion
Cosmopolitan orientation ('we' = humanity or world citizens)	Global Keynesianism, global social justice and/or global democracy	Global free markets and movements, coupled with common institutions such as global money

it has fostered market-freedoms, and in so far as there has been a perception it can become more free-private-market oriented in the future (justifying some ceding of sovereignty). However, by the time David Cameron became leader, the Euro-sceptic right of the party were becoming increasingly restive and the party more broadly ambivalent about their position. This may have been partly because in the aftermath of the global financial crisis of 2008–2009, the EU Commission started to advocate financial taxes and stronger regulation of finance (in 2016 the City of London nonetheless supported 'Remain').

Another shift, from left to right, concerns the nationalist populist parties. In their anti-estab-lishment rhetoric, these parties have every so often defended nationally based welfare-systems for native citizens; but when in position to make decisions, they have characteristically con-sented to neo- or ordo-liberal policies (from option A to B in Table 2). On the left, in turn, the popularity of Plan B and Lexit (both meaning 'left exit') rose rapidly after the dramatic sur-render of Syriza in summer 2015. The Plan B manifesto was signed in late 2015 by many of Europe's best known Left politicians, including Oskar Lafointane and Yanis Varoufakis, but soon there was a split between the nationalists and cosmopolitans.[4] In this Forum, Boris Kagar-litzky advocates the national Lexit-option, assuming that cosmopolitanism necessarily implies neo-liberal elitism and right-orientation.

Shifts over the national/cosmopolitan and left/right divides are dynamic and complex. In their orientation, the liberals and post-Keynesians of Table 1 can be either national or cosmopolitan. In countries considering entering the EU, the cosmopolitan left has been divided, commonly arguing and voting against joining the EU. Once in, they have shifted their position and declared that the point must be to transform the Union, because developments are path-dependent, and because cosmopolitanism can be furthered also through the EU. Cosmopolitans on the right, such as Robert Mundell, can be enthusiastic about the EU, but consistent formulations of free-market globalism are rare.[5] Usually global economic liberalism has been premised (i) on the free movement of goods, services, and capital and (ii) on the national powers to limit the movements of people. Capitalist world economy is also about exclusion.

Gradually since the formation of the Maastricht Treaty, but especially as a response to the flow of crises that started with the financial collapse of 2008–2009, the overall effects of these and other shifts have amounted to diffusion of doubts about, and distrust in, the European integration project. To understand the complex dynamics of various shifts, we need theory-derived but fal-sifiable hypotheses to explain why the overall trend has been towards renationalisation of poli-tics (the main tendency) and towards cosmopolitan left's transformative ideas (a weaker tendency, so far having involved significant electoral success only in Greece and Spain).

From theories of ethico-political learning we can draw, first, the proposition that collective human learning explains the historical quest for democratisation and simultaneously points towards cosmopolitan sentiments. Actors come to understand that collective rules are the product of their autonomy and free, mutual agreement (Kohlberg, 1971, 164 f.; Piaget, 1977, 24 f.). Cosmopolitanism involves a hypothetical attitude, a holistic perspective, and adherence to generalisable and often abstract principles of justification (Habermas, 1976, pp. 69–94). These theories of collective learning indicate that the development of cosmopolitan orientation requires more learning than national orientation and requires a favourable social context. National orientation is compatible with tying identity to given norms and roles of the institutions and traditions of a particular political community; it is also compatible with the reification of those roles, institutions, norms, and traditions.

In functionally differentiated capitalist market societies, economic problems can become threatening to identity (because not only one's earnings but also social worth, rights and duties are tied to a position as an employee, entrepreneur or capitalist) and endanger social integration (because many integrative functions are secured by market-based or tax-revenue dependent public organisations) (Habermas, 1988, pp. 20–31). Problems of social integration and a threatened identity translate into existential insecurity, providing fertile ground for processes such as securitisation of social issues and telling Manichean stories antagonising the situation.[6] Actors can bring about securitisation by presenting something as an existential threat and by dramatising an issue as having absolute or very strong priority. Securitisation is also about identity politics, as is Manichean story-telling about struggle between good (us) and evil (specific or generic others). Thus, emerges a hypothesis about a two-phase causal mechanism, efficacious in contemporary geo-historical context.

The two phases of the mechanism described in Figure 1 are connected causally, but at the level of meanings, they can be largely disconnected. The category 'economic trouble and crisis' involves both subjective experience (trouble) and systemic effects (downturn and crisis). Thus unemployment or its threat, precarisation of work (meaning transformation from permanent employment to less well paid and more insecure jobs) and falling behind due to increasing inequalities, can all translate into 'trouble' from the point of view of those experiencing the hardship.

Social class positioning matters morally (Sayer, 2009), as well as by predisposing actors to particular forms of learning and by generating characteristic (dis)trust to established institutions. Pathologies of socialisation and existential insecurity can expose 'ego' to securitisation and to stories that are composed from older, or transnationally dispersing, elements of meaning, apparently 'explaining' the experiences of vulnerability and insecurity.[7] Commercial and social media play a key role in the dispersion of these kinds of ideas, especially to the extent that they can sustain positive feedback loops and thus generate self-reinforcing processes. Violence dramatically exposed in the media can further inflame the process of othering. To share related sentiments of 'us' vs. 'them' can also be cherished as democratic; as being on the side of the 'people'.

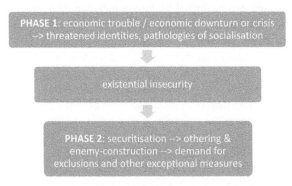

Figure 1. A two-phase causal mechanism leading to other-blaming.

Three Scenarios about the Future of the EU

Varoufakis' reliance on perspective D of Table 1 in his prognosis about the future of the Union does not seem unfounded. Trust in the EU has declined, in part due to a prolonged economic downturn and crisis (with deep roots in the global financialisation process), but in part because of what is perceived to be the undemocratic or unchangeable nature of the EU. From existential insecurities stem also exclusive processes of identity politics, securitisation, and enemy-construction.

The future of the EU depends, however, to a significant degree on future economic developments. In open systems precise predictions are not possible. Even if post-Keynesians are right and the austerity-driven tendency towards low investment and high unemployment is permanent, and new crises are to be expected sooner or later, a lot depends on the precise budget-positions and timing and nature of the next downturn or crisis. Even a relatively short-lived semi-recovery of the European economy would give time for the EU to evolve in novel directions.

The current EU strategy is to tighten the Union under the rubric of enhancing its external competitiveness. In practice this amounts to austerity; further market-based 'reforms'; budget and labour markets discipline (coupled with labour-markets 'flexicurity'); internal devaluation and perhaps also currency devaluation; flimsy banking union; and development of elements of modest common fiscal capacity.

These policies feed into the first phase of the mechanism depicted in Figure 1. The explicit idea, however, is to increase demand for European goods and services in the world markets— at the expense of other countries. World imports and exports cancel out. Although it is not impossible for all countries to simultaneously grow the value of their exports and imports, their overall sum is always zero. In Varoufakis' (2016, p. 240) estimation, 'to escape its crisis in this manner the Eurozone must reach a current account surplus in relation to the rest of the world of no less than 9 per cent of total European income'. This is highly unlikely to succeed, but if it succeeded, it would 'destroy the hopes of America, China, Latin America, India, African and Sout East Asia for stability and growth'. The estimate of 9% may be unreliable, but the argument is sound.

There are more than one possible future for the EU, however. A possibility is an increasingly disciplined and militarised Union. Common external enemies can unify. Perhaps the exit of Britain will facilitate consolidation of the remaining EU via the escalating conflict with Russia, constant 'state of emergency' related to the refugee crisis and terrorist attacks (often by the migrant sufferers of class inequalities), increasingly strained relations with Turkey, economic competition with China and India, and the election of 'America-first' Donald Trump?

The two-phase mechanism presented in Figure 1 can be exploited also to further a common European cause. The identification of threats to 'our European' existence can create unity and acceptance, or at least acquiescence, to the ever more disciplinary rule of the EU. Indeed, from a cosmopolitan perspective, one of the ambiguities of the Union has always been the possibility that it generates a nationalism of its own and evolves into a military great power. What is more, expanding security and military spending could boost the European economy. By pooling part of this spending through the EU institutions, and perhaps by introducing EU taxes, the Union could manage to create some common fiscal capacity.

This scenario may not be the most likely one. The euro crisis has drawn attention away from developing a common European security and defence policy. The US and NATO, together with EU member states, remain the main players also vis-à-vis Russia. The prevailing disintegrative tendencies make it difficult to convince the audience that a united Europe is the best answer to the perceived existential threats; while the process of building an increasingly disciplined and militarised Union would take time. And yet with several propitious circumstances coinciding and coalescing, attempts to construct such a union might eventually succeed. The EU would then be on par with the USA, Russia, and China, a military superpower in the global insecurity community, which has potential of being further destabilised by new downturns and crises in the world economy. This is not a good scenario for the world as a whole.

The third possible future for the EU could result from the success of the left cosmopolitan project to transform the Union. There are various plans to use the resources of the European Central Bank and the instruments of the European Investment Bank to create a public investment programme on a European scale (e.g. Varoufakis, Holland, & Galbraith, 2013); and to relieve national budget constraints for instance by a new application of the so-called Golden Rule, exempting public net investment from the relevant deficit targets (e.g. Truger, 2016). These plans do not necessitate changes in the basic treaties of the EU, so they could be implemented fairly rapidly.

But none of these proposals is on the EU agenda in summer 2016. The first phase of the current plan to 'complete EMU' is due to be completed by summer 2017 and the last phase by 2025. If a will emerges to change the course of EU economic policy, it will take at least a year to start implementing even a modest plan. What is more, the proposed—and even more so, the realistically achievable—scale of the required expansion in public spending appears rather limited. Doubling the level of European Investment Bank lending or adding gradually about 1% of GDP deficit funding to public investments would boost the European economy to a degree, but may well turn out to be too little too late. At best, these plans could buy time.

The realisation of the DiEM25 scheme to democratise the Union would take time too. I know only one way to speed up the process, namely the use of citizens' initiatives and referenda on the euro and related fiscal discipline.[8] In any case, the purported DiEM25 first step is to achieve full transparency in decision-making. Written in autumn 2015, the manifesto demands that this should be realised within a year. More realistically, it is conceivable that full transparency could become one of the main themes of the European Parliament elections in 2019. Its successful implementation is yet another matter—as is whether this is what EU citizens really want and need.

The second demand is to convene 'an Assembly of citizens' representatives' within two years. Nothing like this is on the agenda in summer 2016. The euro crisis and Brexit may have prepared the ground for revisiting and revising the Treaty of the European Union in certain regards, but even in the best of circumstances, to initiate this kind of process will take probably two to three years. Currently, there is no political will to establish a directly elected constitutional assembly. If anything, the EU has become more intergovernmental during the euro crisis. The composing and then signing of the draft for a European Constitution in the early 2000s took almost three years. Nearly a year later, it was rejected in the French and Dutch referendums.

Conclusions

The five presidents' plan to 'complete the EMU' is unlikely to succeed. Its success, on the other hand, would probably be detrimental to the world economy as a whole, especially if others tried to respond in kind. The policies now demanded from the member states strengthen tendencies towards disintegration via the causal mechanism depicted in Figure 1. The alternate scenario about a disciplinary and militarised future EU may not be the most likely one, but with mutually supportive circumstances coinciding and coalescing, it can well happen. Because this kind of Union involves military Keynesianism, it could work economically better than the current EU, but its legitimation basis would be internally shaky and externally dangerous.

The third scenario outlines the left cosmopolitan project to transform the EU. The main problem for this project appears to be time and timing. Even if a strong political drive to transform the EU develops, perhaps as a result of the next economic crisis, it is likely that the transformation process will take many years. Moreover, until such a collective will forms, the process of 'completing the EMU' will proceed in accordance with the scheme of the five presidents' report. This means that the Union must muddle through something like a decade or more before the effects of the transformation will become tangible in the everyday lives of European citizens. Meanwhile new crises are likely to erupt and new shifts in the political landscape to occur. The question is whether the current Union can survive until 2025–2030.

What would the disintegration of the EU tell about the likely future of the world? The option-fields of Tables 1 and 2 and the mechanism depicted in Figure 1 are in no way confined to the European context. The tendencies that are causally efficacious in Europe operate also in other parts of the world political economy, as is evident from the popularity of right-wing populist-nationalist political leaders ranging from Donald Trump via Recep Tayyip Erdoğan to Vladimir Putin. Meanings are context-sensitive and specific substantial developments path-dependent, yet local and regional processes are interwoven in the dynamics of our planetary economy and politics. The scenarios of global politico-economic competition among great powers gradually assembling the conditions for a global military catastrophe are increasingly pertinent (they have become more likely than in my earlier assessments, currently describing the most likely next future; cf. Patomäki, 2010).

The contradictory nature of the plan to 'complete the EMU', and the security dilemma implied by the alternate scenario of militarist EU, indicate that a better EU becomes possible only when it is understood that the relevant whole is not Europe but the world. To succeed, the left cosmopolitan project has to go beyond Europe. This means that it would have to articulate a vision of overcoming the contradictions of the world economy by means of green democratic global Keynesianism (see Patomäki, 2013, ch 8). Even in the best of circumstances, that task, however vital, is going to take still more time than the transformation of the EU.

Notes

1 See DiEM25's website at https://diem25.org/; the long version of the manifesto can be found at https://diem25.org/manifesto-long/.

2 Varoufakis focuses largely on Germany's Finance Minister Dr Schäuble and his authoritarian plans, but officially the main current design for the further development of the Union is the 'The Five Presidents' Report: Completing Europe's Economic and Monetary Union', available at https://ec.europa.eu/priorities/publications/five-presidents-report-completing-europes-economic-and-monetary-union_en.

3 The latest standard Eurobarometer is from autumn 2015, available at http://ec.europa.eu/COMMFrontOffice/PublicOpinion/.

4 Terrorist attacks postponed the first Plan B summit in Paris from November 2015 to January 2016. This first summit was dominated by nationalists, while Varoufakis and many other cosmopolitans abstained from participating (see my report at http://patomaki.fi/en/2016/01/preparing-for-plan-b-in-paris/). However, the second summit in Madrid in February 2016, which I also attended, was open to different positions and aimed at compromise formulations.

5 Optimal currency area theory, pioneered by Mundell (1961), has also been used by EMU opponents (for a critical discussion of the theory and its applicability, see Patomäki, 2013, pp. 60–64). Mundell, himself has trenchantly supported the euro project, and in 2000 predicted that by 2010 50 states would have joined the Eurozone. Several of Mundell's writings on the world currency can be found at http://robertmundell.net/economic-policies/world-currency/.

6 Guzzini (2011) examines securitisation as a non-positivistically conceived causal mechanism. For a related but more future-oriented analysis, making an explicit link between political economy and security, see Patomäki (2015). Aho (1990) remains one of the best summaries of the deep-structural and characteristically Manichean underpinnings of the processes of enemy-construction, based partly on his studies of right-wing extremist movements in the USA.

7 I discuss the processes of unlearning and pathological learning via the generic, yet also context-specific experiences of vulnerability and insecurity in much more detail in Patomäki (forthcoming).

8 Civil society organisations and interested political parties could use the mechanism of citizens' initiative to call simultaneously for referenda in the EU as a whole and within member states. A lot hinges upon the design of the

referendums. A referendum should include multiple choices—the third option being the cosmopolitan Left's alternative—and the voting system could be designed to take into account multiple preferences (there are different methods of doing this). See http://patomaki.fi/en/2016/01/beyond-plan-b-and-c-on-the-use-of-citizens-initiative-and-referenda/.

Disclosure Statement

No potential conflict of interest was reported by the authors.

References

Aho, J. (1990). Heroism, the construction of evil, and violence. In V. Harle (Ed.), *European values in international relations* (pp. 15–28). London: Pinter.

Guzzini, S. (2011). Securitization as a causal mechanism. *Security Dialogue, 42*(4–5), 329–341.

Habermas, J. (1976). *Communication and the evolution of society.* (T. McCarthy, Trans.). Boston, MA: Beacon Press.

Habermas, J. (1988). *Legitimation crisis.* (T. McCarthy, Trans.). Cambridge: Polity Press.

Harmes, A. (2012). The rise of neoliberal nationalism. *Review of International Political Economy, 19*(1), 59–86.

Kohlberg, L. (1971). From is to ought: How to commit the naturalistic fallacy and get away with it in the study of moral development. In T. Mischel (Ed.), *Cognitive development and epistemology* (pp. 151–235). New York, NY: Academic Press.

Mundell, R. (1961). A theory of optimum currency areas. *American Economic Review, 51*(4), 657–665.

Patomäki, H. (2010). Exploring possible, likely and desirable global futures: beyond the closed vs. open systems dichotomy. In J. Joseph & C. Wight (Eds.), *Scientific realism and international relations* (pp. 147–166). London: Palgrave.

Patomäki, H. (2013). *The great Eurozone disaster. From crisis to global new deal.* London: Zed Books.

Patomäki, H. (2014). Can the EU be democratised? A political economy analysis. In R. Fiorentini & G. Montani (Eds.), *The European Union and supranational political economy* (pp. 116–132). London: Routledge.

Patomäki, H. (2015). Absenting the absence of future dangers and structural transformations in securitization theory. *International Relations, 29*(1), 128–136.

Patomäki, H. (forthcoming). *After Brexit: A race between learning and catastrophe?* London: Routledge.

Piaget, J. (1977). *The moral judgement of the child.* (M. Gabain, Trans.). Harmondsworth: Penguin Books (orig. published in 1932).

Tetlock, P. (1999). Theory-driven reasoning about plausible pasts and probable futures in world politics: are we prisoners of our preconceptions? *American Journal of Political Science, 43*(2), 335–366.

Sayer, A. (2009). *The moral significance of class.* Cambridge: Cambridge University Press.

Truger, A. (2016). *The golden rule of public investment—a necessary and sufficient reform of the EU fiscal framework?* (IMK Working Paper No.168). Düsseldorf. Retrieved from https://ideas.repec.org/p/imk/wpaper/168-2016.html

Varoufakis, Y. (2016). *And the weak suffer what they must? Europe, austerity and the threat to global stability.* London: The Bodley Head.

Varoufakis, Y., Holland, S., & Galbraith, J. (2013). *A modest proposal for resolving the Eurozone crisis—version 4.0.* Retrieved from https://yanisvaroufakis.eu/euro-crisis/modest-proposal/

Introduction: Special Forum on Brexit Part 2

JAMIE MORGAN & HEIKKI PATOMÄKI

The Present

Brexit was triggered March 2017 and is formally to be completed by March 2019. It seems increasingly likely that the actual process of leaving the EU will be more protracted, extending into the next decade. The British government seems to have been wrong-footed at every turn. The decision made in 2013 to hold a referendum was never properly thought through and the Cameron-led coalition of that time did not expect to have to fulfil this promise. The unexpected Conservative majority government returned in the general election of 2015 followed, and the Executive approached a referendum based on sharp divisions within Conservative ranks, but with a sense of complacency. Remain never expected to lose.

Nothing since then has been normal, and that includes the result of the general election of June 2017. Again, voters confounded received wisdom, eliminating the slim Conservative majority. Prime Minister Theresa May campaigned based on strength of leadership and a mandate for Brexit, but the campaign made little reference to Brexit and was undone by a failure to address discontent regarding welfare and social policy after almost a decade of austerity. What it means to talk about mandates in this context is deeply ambiguous. More importantly, an unstable minority governing party, dependent on an unofficial coalition with a Northern Irish party whose concerns are parochial, leads negotiations. Theresa May has lost credibility as a leader and members of her Party are positioning to replace her. It remains the case whoever is leading the Conservatives that the UK government may be unable to guarantee acceptance by Parliament of any agreed position with the EU, and that there is a further potential of government collapse. New complications now compound an already complicated situation.

The Future?

Complications are many (see Morgan & Patomäki, 2017). The beginning of formal negotiations crystallised what previously had seemed likely. The UK negotiating team, led by David Davis accepted the EU stipulated sequence of negotiation (settling the guarantee of citizen rights and establishing the liabilities of the UK vis-à-vis the budget, etc. *prior* to negotiation of the UK's post-Brexit relation with the EU). The UK government sought to represent this as a generous concession. It is more accurately a conforming to standpoints already ingrained in reality, since the EU had already set out its collective position (European Commission, 2017a, 2017b, 2017c). Once an EU27 position has been agreed between members, the form of that agreement creates a clear and restricted scope to which its negotiators led by Michel Barnier must abide (and which is difficult to change). So, one might describe the UK part as seeming capitulation based on either wilful misrepresentation or hapless misunderstanding of what was possible. The EU for its part has a collective position but one should not conflate this with unity. A collective position does not require background unity or coincidence of all interests, merely agreement. Different members, for example, will compete to host EU agencies (with attendant benefits) that can no longer be located in the UK; notably the European Banking Authority and the European Medicines Agency. They are likely also to lobby to restrict London's capacity to act as the main clearing centre for the Euro.

The collective position matters, since the EU's fundamental position remains that it is not in the interests of the coherence of the EU for the UK's status outside of the EU to be relatively unchanged in its relation to the EU. This is not the same as intent to hold or exercise ill-will, it need not be considered *personal*. The central idea accords with a moral principle that is widely held: a non-member of the Union that does not have or adhere to the same obligations as a member, cannot have the same rights, and enjoy the same benefits as a member.[1] The idea of symmetry of rights and benefits, on the one hand, and obligations, on the other, thus becomes an implacable institutional constraint. In so far as it manifests in particular consequences as negotiations continue over the coming years, what seems likely to also be revealed is the basic lack of leverage UK negotiators possess. Negotiation, like social reality in general, is a process. However, agreement matters more to the UK than to the EU, and formal deadlines for domestic changes to law within the UK and for detailed negotiation with the EU are tight. Moreover, there remains basic ambiguity concerning what the UK government actually wants and what it can achieve. Differences, dichotomies and simplistic representations abound and the basic splits between soft/hard and left/right exits persist.

Martin Wolf, the economics commentator of the *Financial Times*, has argued in favour of a second referendum after the Brexit negotiations.[2] In his view this would be the most legitimate thing to do from a democratic viewpoint, given that the original vote between 'remain' and 'leave' was between a known existing state of affairs and some unspecified future form, where different voters could imagine their own preferred or non-preferred exits. The leave decision thus disguises difference. Wolf goes so far as to suggest that the UK should pull out from the Brexit process. This may be impossible, however. Many processes are path-dependent and become for-all-intents-and-purposes irreversible. Whereas in June 2016 the 'remain' option was clear, the same option does not seem to be available to the UK anymore. Not only is a reversal constitutionally questionable within the EU as currently structured, any reversal of policy may not include reinstatement of the UK's relatively privileged position of budget rebates and opt-outs within the EU. This conforms to recent comments by Guy Verhofstadt, the

European Parliament's coordinator on Brexit, the French president Emmanuel Macron, and other European politicians. As Verhofstadt stresses, the UK may stay but only as an ordinary member:

> Like Alice in Wonderland, not all the doors are the same. It will be a brand new door, with a new Europe, a Europe without rebates, without complexity, with real powers and with unity. (Quoted in Rankin, 2017)

It remains the case as Wolf argues that the choice in the June 2016 referendum was badly defined. Even slight changes in the framing of questions can result in different answers from the same people. Moreover, as Table 1 below illustrates, it is relatively straightforward to demonstrate how incompatible different leave-options can be. The basic principle of Brexit negotiations is that nothing is agreed until everything is agreed; individual items cannot be settled separately. This opens up possibilities for further twists and turns. If the UK government changes in the course of these negotiations, Table 1 options D or B could change to C or A. Moreover, if no agreement is reached by the deadline, EU Treaties will no longer apply to the UK. This is likely to mean a sudden collapse of the countless collaborative ties between the UK and the rest of the EU. However, it is also conceivable, though much less likely, that it could mean no Brexit after all, followed by negotiations about the precise terms of renewed British membership and a new referendum in the UK. If Brexit becomes real, it is probable that the UK will continue to pay its annual EU contribution (approximately £13 billion annually) for the two years from 2020 to 2021. There will be a three-year transition phase and the UK will have to renegotiate a large number of international treaties. The Brexit process will drag on for several years and well into the 2020s.

As has been made clear to the UK negotiators, the Brexit deal itself covers only the terms of exit; the future relations between the UK and the EU will have to be negotiated separately. As has also become immediately clear, the negotiation process is formalised in all senses, and so is far from the more freewheeling approach that the UK government gave every impression that they expected to pursue prior to the initiation of talks. The first phase consists of four rounds of talks each round to begin four weeks after the last and up until a final round, the second week of October. The talks are broken into three separate strands undertaken by different teams or working groups. Within each four-week cycle the first two weeks consist of preparations by the working group members, followed by a week of talks in Brussels (with Davis and Barniers in attendance), and then a week of reporting back/consultation of each party with their relevant decision-making constituencies (the UK government, etc.) before the next round begins.

Table 1. Four possible British exits from the EU

	Left	Right
Soft	A. Retain close ties to the EU, especially in terms of free movement of labour/people and human and social rights.	B. Retain close ties to the EU especially in terms of the single market in goods, services and capital.
Hard	C. Use the regained autonomy to rebuild democratic welfare state in the UK independently of the neoliberal regulations and policies of Brussels.	D. Use the regained autonomy to exploit maximally the UK possibilities for benefitting from tax and competitiveness war against other states.

However, the formality of talks is not quite the same as an over-determination of content. One should note that the difference between the two soft exits (A and B in Table 1) has become blurred to the extent that there is at least a tentative basis for some agreement to protect migrant EU citizens' post-Brexit rights if they have been resident at least for five years in the UK/EU. One should not confuse the indifference with which this was met in the European Council with disinterest regarding this offer. The Council is a forum for many issues, of which Brexit is now only one among those many, and the Council is not the direct point of inter-face for negotiation, which remains the Commission. Leaders, including the German Chancellor Angela Merkel, recognised May's offer as an opening position (see Rankin, Stewart, & Boffey, 2017). The key question is whether the UK will remain in the European Economic Area (EEA). On purely ideological grounds, one would expect Labour to stress social and human rights and the Conservatives economic freedoms and free markets. Behind this difference lie very different approaches to critique of the EU as-is. The Left has always considered the EU as too neoliberal (the single market as a local expression of global capital) and the Right, not neoliberal enough (Delors' social policy and stealth integration corroding sovereignty where only an economic relation was envisaged, see Jessop, 2017; Worth, 2017). The EEA is a very extensive agreement, however, and this would mean the endorsement of most of the EU's apparatus, deals, and regu-lation without the capacity to shape EU-regulation in the future. A soft exit would thus mean leaving the EU decision-making system, resulting in the UK becoming, in the main, a rule-taker rather than rule-maker.

Clearly, this could make a hard exit (C and D in Table 1) attractive to some, but there are two very different versions of it. The Conservative version of hard exit revolves around the regained autonomy to maximally exploit the possibilities for benefitting from tax competition and broader oppositional competitiveness approaches with other states (D). Tax reductions and other related measures translate readily to austerity, implying cuts to public services and social benefits. The Left version of hard exit aims at the opposite outcome. The point of hard exit would be to use the regained autonomy to rebuild a democratic welfare state in the UK independently of the neolib-eral regulations and policies of Brussels (C). In so far as the EU represents an authoritarian project of neoliberal integration, it is only possible to develop a democratic political system and a social-democratic society outside the EU (e.g. Johnson, 2017). The Labour Party 2017 Manifesto takes a softer line, however, stressing that the UK wants to retain as much of the exist-ing EU agreements and systems as possible. Should there be new general elections in 2017 or 2018 resulting in a Labour government, the softness or hardness of Left Brexit would have to be resolved within the Labour Party. This leaves unresolved a fundamental question: To what extent are different EU agreements and systems compatible with the attempt to develop political and social democracy within the UK? Addressing this would seem likely to manifest divisions within the Labour party no less deep than those that afflict the Conservatives.

Failing Forward or Merely Lurching?

We suspect that neither version of hard exit would be particularly successful even in its own terms, albeit for dissimilar reasons. In many areas such as international trade the Conservative version (D) is ambiguous, because it is not clear how the Conservative understanding of free trade and competitiveness would be different from the currently prevailing EU policies. Clearly a radical reduction of the UK corporate tax rate would go against the spirit of the Com-mission's 2015 proposal for a Common Consolidated Corporate Tax Base (see Morgan, 2016, 2017b). It would serve to intensify an on-going race to the bottom and strengthen disintegrative tendencies in the European and global political economy (Patomäki, in press). Tax war against other states in Europe and elsewhere is a zero-sum game, and in the context of financialisation, which tends to decelerate growth (e.g. Seabrooke & Wigan, in press; Stockhammer, 2004; Treeck, 2009) and has adverse fiscal multiplier effects resulting from austerity and increasing inequalities (e.g. Cynamon & Fazzari, 2015), it can also be a negative-sum game between countries. This makes the world system more susceptible to conflicts. An increasingly less benign international political environment is unlikely to spell a successful future for the UK in terms of social progress, GDP-growth, or security.

The Left version of hard exit, meanwhile, ignores the numerous subtle mechanisms and international treaties and institutional arrangements that underpin neoliberalism and, moreover, is vulnerable to the structural power of transnational capital (mediated by prevailing ideas and forms of agency, see Bell, 2012). While some economic, political, and social progress can be achieved—depending on concrete circumstances—by means of social-democratic economic policies within the confines of a nation-state, it is not easy to reverse the worldwide process of neoliberalisation individually, i.e. independently of what happens elsewhere and without collective actions and new or transformed common institutions. The hard Left exit is constrained by other states' policies and by the possibility of capital exit. The more radical the Labour programme, the more likely it is that transnational capital will resort to investment strikes or move elsewhere (consider France 1981–1983 or, in a much more partial analogy, the UK in 1992). Significant capital outflows would also have a major impact on the exchange rate of Sterling. Although actors know what it is that they are doing, under some perspective, they do not necessarily understand (all) the effects of their actions and policies, not even retrospectively. The dynamic and systemic international (or transnational, regional, or global) impact of the consequences of their actions can in turn have feedback effects, whether acknowledged as such or not. It is, of course, important to approach the significance of Brexit from multiple perspectives. In particular, one should not conflate a UK-centred focus with a UK-centric point of view. What is occurring in the UK has context and is part of broader processes.

The New Essays

Erroneous expectations, forecasts, and anticipations, like unintended consequences of actions and policies, usually arise from false or misleading categories, prototypes, and theories. Steve Keen is a prominent post-Keynesian critic of mainstream economics and its consequences. Keen starts the second part of our Brexit Forum with an explanation of why mainstream economists were wrong in anticipating that a vote to leave the EU would have an immediate significant negative impact on the British economy in 2016–2017. Moreover, he argues that this failure is rooted in a deeper misunderstanding that confuses the role of and possible reasons to engage in trade with an abstract model of free trade, creating in turn a mis-specified underpinning for a discourse of globalisation. According to Keen, when assessing the consequences of economic foreign policy-making, mainstream economists rely largely on the theory of comparative advantage. The concept is so basic because it is for many prominent economists an unquestionable commitment that identifies real or serious economists. As Alan S. Blinder, a leading academic macroeconomist who has also served as Vice-Chairman of the Federal Reserve Board, puts it:

> I have long believed that one true test of whether a person is an economist is how devoutly he or she lives by the principle of comparative advantage. And I don't mean just preaching it, but actually practicing it. (Blinder, 1998, p. 1)

Mainstream economists in general assume that international free trade is beneficial because of gains from specialisation. This underpins basic arguments for free movement of capital and labour and for factor equalisation and so has profound political implications for the policy space of states. And yet the most affluent countries are also the most diverse and complex in their organisation of production and have rarely become successful by simply opening their borders (infrastructure, capital controls of one kind or another and many other policies have mattered). Basing his argument on the results of extensive empirical research, Keen concludes that 'whether trade liberalisation causes a net increase or decrease in productive capacity is a question of investment and effective demand, and not one of relative efficiency' (Keen, 2017a). Brexit, as currently presented has little to say about constructive investment and effective demand. As Keen also notes economists' failure to predict the UK's better-than-expected economic performance since the June 2016 referendum is also in the context of their general failure to forecast anything of importance, including basic features of real economies, such as asset bubbles and financial crises—which are features of, rather than accidents that happen to, economies (Keen, 2017b).

Silke Trommer (2017) continues Keen's theme of trade, but focuses on the reality of the UK's position in terms of trade treaties. She argues that post-Brexit UK trade policy autonomy is a pyrrhic victory, and in many ways illusory, since the UK will be required to conform to existing institutions even as it seeks to develop new terms of trade. Apart from the 'absence of a clearly formulated substantive post-Brexit trade agenda', or any systematic account about the ways in which the EU and UK positions on free trade may differ, there are a number of reasons why 'Britain may find it more difficult to push its own trade agenda internationally than is currently conceded in the debate' (2017). Current free trade negotiations are mostly not about direct or purposeful obstacles to products crossing borders. Rather they concern market access to sectors of services, public procurements, investment protection, and regulatory harmonisation. Free trade negotiations have become complex and unmistakeably political. The UK's relative importance in the world economy has declined and, moreover, it lacks capacity to conduct dozens if not hundreds of negotiations simultaneously. Fragmented and complex trade negotiations 'produce commercial fragmentation and contribute to regulatory clashes' (2017). It seems unlikely that Brexit will turn out to be beneficial to the UK in 'free-trade' terms.

Seabrooke and Wigan (2017a) focus on the likely consequences for tax policy and competition based on Brexit. They situate the potentials as a product of activity in global wealth chains, a concept that builds but diverges from the well-known concept of global value chains (Seabrooke & Wigan, 2017b). Firms and other actors seek to concentrate and protect income and wealth from other claims and this sits in terms of a complex of rules and practices within and between states. They set out the likely consequences of the hard Right exit (D), defined as a strategy of relying on 'highly flexible labour markets, light touch regulation and a hyper competitive low tax regime' (2017a). They argue that Brexit may provide scope for the UK to develop along tax haven lines and so exacerbate trends in financialisation. However, for this to benefit the UK in any meaningful sense, a large number of factors would have to be taken into account as Brexit occurs:

> Occupying space in global wealth chains requires a series of careful balancing acts between making a tax offer attractive to mobile capital and maintaining sufficient revenue, designing a low tax regime and staying within the boundaries of accepted practice established by multilateral rules and norms, and between multiple, often conflicting, goals that Britain must simultaneously pursue as it leaves the European Union. (2017a)

Moreover, this strategy will make the UK ever more dependent on the City of London.

It is important, of course, to emphasise that a hard Right exit is a gamble at the expense of other states and the sustainability of the world economy. It would make world politics ever more competitive and less benign for *all* parties. Jayati Ghosh (2017) takes up this collective theme. Ghosh explores the causes of the 'leave' outcome and draws implications for the possible and likely futures of the EU as a whole. She does so based on a non-Eurocentric perspective: 'Across the world, people have been watching recent political changes in developed countries with a mixture of bemusement and shock' (2017). Ghosh explains these developments first and foremost in terms of growing inequalities and flat or falling incomes for the multitude in the industrialised North. Moreover, 'labour market trends [i.e. flexibilisation] have contributed to feelings of insecurity among workers everywhere' (2017). These two developments are closely connected, since 'countries that have encouraged the growth of part-time and temporary contracts experienced bigger declines in wage shares'. Relying on a large-scale empirical study provided by the McKinsey Global Institute, she shows that many of those people suffering most from these developments are particularly liable to blame foreigners and globalisation for their problems. Moreover, during the euro crisis, the EU—the Commission and the leading member states, particularly Germany—have insisted on strict adherence to the rules and procedures that penalise (and so blame) member states in crisis. Empathy and solidarity, which are supposedly soft features of the EU project, are notoriously absent; and the tendency to localise blame (victimising those who may be victims) is stark. Clearly, the consequences of policies of indifference can be counterproductive for those who pursue them, resulting in popular disaffection that can easily translate into equally or perhaps even more devastating responses than in the UK. As Gosh notes these responses 'could even cause a disintegration of the union' (2017).

The unthinkable, of course, has to be thought in order to be designated as such. Moreover, what is unthinkable is a moving issue that mutates as history unfolds. History itself provides useful points of comparison to explore possibilities. Joachim Becker (2017) concludes our Special Forum by drawing close parallels between the disintegration of Yugoslavia and the present centrifugal tendencies in the EU. In Yugoslavia uneven developments and decentralised structures prepared the ground for the intensification of conflicts in the wake of a debt crisis and several austerity programmes in the early 1980s. The story of the disintegration of Yugoslavia is surprisingly similar in several ways to what seems to be occurring in the EU. This includes at the level of other-blaming rhetoric—though there are, of course, also obvious differences, and actual military conflict seems particularly unlikely. A close parallel is that apart from Slovenia, the Yugoslav successor states have suffered from lasting de-industrialisation. World history never repeats itself in exactly the same way, but we can still draw historical lessons by understanding the mechanisms that can be causally efficacious across different geo-historical contexts. Uneven developments have been repeated in the EU. As Becker states:

> Projects like the Single Market and the euro zone have deepened uneven development patterns because they removed protective mechanisms from the peripheral economies without creating sufficient compensatory mechanisms (like regional industrial policies). [...] In late Yugoslavia, likewise pro-Yugoslav tendencies tended to be relatively strongest in some of the urban centres. And exclusionary nationalism took particularly strong roots in crisis-stricken rural areas and small towns. (2017)

Becker's analysis supports Gosh's main conclusions that 'only a more progressive and more flexible union based on solidarity of peoples is likely to survive' (2017).

Conclusion

For the UK, Brexit has become a reality that is weirdly surreal in its moment-to-moment manifestations. It still carries a sense of unreality for many in the UK, and in terms of its possible consequences continually provokes analyses that emphasise a kind of collective stupidity that has been stumbled into, but from which no one seems capable of withdrawing. It seems highly unlikely that any constituency is going to get what they thought they were voting for (see Morgan, 2017a). Moreover, the Leave grouping that has dominated proceedings in recent months is now starting to acknowledge that no one 'votes to be poorer', and yet the very terms on which 'control' was sold to a voting public created this as a likelihood, if immigration dominated other economic concerns. This is a circle that has yet to be, and may never be, squared by substantive policy for negotiation.

However, again one must not conflate a UK-centred problematic with a purely UK-centric focus of concerns. Brexit is also part of broader processes. It is not hyperbolic to suggest that the survival of the EU is still at stake in the longer term. The election of Macron may seem to have stabilised a Franco–German axis at the heart of the EU and recent improved economic metrics across the EU may provide grounds for an optimistic narrative in the press. However, underlying issues of inequality and lack of democratic representation have not simply disappeared, and global tendencies for growth to occur within unstable processes of financialisation have not been addressed. They are institutionally ingrained. Currently, prevailing modest reform proposals and tentative steps within the existing EU Treaty framework may be too little too late to address underlying issues. This remains to be seen. Without such changes European disintegration and broader global socio-economic crises remain possibilities (Keen, 2017b). For these possibilities not to arise then more fundamental changes are required (see three scenarios for the EU: Patomäki, 2017; in press, chap. 6). More democratic and sustainable futures do not write themselves, they must be conceived and realised.

Disclosure Statement

No potential conflict of interest was reported by the authors.

Notes

1 The philosophical principle actually holds that every meaningful right has a corresponding duty of others to respect that right (e.g. right to free speech means you cannot stop someone else from speaking things out loud that you oppose), or duty of particular others to provide whatever that right promises to deliver (e.g. social rights vis-à-vis the state). The version according to which those who do not live up to the same obligations as a member, cannot have the same rights and enjoy the same benefits as a member, is analogical to the basic principle of (neo)liberal welfare state (e.g. you are only entitled to unemployment or welfare benefits if you are actively seeking for work and have employment normally).

2 See Wolf's FT interview of 16 June 2017 at https://www.facebook.com/financialtimes/videos/10155370220965750/ ; see also his column (Wolf, 2017), which forms the starting point of the interview.

References

Becker, J. (2017). In the Yugoslav mirror: The EU disintegration crisis. *Globalizations*. doi:10.1080/14747731.2017.1330984

Bell, S. (2012). The power of ideas: The ideational shaping of the structural power of business. *International Studies Quarterly, 56*(4), 661–673.

Blinder, A. (1998). *Central banking in theory and practice*. Cambridge, MA: The MIT Press.

Cynamon, B., & Fazzari, S. (2015). Rising inequality and stagnation in the US economy. *European Journal of Economics and Economic Policies: Intervention, 12*(2), 170–182.

European Commission. (2017a, May 5). ANNEX to the recommendation for a COUNCIL DECISION authorising the opening of the negotiations for an agreement with the United Kingdom of Great Britain and Northern Ireland setting out the arrangements for its withdrawal from the European Union. COM 218 final.

European Commission. (2017b, June 12). Position paper on 'Essential Principles on Citizens' Rights' EU position in view of the 1st negotiation round with the UK.

European Commission. (2017c, June 12). Position paper 'Essential Principles on Financial Settlement' EU position in view of the 1st negotiation round with the UK.

Ghosh, J. (2017). Brexit and the economics of political change in developed countries. *Globalizations*. doi:10.1080/14747731.2017.1330985

Jessop, B. (2017). The organic crisis of the British state: Putting Brexit in its place. *Globalizations, 14*(1), 133–141.

Johnson, A. (2017, March 28). Why Brexit is best for Britain: The Left wing case. *New York Times*. Retrieved from https://www.nytimes.com/2017/03/28/opinion/why-brexit-is-best-for-britain-the-left-wing-case.html

Keen, S. (2017a). Trade and the gains from diversity: Why economists failed to predict the consequences of Brexit. *Globalizations*. doi:10.1080/14747731.2017.1345104

Keen, S. (2017b). *Can we avoid another financial crisis?* London: Polity Press.

Morgan, J. (2016). Corporation tax as a problem of MNC organizational circuits: The case for unitary taxation. *British Journal of Politics and International Relations, 18*(2), 463–481.

Morgan, J. (2017a). Brexit: Be careful what you wish for? *Globalizations, 14*(1), 118–226.

Morgan, J. (2017b). Taxing the powerful, the rise of populism and the crisis in Europe: The case for the EU common consolidated corporate tax base. *International Politics*. doi:10.1057/s41311-017-0052-x

Morgan, J., & Patomäki, H. (2017). Introduction: Special forum on Brexit. *Globalizations, 14*(1), 99–103.

Patomäki, H. (2017). Will the EU disintegrate? What does the likely possibility of disintegration tell about the future of the world? *Globalizations, 14*(1), 168–177.

Patomäki, H. (in press). *Exits and conflicts: Disintegrative tendencies in global political economy*. London: Routledge.

Rankin, J. (2017, June 14). Perks will stop if UK ends up staying in EU, says Guy Verhofstadt. Britain is free to change its mind and stay in union, but would have to give up rebate, says EU parliament's Brexit coordinator. *The Guardian*. Retrieved from https://www.theguardian.com/politics/2017/jun/14/perks-end-uk-eu-guy-verhofstadt

Rankin, J., Stewart, H., & Boffey, D. (2017, June 23). Brexit talks 'will not consume EU', Angela Merkel warns Britain. EU leaders dismiss Theresa May's offer on citizens' rights as inadequate while summit seeks to focus on terrorism and defence. *The Guardian*. Retrieved from https://www.theguardian.com/politics/2017/jun/23/eu-leaders-uk-plan-citizens-rights-vague-inadequate

Seabrooke, L., & Wigan, D. (2017a). Brexit and global wealth chains. *Globalizations*. doi:10.1080/14747731.2017.1330987

Seabrooke, L., & Wigan, D. (2017b). The governance of global wealth chains. *Review of International Political Economy, 24*(1), 1–29.

Seabrooke, L., & Wigan, D. (in press). *Global tax battles: The fight to govern corporate and elite wealth*. Oxford: Oxford University Press.

Stockhammer, E. (2004). Financialisation and the slowdown of accumulation. *Cambridge Journal of Economics, 28*(5), 719–741.

Treeck, van T. (2009). *The macroeconomics of 'financialisation', and the deeper origins of the world economic crisis* (IMK Working Paper, 9/2009). Retrieved from http://www.boeckler.de/pdf/p_imk_wp_9_2009.pdf

Trommer, S. (2017). Post-Brexit trade autonomy as Pyrrhic victory: Being a middle power in a contested trade regime. *Globalizations*. doi:10.1080/14747731.2017.1330986

Wolf, M. (2017, June 13). Sleepwalking towards a chaotic Brexit. The likelihood that there will be no deal is now even higher than before the election. *Financial Times*. Retrieved from https://www.ft.com/content/ad75838c-5011-11e7-a1f2-db19572361bb

Worth, O. (2017). Reviving Hayek's dream. *Globalizations, 14*(1), 104–109.

Trade and the Gains from Diversity: Why Economists Failed to Predict the Consequences of Brexit

STEVE KEEN

ABSTRACT   *In this brief article I explain why the expectation amongst economists that Brexit means Britain will experience significant economic losses, thanks to the reversal of the gains from specialisation, is incorrect. The background assumptions regarding comparative advantage are false and cannot inform real-world situations. However, this is not the same as to suggest Britain as a post-Brexit country will follow successful trade policies.*

Introduction

Statisticians distinguish two types of prediction errors: Type I, where a false positive is returned (cancer is diagnosed in someone who does not have it), and Type II, where a false negative is returned (no cancer is detected in someone who does have it). Mainstream economics has delivered significant instances of both errors in recent years: a resounding Type II error with the failure to anticipate the 2008 financial crisis (Keen, 2017), and an embarrassing Type I error when dire predictions that a victory for Brexit would lead to an immediate economic crisis proved false.

It was of course far too early to expect any loss of output from Brexit the day after the vote. But the reversal of the trend to globalisation was a visceral shock to a profession used to getting its way in political decisions about economic policy. Nonetheless, the expectation remains amongst economists that Britain will experience significant economic losses, thanks to the reversal of the gains from specialisation. Their rationale for the British public failing to understand this potential loss was that the gains from specialisation had not been widely shared. There may be other reasons why future British trade policy proves problematic (see Trommer, 2017) but the background role of economic theory warrants clarification.

The hypothesis of gains from specialisation due to free trade is derived from the 'Law of Comparative Advantage', which has been an article of faith amongst economists ever since it was developed by Ricardo in the early 1800s. The basic proposition is that trade enhances growth by allowing countries to specialise in what they are comparatively good at, even if they may be absolutely worse than their competitors at everything. Falling trade barriers will enable countries to specialise more, which will then increase aggregate global output via greater efficiency. The more specialised a country is, the higher its welfare will be, and specialisation via free trade will promote growth in all countries.

Diversification Rather than Specialisation Matters

It is a beautiful story. Unfortunately, disinterested empirical research by data scientists strongly suggests that it is in fact a fantasy: the wealthiest countries are not the most specialised economies, but the most diversified.

The Harvard University-based Atlas of Economic Complexity uses the information in the huge SITC ('Standard International Trade Classification') database of cross-country trade.[1] The sheer mass of data stored in this database—statistics on trade between all countries in over 800 industry classifications since the 1950s—overwhelmed standard statistical techniques. This study began largely as an attempt to see whether modern concepts and analytic methods from big data and complex systems theory could make sense of the information it contained.

The Atlas developed two key measures—ubiquity and diversity—to measure how complex a given product is, and how complex a country's industrial structure is, proxied by its export/import data. Ubiquity is a measure of how many countries produce a given product: the higher the number, the higher the ubiquity score. Diversity is based on how many products a given country exports: the more products, the more diverse. The two measures are then combined in an iterative process to generate a numerical index of complexity, which as of 2014 varied between a maximum of 2.209 for Japan and a minimum of minus 2.32 for Angola.

The theory of Comparative Advantage implies that most countries would in general score low on ubiquity *and* low on diversity. This was indeed the case for developing countries like Ghana, which produced some products, which were only exported by a few others (such as cocoa, which made up 29% of Ghana's exports in 2014), and where there was only a small number of products in its export catalog (Figure 1).

But developed countries like Germany scored low in the ubiquity of key exports and *high* on diversity: while they do export goods that few other countries can produce (18% of Germany's exports are nuclear reactors and boilers), they also export a much wider range of goods—including those which Comparative Advantage asserts they should import from other countries instead (Figure 2).

Are they simply not taking sufficient advantage of specialisation, and thereby foregoing potential growth? No, because the index of complexity was strongly correlated with *higher* growth, not lower. As *The atlas* puts it:

> We regress the growth in per capita income over 10-year periods on economic complexity, while controlling for initial income and for the increase in real natural resource income experienced during that period. We also include an interaction term between initial income per capita and the ECI. The increase in the explanatory power of the growth equation that can be attributed to the Economic Complexity Index is at least 15 percentage points, or more than a third of the variance explained by the whole equation. Moreover, the size of the estimated effect is large: an increase of one standard deviation in complexity, which is something that Thailand achieved between

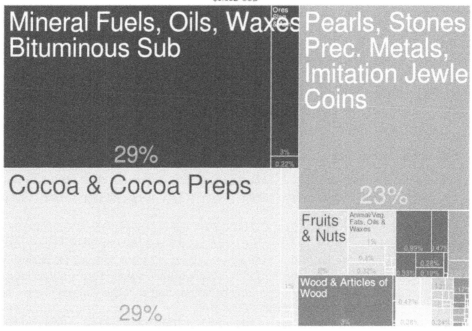

Figure 1. Ghana's exports in 2012 at the medium level of detail.

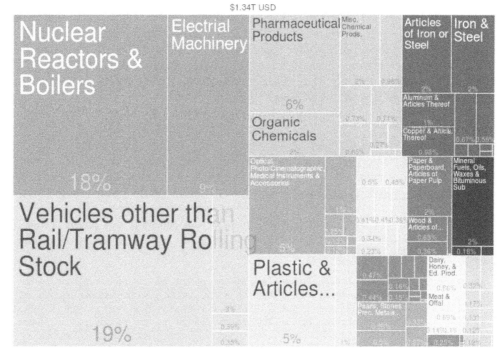

Figure 2. Germany's exports in 2012 at the medium level of detail.

1970 and 1985, is associated with a subsequent acceleration of a country's long-term growth rate of 1.6 percent per year. This is over and above the growth that would have been expected from mineral wealth and global trends. (Hausmann et al., 2011, p. 27)

The apparent paradox that significant growth comes from diversity—in essence, the opposite of specialisation—is easily explained. The growth that the theory of comparative advantage promises comes from using existing resources more efficiently in existing industries; growth in the real world comes predominantly from creating entirely new industries. Another of the Atlas's measures—proximity—indicates that new industries are formed primarily by combining concepts from existing ones. This is easier with a diversified industrial base rather than a specialised one. As *The atlas* puts it:

> new capabilities will be more easily accumulated if they can be combined with others that already exist. This reduces the need to coordinate the accumulation of several new capabilities simultaneously ... For this reason, countries are more likely to move into products that make use of the capabilities that are already available. These capabilities are available, however, because they are being used to make other products. An implication of this is that a country will diversify by moving from the products they already produce to others that require a similar set of embedded knowledge. (Hausmann et al., 2011, p. 44)

A good example here is the invention of sailboards: this is much more likely to occur in a country (or indeed a city) where both sails and surfboards are already being manufactured. In the dynamic, evolutionary world in which we actually live, diversity, rather than specialisation, empowers growth.

The False Assumptions of Comparative Advantage

This empirical challenge to the theory of comparative advantage—that diversity, and not specialisation, is the preferred industrial strategy for export success—is not the only basis on which the argument that there are net gains from trade liberalisation can be challenged. Neoclassical macroeconomists are finally conceding, after failing to anticipate the global financial crisis, and systemically over-forecasting post-crisis growth for a decade, that 'we simply do not have a settled successful theory of the macroeconomy' (Kocherlakota, 2016), and that amongst the reason these models have failed is that 'They are based on unappealing assumptions. Not just simplifying assumptions, as any model must, but assumptions profoundly at odds with what we know about consumers and firms' (Blanchard, 2016, p. 1). It is time that trade theorists admitted the same.

There are many assumptions in Comparative Advantage that are not just 'profoundly at odds with what we know about consumers and firms', but what we know about physical reality as well. The key issue here is the nature and role of machinery in production. The theory is predicated on the capacity to costlessly move 'factors of production' from a less to a more competitive industry in one country in response to a reduction in trade barriers. This is manifestly impossible for machinery, but it has been the practice of international trade theory to ignore this issue since its inception in Ricardo's original example of wine and cloth production in England and Portugal:

> England may be so circumstanced, that to produce the cloth may require the labour of 100 men for one year; and if she attempted to make the wine, it might require the labour of 120 men for the same time ...
>
> To produce the wine in Portugal, might require only the labour of 80 men for one year, and to produce the cloth in the same country, might require the labour of 90 men for the same time. (Ricardo, 1817, Chapter 7, Section 15)

While it is feasible to contemplate unskilled labour moving from one industry to another, as Ricardo did, it is not feasible to do the same with machinery. Unskilled labour in Ricardo's example of cloth and wine are respectively shepherds and grape pickers; one can arguably be retrained to become the other.[2] The same does not apply to a machine, which in its essence is a device used to harness energy to perform useful work in a specific production process. Key machines in Ricardo's example are the 'Spinning Jenny' and the wine press, and there is no way that one can be turned into another. The process of 'moving capital' from one industry to another consequent upon a reduction of trade barriers assumed by the theory simply cannot happen in reality.

If trade liberalisation makes a given industry unprofitable thanks to cheaper imports being available, the immediate consequence is a decline in the financial valuation of companies in the import-competing industries, and an increase in the financial value of companies in the exporting industries. If free trade is to lead to an increase in physical output of both goods in both countries, then there must be significant under-utilised machinery in those industries—and this is normally the case, since most companies operate with significant excess capacity (Blinder, 1998, Chapter 4). But this increase in output is due to the higher utilisation rate of existing machinery in the exporting industries counteracting the lower utilisation rate (or outright mothballing) of machinery in the import-exposed industry. It is not due to the more efficient allocation of capital within the country, which is what comparative advantage assumes.

Often, nothing moves at all within a country. The US phenomenon of the 'Rust Belt', after all, is named after the many factories that are disused and rusting through neglect after their operations were terminated. Physical capital is not re-deployed more productively, but scrapped. If machinery is moved, it is not from one industry to another within one country, but in the same industry from one country to another, either by sale for near scrap value by firms in one country to those in another, or by transfer within the one transnational firm via the relocation of production. Ricardo himself both asserted and hoped that this would not happen:

> It would undoubtedly be advantageous to the capitalists of England, and to the consumers in both countries, that under such circumstances, the wine and the cloth should both be made in Portugal, and therefore that the capital and labour of England employed in making cloth, should be removed to Portugal for that purpose . . .
>
> Experience, however, shews, that the fancied or real insecurity of capital, when not under the immediate control of its owner, together with the natural disinclination which every man has to quit the country of his birth and connexions, and intrust himself with all his habits fixed, to a strange government and new laws, check the emigration of capital. These feelings, which I should be sorry to see weakened, induce most men of property to be satisfied with a low rate of profits in their own country, rather than seek a more advantageous employment for their wealth in foreign nations. (Ricardo, 1817, pp. 136–137)

Ricardo cannot be criticised for failing to anticipate the development of modern shipping and transnational corporations—though he can be criticised for postulating that consumers in both countries would be better off were all production relocated from England to Portugal, without considering what this would mean for the incomes of consumers in both countries. Those who continue promoting the theory of comparative advantage without considering these modern-world issues that were unknown to Ricardo and the macroeconomic issues he ignored can of course be criticised on both fronts. We need a realistic model of the effects of trade liberalisation, and that necessarily has to be a monetary and macroeconomic theory, not a microeconomic one with a fantasy treatment with the confusion of fungible monetary capital with physical non-fungible machinery. Globalisation *and* Brexit need to take this seriously in order to avoid the ills that create dissent.

Conclusion: Why Mainstream Economics Failed to Predict the Costs of Brexit

Whether trade liberalisation causes a net increase or decrease in productive capacity is a question of investment and effective demand, and not one of relative efficiency. Trade theory may have moved on in some ways since Ricardo, but approaches such as Paul Krugman's New Trade Theory, with its emphasis on economies of scale and monopolistic competition, do not go far enough. The key question remains: Does the reduction in trade barriers spur investment in the exporting industries that outweighs the destruction of productive capacity in the import-competing industries? This is a question of macroeconomics, not the microeconomics that has dominated international trade theory since its inception. The gains from trade *for everyone and for every country* that could supposedly be shared more fairly simply are not there in the first place. Of course trade occurs, but genuinely successful trading countries think about the range of products and services they produce and also how to control access to, rather than simply open up, their domestic economy. It remains to be seen if this is an issue that British policy adequately addresses. Brexit remains a complex problem (see Morgan & Patomäki, 2017).

Disclosure Statement

No potential conflict of interest was reported by the author.

Notes

1   Atlas of economic complexity (http://atlas.cid.harvard.edu/) 'SITC' database of cross-country trade (see https://unstats.un.org/unsd/cr/registry/regcst.asp?Cl=28).
2   Though for any real-world modern economy the characteristics of labour are more complex, creating problems; labour too cannot easily retrain, move or transform itself, and so reference to an idealised economic agent of infinite malleability in mainstream theory is often unhelpful (if nothing else it tends to blame the victim).

References

Blanchard, O. (2016). *Do DSGE models have a future?* Retrieved from https://piie.com/system/files/documents/pb16-11.pdf

Blinder, A. S. (1998). *Asking about prices: A new approach to understanding price stickiness.* New York, NY: Russell Sage Foundation.

Hausmann, R., Hidalgo, C. A., Bustos, S., Coscia, M., Chung, S., Jimenez, J., . . . Yildirim, M. (2011). *The atlas of economic complexity: Mapping paths to prosperity.* Cambridge: MIT Press.

Keen, S. (2017). *Can we avoid another financial crisis? (The future of capitalism).* London: Polity Press.

Kocherlakota, N. (2016). *Toy models.* Retrieved from https://docs.google.com/viewer?a=v&pid=sites&srcid=ZGVmYXVsdGRvbWFpbnxrb2NoZXJsYWtvdGEwMDl8Z3g6MTAyZmIzODcxNGZiOGY4Yg

Morgan, J., & Patomäki, H. (2017). Introduction: Special forum on Brexit. *Globalizations, 14*(1), 99–103.

Ricardo, D. (1817). *On the principles of political economy and taxation*. Indianapolis, IN: Library of Economics and Liberty.

Trommer, S. (2017). Post-Brexit trade policy as pyrrhic victory: Being a middle power in a contested trade regime. *Globalizations*. http://www.tandfonline.com/doi/full/10.1080/14747731.2017.1330986.

Post-Brexit Trade Policy Autonomy as Pyrrhic Victory: Being a Middle Power in a Contested Trade Regime

SILKE TROMMER

ABSTRACT   *The Leave camp and prominent Brexiteers typically present regaining political control over international trade policy after Brexit as one advantage of leaving the European Union. A newly autonomous UK government, so the argument goes, will be free to negotiate wide-reaching and ambitious trade agreements with the world and will not be restricted by the compromise-culture inherent in supranational, Brussels-based deliberations. In the absence of clear formulations of Britain's post-Brexit trade political agenda, much of the debate remains hypothetical at this point. Yet, from a global governance perspective, it is clear that the institutional and legal architecture for international trade cooperation is currently fragmented. Given WTO negotiating deadlocks, the institutional strain resulting from parallel country-by-country negotiations, regulatory clash in the existing network of preferential trade agreements, and the UK's new position as a middle power in the trade regime, this essay argues that Britain may find it more difficult to push its own trade agenda internationally than is currently conceded in the debate. With the global trade regime currently shifting back towards more power-based forms of international interactions, regaining trade policy autonomy post-Brexit may turn out to be a pyrrhic victory for the new trade middle power Britain.*

As the United Kingdom (UK) and the European Union (EU) engage in Brexit negotiations, international trade remains at the centre of public and policy debates (for other issues, see e.g. Jessop, 2017; Wahl, 2017). At the time of writing, it seems as though the UK government has acknowledged that the EU will not give heed to Britain's desire for simultaneous talks on Brexit and the new UK–EU trading relationship (Giles, 2017). Within the UK, the trade debate rages between those who warn of economic havoc if Britain should lose access to the EU's single market, and those who point to potential gains to be made from new trade deals struck with the rest of the world. For now, the debate remains hypothetical and largely abstract. EU trade policy-making is a supranational process involving European institutions, transnational interest groups, and an EU-wide epistemic community on trade. Both the UK and the EU trade policy positions will likely shift after Brexit, as British political actors focus their attention on formulations of UK trade policy and cease to play a key role in EU trade policy. In the absence of a clearly formulated substantive post-Brexit trade agenda, the UK government highlights the trade political potentials of Brexit as policy autonomy over international trade returns to London. In its line of argument, Brexit should allow Britain to become a global free trade champion through preferential trade deals made with the world's leading established and emerging economies.

Visions of 'bold and ambitious' free trade agreements (May, 2017) with an array of economies in the proverbial 'queue' for a deal with Britain (Tolhurst, 2017) populate the UK's political discourse on post-Brexit trade. In his 'Free Trade Speech' delivered in September 2016, the UK's International Trade Secretary Liam Fox argued that 'technological advances dissolving away the barriers of time and distance' have led to what he calls a 'post geography trading world'. Britain is thought to be 'much less restricted in having to find [trading] partners who are physically close to us' (Fox, 2016). As a result of the transport, communication, and technology revolution of the late twentieth century, as well as service trade and capital control liberalisation, global production chains are a salient feature of today's global economy. This has in fact altered the conduct of global trade politics, but in different ways than the UK government publicly acknowledges.

First, trade liberalisation traditionally meant reduction of tariffs and tariffication of quotas in trade in goods. In this context, the term 'free trade' in essence refers to removing all duties or other obstacles to products crossing borders. Along with the growth of global production chains, the global trade agenda has started expanding substantially to include behind-the-border issues, services, intellectual property rights, and investment, while average tariff levels are at an all-time low. Phrases such as 'free trade' and 'trade liberalisation' have lost precision as a result, because any rule or regulation across virtually all public policy domains can be construed to constitute a barrier to the free flow of goods and services in the global economy. Seen through the lens of global trade policy elites, 'the crux of the issue is the regulatory environment under which firms located in Britain operate' (Bishop, 2017). When promising bold and ambitious free trade agreements, the reference to 'free trade' is ideological. In negotiations, contemporary trade negotiators typically pursue any mix of improved market access, investment protection, and regulatory harmonisation clauses that they deem suitable for attracting or retaining profitable parts of production chains in their territory, with the precise trade measures depending on the specific economic operators they want to attract or retain.

Second, innovation and deregulation may well have empowered corporations to produce transnationally. The conduct of global trade negotiations, however, remains an international affair. In the world of trade policy-making, countries' economic characteristics and negotiating capacity, as well as domestic and international institutional design and politics continue to be key determinants for the outcomes of state-based negotiations. The question of whether Britain should pursue its trade interests only preferentially or also through multilateral initiatives at the World Trade Organization (WTO) is not explicitly posed in the post-Brexit trade debate for the time being. Yet, the global trade governance architecture contains 270 Preferential Trade

Agreements (PTA) currently in force, that are set up on a multilateral baseline of WTO rules (WTO, 2017a). Far from being transparent, the existing sets of global trade rules and venues for the conduct of world trade politics are fragmenting and complex. This raises further institutional and political challenges for the UK government to successfully pursue its trade agenda as a stand-alone negotiator.

This essay asks what options the UK government has to pursue its trade agenda in the post-Brexit era, given the fragmented nature of the institutional landscape for world trade politics. Trade scholars have thus far dealt with the questions of Britain's post-Brexit trade levels (Dhingra, Ottaviano, Sampson, & Reenen, 2016); WTO status (Bartels, 2016); and trade policy towards developing countries (Mendez-Parra, te Velde, & Winters, 2016). They have pointed out that Britain needs to negotiate on several terrains, namely at the WTO, with the EU, with countries with which the EU has existing free trade agreements, and new commercial partners (Holmes, Rollo, & Alan Winters, 2016). And they have provided basic principles and strategic advice for trade negotiations (Sampson, 2016).

This essay investigates British post-Brexit trade policy through the lens of the current global trade governance architecture. It takes the UK government's declared, if vague, ambitions to be a global free trade champion as the starting point of the analysis, and asks how current centrifugal dynamics in the global legal and political infrastructure for trade cooperation affect Britain's chances of pursuing its agenda successfully. As such, the essay does not engage admittedly important questions of whose interests Britain's post-Brexit trade policy should serve, or whether it is possible to pursue progressive trade policy goals through existing preferential or multilateral channels for global trade cooperation. Instead, it assumes that in line with dominant thinking among global trade policy elites, Britain will eventually likely attempt forging trade rules that improve the regulatory environment in which British corporations operate. The essay depicts a newly autonomous UK as a middle power in a legally, politically and economically fragmented global trading system. It shows that given this position, the UK will be faced with a choice of engaging in cumbersome preferential trade talks and/or a politically deadlocked WTO. The chapter argues that neither of these avenues will likely lend itself to regulatory optimisation. In trade governance terms, Brexit may turn out to be a pyrrhic victory for the self-proclaimed global free trade champion.

A New Middle Power in a Shifting Global Trade Regime

For those critiquing EU membership in Britain (and beyond), the prospect of regaining a free hand in setting trade measures and commercial policy according to national interests has played an important role in making the case for leaving the EU. In terms of foreign policy, the UK has perhaps the biggest measure of political autonomy to regain in the field of trade. Since the start of the European project, political competences over international trade have resided at the supranational level. As a customs union, the EU has a liberalised internal market and a unified set of commercial policies with the outside world. Under EU trade policy-making procedures, national governments have to compromise in order to reach a coherent position that the European Commission pursues in international trade talks (Keukeleire & Delreux, 2014). Post-Brexit Britain, so the argument goes, will be free from these constraints on its negotiating position and can negotiate trade agreements in its own interests. Brexiteers might read historical precedent and current developments in Washington as signalling the UK's ability to successfully pursue its post-Brexit trade agenda, potentially with US support. Historically, the UK government has been able to influence the design of the international trade regime, either in cooperation with the United States (US) or as part of a European alliance. In the twentieth century, transatlantic initiatives have typically set the global trend in international trade cooperation. In the 1930s, European trading nations ratcheted up tariff barriers following the US Smoot–Hawley Tariff Act. Under US political and economic hegemony, industrialised countries shaped the multilateral trade regime of the General Agreement on Tariffs and Trade (GATT) and the WTO (Wilkinson, 2014). The adoption of the competitive liberalisation doctrine under United States Trade Representative Robert Zoellick in 2001 and the Global Europe strategy introduced under Director-General for Trade Peter Mandelson in 2006 consolidated the institutional shift in global trade governance towards the current era of coexisting trade multilateralism and bila-teralism (Heron & Siles-Brügge, 2012). Since then, the world's most powerful trade bureaucracies in Washington and Brussels have actively pursued preferential deals as alternative policy forums to a WTO that they have been increasingly unable to control through the traditional 'quadrilateral group' (or 'Quad') that dominated decision-making in the GATT (WTO, 2017b).

At the time of writing, the UK government's discursive focus on negotiating individual trade deals with third countries post-Brexit mirrors current rhetoric across the Atlantic. The US admin-istration has recently announced its intention to review all of its existing international trade com-mitments and negotiate country-by-country agreements with one commercial partner at a time (Mauldin, 2017). Under the influence of economic nationalist perspectives, the US appears to be withdrawing from so-called 'megaregional' initiatives in trade governance, such as the Trans-Pacific Partnership or the Trans-Atlantic Trade and Investment Agreement. The US administration's nonchalant stance towards WTO rules is perceived as a threat to the multilateral trade regime (Bacchus, 2017).

However, in an international political sense, the UK government will re-enter a transformed world which brings inherent challenges for its ability to pursue its trade political agenda. The global economy and global trade governance architecture have undergone significant changes since the UK last negotiated international trade rules on its own behalf under the GATT Kennedy Round (1964–1967). In 1967, the UK was the fourth biggest world economy. Its GDP stood at 111 billion current USD and was almost on par with the then second and third biggest world economies, Japan and France. It was a mere eight times smaller than the world's leading economy, the US (World Bank, 2017). Table 1 shows global GDP and merchan-dise exports rankings for 2015 in USD. The EU is not included in WTO statistics on merchandise exports, however, according to its own calculations was the third biggest exporter in 2015, exporting €3517 billion worth of products to the rest of the world (Eurostat, 2017).

In terms of GDP and global exports, the UK has dropped some ranks over the past 50 years. More importantly, however, economic power relations have changed to the point where the UK's GDP and export figures are today dwarfed by those of the US, the EU, and China. In terms of economic weight alone, the UK finds itself in the position of a middle power, along with countries such as Canada and Japan, but also India and Brazil, which it comfortably out-performed by significant margins in the 1960s.

The fact that political power relations in global trade governance have also shifted since the UK last negotiated agreements on its own behalf compounds the significance of these changes. From the GATT days to the WTO's Cancún Ministerial Conference in 2003, the Quad effec-tively governed the multilateral trade regime (Jawara & Kwa, 2003). The group consisted of the US, Canada, Japan, and the European Communities, including the UK from 1973 onwards. Prior to its accession to the European Communities, Britain could use its position in the GATT to draw economic benefits from acting as a broker among the big traders (Lee, 1998). Those big traders were predominantly other Western countries of comparable levels of

Table 1. Global GDP and merchandise exports, 2015

	GDP (in billion USD)	Exports (in billion USD)
1	US (18,037)	China (2275)
2	EU (16,312)	US (1505)
3	China (11,008)	Germany (1329)
4	Japan (4383)	Japan (625)
5	Germany (3363)	Netherlands (567)
6	UK (2858)	South Korea (527)
7	France (2419)	Hong Kong (511)
8	India (2095)	France (506)
9	Italy (1821)	UK (460)
10	Brazil (1775)	Italy (459)
11	Canada (1551)	Canada (408)

Source: Authors compilation from World Bank (2017) and WTO (2017c).

social and economic development to the UK, that by and large shared the UK's trade political outlook.

Today, countries at varying levels of development expect to be involved in the negotiations of multilateral trade rules and have acquired the negotiating capacity and skill to do so (Narlikar, 2003). Brazil and India have pushed into the Quad to replace Canada and Japan. China has become a WTO decision-making power (Scott & Wilkinson, 2013). South Africa has demonstrated its ability to shape multilateral trade negotiations (Efstathopoulos, 2015). Although many of these countries have a history of being vocal in multilateral trade talks, developing countries today 'cannot so easily be pressured, marginalized or ignored by richer members' in WTO talks (Aggarwal & Evenett, 2013, p. 6).

The Doha Round has exposed the WTO as a negotiating forum that is struggling to promote an inclusive global trade regime (Capling & Trommer, 2017). Middle powers Norway, New Zealand, Kenya, Indonesia, Chile and Canada formed the 'Oslo group' following the suspension of the WTO Doha Round in 2006 to foster compromise among the new big four, to no avail (WTO, 2017b). With multilateral trade negotiations absorbed in their own political conundrums that middle powers can likely not resolve (anymore), the UK government's best option for pursuing its post-Brexit trade agenda seems to lay in country-by-country deals. Yet, there are institutional limitations to negotiating networks of overlapping PTAs which make this process more cumbersome, and potentially unable to attract public legitimacy.

Negotiating Country-by-Country Deals and Its Discontents

It is a rarely acknowledged fact that governing trade through country-by-country deals is heavy on the human and financial resources of state and non-state stakeholders. In multilateral trade cooperation, one admittedly large team of bureaucrats and legal and economic experts is able to engage with virtually the entire world's trading nations at the same time. PTA-based global trade governance has no physical epicentre, but is entirely conducted on a one-on-one basis. PTAs also by and large remain international treaties, and do not set up international bureaucracies that oversee the application and enforcement of rules. PTA negotiations are thus constrained by institutional capacity and have political drawbacks in terms of outcomes, transparency, and enforceability. They move trade governance towards ever more power-based forms, with all the implications this entails for a global trade middle power.

In a one-country-one-deal approach, the financial and human resources of trade bureaucracies invariably become stretched by the simple fact that several teams of negotiators need to work on separate sets of negotiations. Even the world's leading trade nations today allocate fewer personnel to multilateral trade governance, due to the fact that negotiating preferential deals absorbs institutional resources (Trommer, 2017). This has implications for how many deals can be negotiated at the same time, and for the quality of information and dialogue among potential trade partners. Because commitments in different agreements can be and often are overlapping, there are risks that a trade bureaucracy loses oversight over how commitments in different agreements relate to each other (Estevadeordal & Suominen, 2009). Because PTAs are negotiated one by one, there is no physical epicentre akin to Geneva in which the global trade policy community can meet on a daily basis to exchange views and information. Yet, information and exchange of views are vital in all aspects of international cooperation, whether in agenda-setting, negotiation, implementation, monitoring, or enforcement of rules (Hoekman & Kostecki, 2001).

Stretching a trade bureaucracy's resources brings growing issue uncertainty, and resource-constrained information and dialogue. Signs of resource-constrained post-Brexit trade talks have arguably already become visible. While reportedly having visited 55 countries by January 2017, Liam Fox announced that his department was in informal consultations with 12 (Express, 2017). While Fox provided no reason for limiting the amount of informal consultations to 12 (or for why this constitutes a strategy of 'going global'), this shows that the queue for British trade deals exists in a very literal sense. There are institutional limits to how many trading partners a trade bureaucracy can negotiate a one-on-one trade agreement with at the same time. Resource-constrained negotiations further affect smaller trading nations more adversely than big global trading powers. The world's leading trade economies are better equipped to summon the institutional capacity required for making sense of, and participating in, the fragmented governance architecture for global trade.

Second, PTAs entrench commercial fragmentation by the fragmented preference structure they create, and hence leave business constituencies less happy in the long run than might at first be surmised. The network of 270 PTAs today contains hub-and-spoke patterns, where certain countries maintain preferential deals with third countries that do not have preferential arrangements among themselves. Typically, hub countries in these patterns impose their sets of preferred trade rules and regulations on the smaller trading partner (Busse, 2000). Because global trade powers have differing regulatory preferences in certain areas, for example, banking regulation, food safety, or intellectual property, hub-and-spoke PTA patterns contain the risk of regulatory clashes (Cho, 2006). How the UK government intends to reconcile its agenda for ambitious twenty-first-century trade agreements with the world's leading economies on the one hand, and pressures to comply with incoherence in their regulatory frameworks on the other hand, given its middle power status, remains unclear.

As Bernard Hoekman further points out, 'rules of origin, regulatory convergence and mutual recognition among mega PTA members may create incentives for companies to locate in a bloc, or to source from firms located within a bloc' (2014, p. 243). This phenomenon produces pressure on companies to comply with the regulatory frameworks set out in each and every PTA and can shape the contours of global production chains. From the perspective of transnational corporations, this is a drawback as fragmented regulatory regimes for global trade add trade costs to their transnational operations, irrespective of geographical distance (Trommer, 2017). Complex networks of overlapping PTAs come at a cost to business, who hire expensive consultants to make sense of the legal rules applicable to their cross-border transactions (*The Economist*, 2009), or simply trade under WTO rules even where more preferential arrangements could have been accessible under existing PTAs.

Third, for small non-state actors, such as small and medium-sized businesses, civil society organisations and trade unions, keeping track of the latest trade rules agreed across all PTAs can be an impossible task (Trommer, 2017). This negatively affects dialogue among trade bureaucracies and smaller societal actors. The accountability and transparency gains made in the global trade regime since WTO's legitimacy crisis in the late 1990s are undermined. At the same time, the trade agenda keeps expanding under preferential deals. While WTO rules mainly cover trade in goods, trade in services, intellectual property and dispute settlement, PTAs today go much further. Liberalisation commitments in services are more extensive, intellectual property rules more stringent, and agreements often incorporate a wide range of WTO+ and WTO-X clauses from government procurement and investment to competition policy and regulatory harmonisation. These clauses have implications for the domestic regulation of non-trade areas of public policy. As in the case of the Comprehensive Economic Partnership Agreement and the Trans-Atlantic Trade and Investment Partnership, broad domestic opposition from non-governmental organisations and social movements can be expected to resist the implementation of this new trade agenda (De Ville & Siles-Brügge, 2016). In addition to dealing with resource-constrained international negotiations across fragmented regulatory regimes, the UK government is likely to face domestic battles with all trade political constituencies over its new envisaged role as global free trade champion that have in previously years been channelled to the supranational level of EU policy-making. The problem also extends to ideological conflict beyond trade issues (see Guldi, 2017; Worth, 2017).

Finally, dispute settlement and arbitration under PTAs are more diplomatic in character than under the WTO. Contentious areas are typically excluded from PTA dispute settlement (Froese, 2016). In addition, the WTO Secretariat and political organs provide institutional support infrastructures for dispute settlement. Most importantly for middle powers like Britain, WTO rules have tasked the WTO Secretariat and political organs with setting up individual WTO disputes and making sure a dispute moves through the stages. These third-party brokers make it considerably more difficulty for even the wealthiest and most powerful countries in the trade regime to block proceedings. WTO dispute settlement proceeds in four stages: consultation, adjudication, appeal, and sanctions. According to Article 27 DSU, the WTO Secretariat assists members in dispute settlement proceedings at their request, including proposing nominations for panellists. If the parties to a dispute cannot agree on the composition of the panel, which is often the case, either party may ask the WTO Director-General to determine the composition of the panel, again undermining members' ability to prevent a dispute from being adjudicated (WTO, 2016).

WTO dispute settlement can bring benefits to smaller members in trade disputes with big global trade powers because the former may 'not always possess the necessary bargaining power to force the latter to withdraw ... WTO-incompatible policies' (Chaisse & Chakraborty, 2014, p. 157). Although PTA dispute settlement clauses are often modelled on the WTO Dispute Settlement Mechanism, they generally do not create the institutional infrastructure to support the day-to-day operation of trade courts. Capacity asymmetries in dispute settlement, systemic exclusions of trading nations and of trade topics and resource-constrained adjudication hamper the effectiveness, accessibility, and reliability of legal recourse in international trade relations. The developments can be expected to affect small traders more adversely than large trading nations and ring in a return to resolving trade disputes through power politics, rather than, however imperfect, third-party adjudication through the WTO.

Conclusion

In the post-Brexit trade policy debate, opportunities of new preferential trade deals are often presented as off-setting potential losses if the UK was to forgo EU single market access. This essay has argued that the position betrays a lack of understanding how global trade governance has changed economically, politically, and institutionally since the UK last negotiated trade agreements on its own behalf. Free trade does not constitute a liberalising of trade in goods any more, but in common trade negotiator language refers to optimising the transnational regulatory environment with a view to facilitating the operation of global production chains. Multilateral trade talks under the WTO have been stumbling from one crisis to the next. *Financial Times* Reporter Alan Beattie has mused the WTO's Doha Round talks are reminiscent of the Irish playwright Samuel Beckett's famous dialogue: 'let's go—we can't—why not?—we're waiting for Doha' (Beattie, 2009). Beyond re-establishing its autonomous membership status and joining existing plurilateral initiatives under the Environmental Goods Agreement or the Trade in Services Agreement, the UK will have few opportunities for pushing bold and ambitious trade deals through the WTO.

Negotiating country-by-country trade deals is attractive from the perspective of those actors who deem themselves politically powerful in the global economy. However, due to human and financial resource constraints in trade bureaucracies and among stakeholders, achieving a coherent trade rule book of quasi worldwide coverage that can gain public legitimacy is virtually impossible through country-by-country deals. Complex networks of trade deals that are negotiated behind closed doors are heavy on institutional resources and score poorly on transparency and accountability. They produce commercial fragmentation and contribute to regulatory clashes. With trade rules predominantly being about behind-the-border issues today, social forces that see their non-trade interests curtailed through secretive trade talks will continue to monitor and challenge government initiatives. Although Britain can strike deals with the world's leading industrialised and industrialising economies after Brexit, whether these rules and norms will find application may ultimately depend on the power balances among countries at the moment when the rules will be tested and this has broader context in terms of power relations and consequences, including for the EU (see Galbraith, 2017; Pato-mäki, 2017). Whether the new middle power Britain will be able to live up to its global free trade fantasies in a contested world trade regime may be more questionable than Brexiteers like to concede.

Disclosure Statement

No potential conflict of interest was reported by the author.

Funding

This work was supported by the Australian Research Council [Discovery Grant 120101634].

References

Aggarwal, V., & Evenett, S. (2013). A fragmenting global economy: A weakened WTO, mega-FTAs, and murky protectionism. *Swiss Political Science Review*, *19*, 550–557.

Bacchus, J. (2017, January 4).Trump's challenge to the WTO. *The Wall Street Journal*.

Bartels, L. (2016). *The UK's status in the WTO after Brexit*. Retrieved March 28, 2017, from https://ssrn.com/abstract=2841747

Beattie, A. (2009, October 12). Misadventures of the most favoured nations. *Financial Times*.

Bishop, M. (2017). *Brexit and free trade fallacies*. Retrieved April 20, 2017, from http://speri.dept.shef.ac.uk/2017/01/11/brexit-and-free-trade-fallacies-part-one/

Busse, M. (2000). The hub and spoke approach of EU trade policy. *Intereconomics*, *35*(4), 153–154.

Capling, A., & Trommer, S. (2017). The evolution of the global trade regime. In J. Ravenhill (Ed.), *Global political economy* (5th ed., pp. 111–140). Oxford: Oxford University Press.

Chaisse, J., & Chakraborty, D. (2014). Implementing WTO rules through negotiations and sanctions: The role of trade policy review mechanism and dispute settlement system. *University of Pennsylvania Journal of International Law*, *28*(1), 153–185.

Cho, S. (2006). Defragmenting world trade. *Northwestern Journal of International Law and Business*, *27*(1), 39–88.

De Ville, F., & Siles-Brügge, G. (2016). Why TTIP is a game changer and its critics have a point. *Journal of European Public Policy*. doi:10.1080/13501763.2016.1254273

Dhingra, S., Ottaviano, G., Sampson T., & Reenen, J. V. (2016). *The consequences of Brexit for UK trade and living standards*. Paper Brexit 02. London: Centre for Economic Performance and London School of Economics.

Efstathopoulos, C. (2015). *Middle powers in world trade diplomacy: India, South Africa and the Doha development agenda*. Basingstoke: Palgrave Macmillan.

Estevadeordal, A., & Suominen, K. (2009). *The sovereign remedy? Trade agreements in a globalizing world*. Oxford: Oxford University Press.

Eurostat. (2017). *International trade in goods*. Retrieved March 29, 2017, from http://ec.europa.eu/eurostat/statistics-explained/index.php/International_trade_in_goods

Express. (2017). *Dozens of countries lining up to do free trade deal with UK says Liam Fox*. Retrieved March 30, 2017, from http://www.express.co.uk/news/politics/756237/politics-brexit-liam-fox-free-trade-deals-global-britain

Fox, L. (2016, September 29). Speech delivered by International Trade Secretary Liam Fox at the Manchester Town Hall. Retrieved March 28, 2017, from https://www.gov.uk/government/speeches/liam-foxs-free-trade-speech

Froese, M. (2016). Mapping the scope of dispute settlement in regional trade agreements: Implications for the multilateral governance of trade. *World Trade Review*, *15*(4), 563–585.

Galbraith, J. (2017). Europe and the world after Brexit. *Globalizations*, *14*(1), 164–167.

Giles, C. (2017, April 13). The UK's negotiating position on Brexit is a fantasy. *Financial Times*.

Guldi, J. (2017). The case for utopia: History and the possible meanings of Brexit a hundred years on. *Globalizations*, *14*(1), 150–156.

Heron, T., & Siles-Brügge, G. (2012). Competitive liberalization and the 'global Europe' services and investment agenda: Locating the commercial drivers of the EU-ACP economic partnership agreements. *Journal of Common Market Studies*, *50*(2), 250–266.

Hoekman, B. (2014). Sustaining multilateral trade cooperation in a multipolar world economy. *Review of International Organizations*, *9*(2), 241–260.

Hoekman, B., & Kostecki, M. (2001). *The political economy of the world trading system: WTO and beyond*. Oxford: Oxford University Press.

Holmes, P., Rollo, J., & Alan Winters, L. (2016). Negotiating the UK's post-Brexit trade arrangements. *National Institute Economic Review*, *238*(1), R22–R30.

Jawara, F., & Kwa, A. (2003). *Behind the scenes at the WTO: The real world of international trade negotiations. The lessons of Cancun*. London: Zed Books.

Jessop, B. (2017). The organic crisis of the British state: Putting Brexit in its place. *Globalizations*, *14*(1), 133–141.

Keukeleire, S., & Delreux, T. (2014). *The foreign policy of the European Union*. Basingstoke: Palgrave Macmillan.

Lee, D. (1998). Middle powers in the global economy: British influence during the opening phase of the Kennedy trade round negotiations, 1962-4. *Review of International Studies*, *24*(4), 515–528.

Mauldin, W. (2017, January 27). Trump's big gamble: Luring countries into one-on-one trade deals. *The Wall Street Journal*.

May, T. (2017, January 17). Theresa May's Brexit speech in full. *The Telegraph*.

Mendez-Parra, M., te Velde, D. W., & Winters, L. A. (2016). *The impact of the UK's post-Brexit trade policy on development: An essay series*. London: Overseas Development Institute and UK Trade Policy Observatory.

Narlikar, A. (2003). *International trade and developing countries: Bargaining together in the GATT and WTO*. London: Routledge.

The noodle bowl: Why trade agreements are all the rage in Asia. (2009, September 3). *The Economist*.

Patomäki, H. (2017). Will the EU disintegrate? What does the likely possibility of disintegration tell about the future of the world? *Globalizations, 14*(1), 168–177.

Sampson, T. (2016). *Four principles for the UK's Brexit negotiations*. British Politics and Policy Blog. London School of Economics. Retrieved March 28, 2017, from http://blogs.lse.ac.uk/politicsandpolicy/four-principles-for-the-uks-brexit-trade-negotiations/

Scott, J., & Wilkinson, R. (2013). China threat? Evidence from the WTO. *World Trade Review, 47*(4): 761–792.

Tolhurst, A. (2017, February 15). Front of the queue: Canada first in long line for post-Brexit trade deal with Britain after EU passes long-awaited CETA agreement. *The Sun*.

Trommer, S. (2017). The WTO in an era of preferential trade agreements: Thick and thin institutions in global trade governance. *World Trade Review*. doi:10.1017/S1474745616000628

Wahl, P. (2017). Between eurotopia and nationalism: A third way for the future of the EU. *Globalizations, 14*(1), 157–163.

Wilkinson, R. (2014). *What's wrong with the WTO? And how to fix it*. Cambridge: Polity Press.

World Bank. (2017). *World Bank open data*. Retrieved March 30, 2017, from http://data.worldbank.org/

Worth, O. (2017). Reviving Hayek's dream. *Globalizations, 14*(1), 104–109.

WTO. (2016). *The process: Stages in a typical WTO dispute settlement case*. Retrieved March 30, 2017, from https://www.wto.org/english/tratop_e/dispu_e/disp_settlement_cbt_e/c6s2p1_e.htm

WTO. (2017a). *Regional trade agreements*. Retrieved March 28, 2017, from https://www.wto.org/english/tratop_e/region_e/region_e.htm

WTO. (2017b). *Membership, alliances and bureaucracy*. Retrieved March 29, 2017, from https://www.wto.org/english/thewto_e/whatis_e/tif_e/org3_e.htm

WTO. (2017c). *World trade statistical review 2016*. Geneva: Author.

Brexit and Global Wealth Chains

LEONARD SEABROOKE & DUNCAN WIGAN

ABSTRACT   *One vision of a post Brexit Britain is of a political economy sustained by highly flexible labour markets, light touch regulation, and a hyper competitive low-tax regime. This article focuses on the tax element, evaluating the prospects of this vision's realization on the basis of the attributes of the British political economy, the substance of the Britain's new found freedoms and the forces at play in the European and international regulatory environment. Britain is seeking a smooth transition via a strategy of upgrading and expanding national position in global wealth chains (GWCs). Occupying space in GWCs requires a series of careful balancing acts between making a tax offer attractive to mobile capital and maintaining revenue, designing a low-tax regime and staying within the boundaries of accepted practice established by multilateral rules and norms, and between multiple, often conflicting, goals that Britain must simultaneously pursue as it leaves the European Union. With hard Brexit, Britain will pursue this vision, but these balances are likely to prove illusive.*

Introduction

One vision that has animated political and public imaginations of a post Brexit Britain is that of a lean free market economic fighting machine built on highly 'flexible' labour markets, light touch regulation, and a hyper competitive low-tax regime. It is a vision that foresees a Britain much akin to former colonial territories such as Hong Kong and Singapore, an offshore financial centre serving as touchdown platform for mobile capital in the hands of corporations and wealthy elites. In conversation with the German newspaper *Welt Am Sonntag*, Philip Hammond, UK Chancellor of the Exchequer, threatened that the UK would choose this path if it did not secure a favourable exit deal:

> If we have no access to the European market, if we are closed off, if Britain were to leave the European Union without an agreement on market access, then we could suffer from economic damage at least in the short-term. In this case, we could be forced to change our economic model and we will have to change our model to regain competitiveness. And you can be sure we will do whatever we have to do. The British people are not going to lie down and say, too bad, we've been wounded. We will change our model, and we will come back, and we will be competitively engaged. (Hammond, 2017)

Theresa May was quick to double down on the threat, stating through her official spokeswoman, 'We would want to remain in the mainstream of a recognizable European-style taxation system, but if we are forced to do something different if we can't get the right deal then we stand ready to do so' (*LA Times*, 2017). It would seem that this iteration of the 'Hayekian dream' (see Worth, 2017) chimes with a large part of the Brexit constituency with a poll finding that 36% of respondents supported the idea of Britain competing with the EU on tax and 22% opposed (TJN, 2017). These are the opening salvos of a major skirmish in ongoing and recently intensified 'global tax battles' (Seabrooke & Wigan, 2018). The 2008 global financial crisis (GFC) spurred seemingly strong multilateral commitment to tackle the problem of harmful tax competition with a G20 communique announcing the intention 'to take action against non cooperative jurisdictions, including tax havens' (G20, 2009, p. 4) and the G8 announcing at Lough Erne a commitment to country-by-country reporting (CBCR) for corporations, the automatic exchange of tax information between national authorities on bank accounts, and full transparency with regard to the beneficial owners of companies and trusts (G8, 2013).

Since the GFC, a host of policy innovations have been launched with the aim of curbing 'global tax battles', starting with the United States acting unilaterally on tax evasion with the Foreign Account Tax Compliance Act and more recently the Organization of Economic Cooperation and Development (OECD) completing avoidance work with the base erosion and profit shifting (BEPS) initiative (OECD, 2015; Palan & Wigan, 2014). The European Union (EU) has been particularly active on the issue reinforcing its armoury against tax avoidance and evasion and continuing to pursue a major overhaul of the corporate tax system in the form of a Common Consolidated Corporate Tax Base (CCCTB). It is in this context of invigorated regulatory activism that the prospect of a post Brexit Britain committed to a strategy of tax war should be evaluated. Morgan notes,

> The temptation will be to pursue policies advantageous to rising profit shares: that is, allowing more wealth capture from wealth creation. Typical means to these ends include: lowering corporation tax ... modern corporations operate long supply chains with complex production processes in different locales. Being outside of a trading bloc disrupts one's capacity to be part of the chain. This is likely to intensify the need for concessions to attract corporate investment, and also further a temptation to attract reporting of revenues rather than actual economic activity—a tax haven effect. (2017, pp. 122–123)

In a corner, Britain promises to come out fighting with the sovereign capacity to write tax law.

One way of thinking about Britain's tax competition exit strategy is through the concept of 'global wealth chains' (GWCs). The work on GWCs provides a systematic way to view how accounting, finance, law, and regulatory governance interact to produce five different ideal types of how wealth is created and protected in multi-jurisdictional environments (Seabrooke & Wigan, 2014, 2017). The purpose of GWC research is to understand corporate form, taxation issues, and regulatory arbitrage opportunities as a system rather than as discrete topics within their own silos. In this manner, GWCs research draws on global value chains research (cf. Gereffi, 1994; Gereffi, Humphreys, & Sturgeon, 2005) that depicts the journey of a commodity through an internationally dispersed production process conditioned by a series of buyer and supplier relationships. GWCs complement its focus on who does what in global production, by following the money. Mirroring work by Gereffi et al. (2005), the GWC frame distinguishes five ideal types of chain—*market, modular, relational, captive,* and *hierarchy*—on the basis of relations between clients, suppliers, and regulators, with the state often playing a dual role as both supplier and regulator (Finér & Ylönen, 2017; Seabrooke & Wigan, 2017). The framework also permits insights into the sources of global inequalities (Quentin, 2017).

Which chain a particular service or product is situated in is a function of the complexity of information and knowledge regarding the product or service being supplied, the liability of the service or product to regulatory intervention, and the capabilities of suppliers to furnish solutions to fend off challenges to the product or service by regulators (Seabrooke & Wigan, 2017). Market chains, for example, will involve arm's-length transactions and simple off-the-shelf products such as offshore shell companies, with the client shielded from the regulator by secrecy provided by the supplier. Relational chains include private wealth managers who closely coordinate with clients, often high net worth individuals, to provide more complex multi-jurisdictional investment solutions that regulators find difficult to track. Hierarchy chains involve the most complex products, including structured finance and corporate reorganizations, where close coordination, or complete integration, between client and supplier ensures that the regulator has little capacity to intervene (Seabrooke & Wigan, 2017). Despite David Cameron's Lough Erne announcement and accelerated regulatory innovation noted above, the threat of a tax war exit strategy promises that a post Brexit Britain will play an even greater role in maintaining and operating GWCs, exporting to Europe the symptoms of a tax curse as it has in the past exported those of a 'finance curse' (Christensen, Shaxson, & Wigan, 2016). Britain certainly occupies a position in the world economy that indicates that this is a credible threat.

The Battle Field

The role of Britain in GWCs has a long lineage. The emergence of the Euro dollar and bond markets in London between 1957 and 1961 effectively created an infrastructure for offshore 'global' finance in the heart of the Bretton Woods system, placing trades between non-residents outside the regulatory net and marking

> a fundamental shift in international financial relations, from one directed towards the furtherance of distinct 'national' regimes of accumulation, based on a system that was almost wholly regulated, to one that is today mostly responsive to the demands of global speculation and almost wholly unregulated. (Burn, 1999, p. 226)

At the same time, UK authorities were often active in the process whereby many of its former colonial possessions used powers afforded by frequently partial independence to pursue an offshore strategy, with the Bank of England and Ministry of Overseas Development sometimes pitted against the Inland Revenue and Treasury in the face of an emergent 'British tax haven empire' (Sagar, Christensen, & Shaxson, 2013).

The British offshore imprint is substantial. Haberly and Wójcik suggest with regard to foreign direct investment (FDI) that of the approximately '30–50 percent of global FDI accounted for by networks of offshore shell companies created by corporations and individuals for tax and other purposes' the metropolitan core of the former European colonial system is, 'clearly the centre of the global offshore network, with Britain's offshore second empire of singular importance' (2015, pp. 251, 272). London is the key hub in this network with capital channelled from the second empire, facilitated by a shared common law tradition. This legal tradition permits ample amounts of what Sol Picciotto refers to as legal indeterminacy, an indeterminacy that empowers legal elites to facilitate wealth chains by keeping the regulator at bay with linguistic word play and normative judgements over what exactly tax law means (Picciotto, 2015). Brexit empowers this aspect of London-focused financial capitalism and the likelihood of Britain becoming even more like a 'tax haven'. The power of judges and lawyers to guard against regulators infringing on different legal structures that underpin wealth chains is well known, and highly protected (Quentin, in press).

The Tax Justice Network (TJN) produces a Financial Secrecy Index (FSI), which compares the offshore footprint of jurisdictions according to the level of secrecy provided to international capital and holders of capital weighted by a jurisdiction's share in global financial services exports. According to the 2015 FSI, Britain taken alone ranks 15th in the world on the basis of the size of its hold in global financial markets (TJN, 2015). Taken together with its Crown Dependencies and Overseas Territories, such as Jersey, the Caymans Islands, and the Isle of Man, Britain would top TJN's list of secrecy jurisdictions. Given legal control over Crown Dependencies, Overseas Territories, and Commonwealth countries—for each London's privy council is the ultimate legal authority—Britain's offshore network would seem to offer an ideal institutional basis from which to wage its tax battle and make a claim on a greater share of the business conducted through GWCs.

At the same time, the United States has occupied a much more aggressive battle position since the election of Donald Trump. The implementation of the Foreign Account Tax Compliance Act has unfolded in such a way as to exclude partner countries from the potential benefits of receiving information on the bank accounts of its nationals. Trump has also committed to slash the U.S. headline corporate tax rate of 35% to 15%, introduce a territorial tax system in the United States, which would only tax U.S. multinationals on income generated in the United States, and provide a repatriation holiday, allowing the $2.5 trillion accrued by Fortune 500 firms offshore to return at a preferential tax rate (USPIRG, 2016; White House, 2017). A roll back on the tax transparency provisions in the 2010 Dodd-Frank Bill and U.S. reluctance to participate in the OECD's multilateral information exchange system suggest that the United States may join a low-tax Anglo-American alliance.

Britain's prospects in this fight could be considered favourable. Hampered by that direct taxation remains a closely guarded EU member state competency and a proposal concerning direct taxes requires unanimity at the Council of Ministers and the de facto revision of the treaties, the EU long failed to progress on issues of direct taxation (Wigan, 2014). While the Community adopted a significant body of legislation on VAT and excise duties in the early 1990s, this 'only highlighted the absence of a coherent policy on direct taxation' (European Commission, 2001, p. 3). EU power has traditionally been limited to indirect taxes such as VAT and excise duties, seen to hinder aspirations for the single market. However, more recently, Algirdas Šemeta and Pierre Moscovici, successively European Commissioners for Taxation and Customs Union, Audit, and Anti-Fraud, have been more active with Šemeta on the heels of the G20 declaring war in 2012:

> Let there be no illusion: tax evaders steal from the pockets of ordinary citizens and deprive Member States of much-needed revenue. If we want fair and efficient tax systems, we must stamp out this

activity. The political will to intensify the battle is there. Now it is time to translate that into action. (quoted in European Commission, 2012, p. 1)

The prospects of Britain's effort to win market share in GWCs are in part conditioned by the coherence of EU policy and concomitant political will to act against British incursions.

The signs point to a Europe more committed to a coherent policy on taxation and less likely to tolerate a Britain acting as offshore satellite. The earlier innovation of the Savings Tax Directive and ongoing policy developments within the EU in terms of the update to the Savings Tax Directive, state aid investigations under the authority of the Competition Commissioner Vestager, the Directive on Administrative Cooperation, the incorporation of the OECD's newly minted multilateral Automatic Exchange of Information standard into European regulation, versions of CBCR in the Capital Requirements Directive IV and the Accounting and Transparency Directives that impact all large multinationals operating in the Union, and the adoption of a directive requiring member states to provide information on the beneficial ownership of companies mean that the European tax regime is evolving rapidly and takes the lead internationally. At the same time, the OECD has taken steps to strengthen the multilateral regulatory architecture against tax abuse in its BEPS initiative, which is promulgating new rules to increase transparency and restrict opportunities for tax arbitrage, including a demand for the automatic exchange of tax information between tax authorities and a form of CBCR by companies (OECD, 2015).

The international tax system (so far as we can usefully nominate one) sits at a juncture, in one direction is increased cooperation and tighter rules, in the other, increased tax competition and greater divergence between nationally circumscribed tax rules. Britain's threat to become a low-tax offshore satellite of the EU in consequence faces countervailing forces. It also faces the apparently weaker hand that Britain holds in negotiating exit terms with the Union. Passporting rights for financial services—the right to sell financial product Europe wide—depends on the acquiescence of Britain's European negotiating partners (cf. Toly, 2017). Initial salvoes in the exit negotiations suggest that Britain will not be given an easy ride, and in choosing a turbo charged tax competition strategy may need to sacrifice other cherished goals, in particular the maintenance of a political economy almost uniquely shaped around London's financial centre (Gifford, 2016, pp. 784–785).

The Battle

Occupying space in GWCs requires a series of careful balancing acts between making a tax offer attractive to mobile capital and maintaining sufficient revenue, designing a low-tax regime and staying within the boundaries of accepted practice established by multilateral rules and norms, and between multiple, often conflicting, goals that Britain must simultaneously pursue as it leaves the EU. Ultimately, these balances may prove more illusory than the bravado behind Britain's threat of post Brexit tax war suggests.

VAT has been harmonized in the EU since 1977 due to the barrier to free trade implied by multiple and varied national sales tax regimes. Britain's exit will provide it with free rein in this regard. However, VAT represents a significant portion of Britain's fiscal income, one fifth of the total, and making dramatic cuts to its rate would entail budgetary consequences the Treasury would be unlikely to support. Instead, Brexit might see some minor tinkering with the VAT system, on the one hand to pander to voters (consider the row over the governments wish to remove VAT from women's sanitary products), and on the other, to ensure that the British system is sufficiently aligned to that of Europe to avoid costs for UK businesses trading in European countries. Import VAT on goods entering the UK and goods from the UK entering Europe, although recoverable, will add cash flow costs to many businesses. VAT then is not a heavy weapon in the British armoury.

Britain has ostensibly more room for manoeuvre in wealth chain markets built around direct taxation, particularly market and hierarchy chains hosting wealthy individuals and large multinational corporations. On corporate taxation, Britain prior to the vote to leave already had journeyed some way down this path. In March 2016, the then Chancellor announced the intention to bring the corporate tax rate down to 17% by 2020. Theresa May, in late 2016, promised business leaders to maintain 'the lowest corporate tax rate in the G20' to match Trump's promise of a 15% rate in the U.S. May's suggestion was warmly welcomed by the former Chancellor, George Osborne, who tweeted, 'Good to see briefing that corporation tax should be cut again. We got it from 28 per cent to 17 per cent. Next step let's go to 15 per cent and show UK open to business' (Houlder, 2016). Notably, this path was well trodden long before the Brexit vote as direct tax rates are a member state competence and successive British governments have sought competitive advantage on the basis of reducing corporate tax levels. It is not beyond imagination that the final destination is a 0% corporate tax rate with foreign shareholders, and corporate issuers, flocking to London in search of tax-enhanced returns. Domestic shareholders may bear the brunt of the cost though, as the revenue that previously came directly from corporates is substituted by revenue coming from British-based shareholders (Murphy, 2017). The vulnerability of this strategy lies more in Britain's international reputation with a leaked memo from the OECD stating, 'A further step in that direction would really turn the UK into a tax haven type of economy' (Houlder, 2016).

On point of Brexit, EU Directives and regulation will no longer apply in Britain. The wind blows both ways here. That British companies will no longer be subject to the Parent-Subsidiary and Interest and Royalty Directives is a potential loss for the UK and those companies. These Directives exempt dividend, interest, and royalty payments from withholding taxes on intra-Union transfers. After Brexit, member states could apply withholding taxes on these payments to Britain. Britain has a double tax treaty with every member of the EU and in many cases, these treaties eliminate taxes on such payments between signatories. However, not all double tax treaties with member states in place carry provisions that eliminate taxes on these transfers (Mazurs, 2016). Revisions to treaty agreements will depend on member states' acceptance of British tax policy more broadly, and its adherence to OECD norms particularly, so that insofar as Britain seeks to leverage an aggressive tax competition strategy, member states may be less willing to make concessions on such issues.

On the other hand, release from EU Directives may provide space in which Britain can redesign its tax system in the way envisioned by George Osbourne, Philip Hammond, and Theresa May. Release from the strictures of agreement to the Code of Conduct on Business Taxation and the reach of EU competition law, deployed concertedly to curtail perceived egregious tax avoidance by the present EU Competition Commissioner, Margrethe Vestager, affords some room for manoeuvre. The Code of Conduct on Business Taxation is soft law, used in the EU when lack of political consensus blocks policy progress. Adopting the code, member states committed to roll back existing tax measures that constituted harmful tax competition and refrain from introducing any further such measures (Cattoir, 2006, pp. 3–4). While the code recognizes the benefits of tax competition, it also provides grounds for a shared understanding of harmful competition, requiring the participation of EU-dependent territories, and leading to confrontation with jurisdictions seeking to compete by distinguishing between resident and non-resident companies for tax purposes. The removal of the strictures of the Code from Britain and its dependencies ostensibly affords Britain greater freedom in designing its tax system in a way of its own choosing. So too does escape from the reaches of EU Competition law.

Post Brexit, the removal of EU state aid rules and the uncertainty over advanced tax rulings that the Competition Commissioner's activism in this area has generated may provide Britain greater scope in its pursuit of aggressive tax competition. State aid investigations into transfer pricing rulings given to multinational companies such as Starbucks, Fiat, McDonalds, and Apple have put a cooler on intra-EU tax competition and infamously resulted in a demand that Ireland collects €13 billion from Apple. This demand is being contested both by the company, and perhaps ironically, by the government under which the revenue authority set to make a windfall gain operates (for the Apple case, see Bryan, Rafferty, & Wigan, 2017). In theory then, out of the reach of EU competition regulation, Britain could provide state aid to resident companies and offer a host of reliefs, benefits, and deductions otherwise not available in the Union. It is important though that the Anti Tax Avoidance Directive passed by the Council in June 2016 foresees the EU compiling a blacklist of non-cooperative third countries, which are susceptible to sanctions. For Britain, if deemed a third country post Brexit, exploiting its new founds freedom may not be costless.

The EU in the absence of Britain at the table may well be able to push further forward on direct taxation issues. The proposed CCCTB envisions a formulary apportionment approach to taxing multinational firms operating in Europe. This involves establishing a common tax base or harmonizing corporate tax rules across all European jurisdictions and allocating corporate group profits to each member state according to a formula including, for instance, sales, labour force, and capital. This has the potential to greatly reduce the space corporations have enjoyed to shift profits to low- or no-tax jurisdictions and losses to high-tax jurisdictions via transfer pricing or intra-firm financing (Morgan, 2016; Seabrooke & Wigan, 2016). Insofar as this form of tax reporting provides a gauge of what might be a reasonable allocation of profits to Britain by a multinational operating in Europe, such allocations will become open to dispute, and disproportional or diverted profits in Britain may lead member states and the Commission to seek redress through blacklisting on the basis of contravention of OECD norms, particularly those promulgated under the BEPS initiative. Similar retaliation can be expected should Britain backslide on commitments to transparency measures on the beneficial ownership of trusts, a long-term British speciality, and an issue that Europe is likely to continue its push forward on given that Britain has long blocked progress.

At the same time, as Britain loses influence in Europe its dependencies and overseas territories, an important source of funding for London's financial markets, may become more vulnerable to sanctions from Europe. In the eventuality that Britain pursues an aggressive tax competition strategy, member states and the Commission will be incentivized to act decisively against these jurisdictions. Having taken a central role in the development of the OECD BEPS initiative, which has established a host of new international tax norms, including the automatic exchange of tax information between authorities, CBCR for corporations and stricter guidelines on the design of financing arrangements, Britain may find it difficult to head full steam in the other direction. 'The tension between tax competitiveness and opposition to tax avoidance will not be removed by Brexit' (Freedman, 2017).

Conclusion

A post Brexit Britain that follows up on the threats issued by Hammond and May will be a Britain excluded from the economic benefits of the trade in goods and services with EU member states, and a Britain facing the atrophy of what is (erroneously) considered the goose that lays the golden eggs, the City of London. Brexiteers dreaming of fighting back with low wages, light regulations, and aggressive tax policies are imagining that these benefits can be substituted by corporate and elite wealth flows. Notwithstanding the fact that wealth flows in and of themselves will be insufficient to propel a major political economy and the welfare and employment requirements attendant to that, this is a recipe for long-term decline. Wealth flows are by nature fickle and a Britain effectively excluded from its giant neighbouring market will unlikely remain attractive. Large international banks are already relocating staff to Ireland and Luxembourg to capture the European market that will be lost to British business. London's financial pre-eminence attracts global professional services firms, law firms, and accounting and taxation specialists. This skills nexus may in turn become fragile and feed back into a frustrated plan. Such a consequence will change how GWCs articulated via the City are formed, changing into more and more aggressive forms of tax planning that are veiled in legal indeterminacy. Should that be the case, we are going to need some analytical tools to handle this transition as Britain and Europe diverge in how they treat corporate form. GWCs provide a fruitful means of integrating how we understand law, accounting, finance, and regulatory changes as a system. Brexit may concentrate the dependence of London-based elites on these systems even more. Knowing how to unbundle and analyse these networks becomes more important, as relations between suppliers, clients, and regulators continue to morph under force of intervention, innovation, and political (mal)intent.

Disclosure Statement

No potential conflict of interest was reported by the authors.

References

Bryan, D., Rafferty, M., & Wigan, D. (2017). Capital unchained: Finance, intangible assets and the double life of capital in the offshore world. *Review of International Political Economy, 24*(1), 56–86.

Burn, G. (1999). The state, the city and the Euromarkets. *Review of International Political Economy, 6*(2), 225–261.

Cattoir, P. (2006). *A history of the 'tax package': The principles and issues underlying the community approach* (Working Paper No. 10). Taxation Papers.

Christensen, J., Shaxson, N., & Wigan, D. (2016). The finance curse: Britain and the world economy. *The British Journal of Politics and International Relations, 18*(1), 255–269.

European Commission. (2001). *Communication from the commission to the council, the European parliament and the economic and social committee: Tax policy in the European Union—Priorities for the years ahead.* COM(2001) 260 final.

European Commission. (2012). *Tackling tax fraud and evasion: Commission sets out concrete measures.* June 27, 2012. Press Release IP/12/697. Retrieved June 29, 2013, from http://europa.eu/rapid/press-release_IP-12-697_en.htm

Finér, L., & Ylönen, M. (2017) Tax-driven wealth chains: A multiple case study of tax avoidance in the Finnish mining sector. *Critical Perspectives on Accounting.* doi:10.1016/j.cpa.2017.01.002

Freedman, J. (2017). Tax and Brexit. *Oxford Review of Economic Policy, 33*(S1), S79–S90.

G20. (2009, April 2). *Global plan for recovery and reform.* Statement Issued by the G20 Leaders, London. Retrieved from http://www.cfr.org/financial-crises/g20-global-plan-recovery-reformapril-2009/p19017

G8. (2013). *2013 Lough Erne G8 Leaders' Communique.* Retrieved from https://www.gov.uk/government/publications/2013-lough-erne-g8-leaders-communique

Gereffi, G. (1994). The organisation of buyer-driven global commodity chains: How US retailers shape overseas production networks. In G. Gereffi & M. Korzeniewicz (Eds.), *Commodity chains and global capitalism* (pp. 95–122). Westport: Praeger.

Gereffi, G., Humphreys, J., & Sturgeon, T. (2005). The governance of global value chains. *Review of International Political Economy, 12*(1), 78–104.

Gifford, C. (2016). The United Kingdom's Eurosceptic political economy. *The British Journal of Politics and International Relations, 18*(4), 779–794.

Haberly, D., & Wójcik, D. (2015). Regional blocks and imperial legacies: Mapping the global offshore FDI network. *Economic Geography, 91*(3), 251–280.

Hammond, P. (2017, January 15). *Philip Hammond issues threat to EU partners.* Welt Am Sontag. Retrieved from https://www.welt.de/english-news/article161182946/Philip-Hammond-issues-threat-to-EU-partners.html

Houlder, V. (2016, November 21). *Business wary over further cuts to UK corporation tax. Financial Times.* Retrieved from https://www.ft.com/content/245bde5a-affa-11e6-9c37-5787335499a0

LA Times. (2017, January 16). British Prime Minister May signals European Union clean break: 'No half-in, half-out'. *Los Angeles Times.* Retrieved from http://www.latimes.com/world/la-fg-britain-brexit-20170116-story.html

Mazurs (2016, June) Brexit: Preparing for change – the tax implications. Retrieved from http://www.mazars.co.uk/Home/News/Latest-news/News-Archive-2016/Brexit-Implications-for-global-mobility-management

Morgan, J. (2016). 'Corporation tax as a problem of MNC organizational circuits: The case for unitary taxation'. *The British Journal of Politics and International Relations, 18*(2), 463–481.

Morgan, J. (2017). Brexit: Be careful what you wish for? *Globalizations, 14*(1), 118–126.

Murphy, R. (2017). *Singapore on Thames?* City Political Economy Research Centre.

OECD. (2015). *BEPS 2015 final reports.* Paris: Author. Retrieved from http://www.oecd.org/tax/beps-2015-final-reports.htm

Palan, R., & Wigan, D. (2014). Herding cats and taming tax havens: The US strategy of 'not in my backyard'. *Global Policy, 5*(3), 334–343.

Picciotto, S. (2015). Indeterminacy, complexity, technocracy and the reform of international corporate taxation. *Social & Legal Studies, 24*(2), 165–184.

Quentin, D. (2017). Corporate tax reform and 'value creation': Towards unfettered diagonal re-allocation across the global inequality chain. *Accounting, Economics, and Law: A Convivium.* doi:10.1515/ael-2016-0020

Quentin, D. (in press). Legal opinion in global wealth chains. In L. Seabrooke & D. Wigan (Eds.), *Global wealth chains: Asset strategies in the world economy.* Oxford: Oxford University Press.

Sagar, P., Christensen, J., & Shaxson, N. (2013). British government attitudes to British Tax havens: An examination of Whitehall responses to the growth of tax havens in British dependent territories from 1967–75. In J. Leaman & A. Waris (Eds.), *Tax justice and the political economy of global capitalism 1945 to the present* (pp. 107–132). New York, NY: Berghahn Books.

Seabrooke, L., & Wigan, D. (2014). Global wealth chains in the international political economy. *Review of International Political Economy, 21*(1), 257–263.

Seabrooke, L., & Wigan, D. (2016). Powering ideas through expertise: Professionals in global tax battles. *Journal of European Public Policy, 23*(3), 357–374.

Seabrooke, L., & Wigan, D. (2017). The governance of global wealth chains. *Review of International Political Economy, 24*(1), 1–29.

Seabrooke, L., & Wigan, D. (2018). *Global Tax battles: The fight to govern corporate and elite wealth.* Oxford: Oxford University Press.

TJN. (2015). *Financial Secrecy Index – Narrative report on the United Kingdom.* Tax Justice Network. Retrieved from http://www.financialsecrecyindex.com/PDF/UnitedKingdom.pdf

TJN. (2017, February 6). *What does the public think about tax haven plans?* Tax Justice Network. Retrieved from http://www.taxjustice.net/2017/02/06/brexit-britain-public-think-tax-haven-plans/

Toly, N. (2017). Brexit, global cities, and the future of world order. *Globalizations, 14*(1), 142–149.

USPIRG. (2016). *Offshore Shell Games 2016: The use of offshore tax havens by Fortune 500 Companies.* United States Public Interest Research Group, Citizens for Tax Justice, Institute on Taxation and Economic Policy. Retrieved from http://www.uspirg.org/sites/pirg/files/reports/USP%20ShellGames%20Oct16%201.2_FINAL.pdf

White House. (2017). *Tax reform for economic growth and American jobs: The biggest individual and business tax cut in American history.* Washington, DC: Author. Retrieved from http://www.washington.edu/federalrelations/files/2017/04/WHfactsheet04262017.pdf

Wigan, D. (2014). Offshore financial centres. In M. Daniel (Ed.), *Europe in global finance* (pp. 156–171). Oxford: Oxford University Press.

Worth, O. (2017). Reviving Hayek's dream. *Globalizations, 14*(1), 104–109.

Brexit and the Economics of Political Change in Developed Countries

JAYATI GHOSH

ABSTRACT   *The economic forces underlying Brexit—and the election of Donald Trump in the US—are similar, but they are also well advanced in many European countries, where much of the population faces similar material insecurity and stagnation. These frustrations can easily be channelled by right-wing xenophobic forces. To combat this, the EU needs to undo some of its design flaws and particularly its adherence to fiscal austerity rules. Only a more progressive and more flexible union based on solidarity of peoples is likely to survive.*

Across the world, people have been watching recent political changes in developed countries with a mixture of bemusement and shock (e.g. Ghosh, 2017). From the vote in the UK in favour of leaving the European Union, to the anointment of Donald Trump as the US President, to the rise and spread of blatantly racist anti-immigration political parties and movements in mainland Europe, it is clear that there are tectonic shifts under way in the political discourse and practice in these countries. It is now obvious that increasing inequality, stagnant real incomes of working people and the increasing material fragility of daily life have all played roles in creating a strong sense of dissatisfaction among ordinary people in the rich countries (see Fullbrook & Morgan, 2017). While even the poor amongst them still continue to be hugely better off than the vast majority of people in the developing world, their own perceptions are quite different, and they increasingly see themselves as the victims of globalisation. This is driving the changing political discourse in the developed world, even if the eventual outcomes of political changes and the economic processes they generate are such as to make the material situation of the poor even worse than before.

Inequality Within the Advanced Countries

While growing inequality within the rich countries is now widely recognised, the full extent of very recent economic trends is probably less well known. There are many sources of evidence one might draw on here. However, one of the more recent and comprehensive is provided by the McKinsey Global Institute (2016). The report is based on three sources: income distribution data from 25 developed countries; a dataset providing more detailed information on 350,000 people from France, Italy and the US and the UK; and a survey of 6000 people from France, the UK and the US. The latter also checked for perceptions about the evolution of their incomes, and provides some evidence that goes beyond standard indicators.

The results are probably not surprising in terms of the basic trends identified, but the sheer extent of the change and the deterioration in incomes still comes as a surprise. In 25 advanced economies, between 65% and 70% of households (amounting to around 540–580 million people) were in income segments that experienced flat or falling incomes between 2005 and 2014. By contrast, in the previous period between 1993 and 2005, less than 2% (fewer than 10 million people) faced flat or falling incomes. The situation was much worse in particular countries. In Italy, 97% of the population had stagnant or declining real incomes between 2005 and 2014, while the ratios were 81% for the US and 70% in the UK. This confirms established work by Galbraith (2012), Stockhammer (2013) and, subject to caveats, Piketty (2014).

The results in the report refer to market incomes, and it is true that government tax and transfer policies can change the final disposable income of households, in some cases improving it. Policy matters. Indeed, for the 25 countries taken together, only 20–25% experienced flat or falling disposable incomes. In the US, government taxes and transfers turned a decline in market incomes for 81% of households into an increase in disposable income for nearly all of them. Similarly, government policies to intervene in labour markets also made a difference. In Sweden, the government intervened with measures designed to preserve jobs, so market incomes fell or were flat for only 20%, while tax and transfer policies ensured that disposable income advanced for almost everyone. But in most of the countries examined in the study, government policies were not sufficient to prevent stagnant or declining incomes for a significant proportion of the population, and labour market trends contributed to feelings of insecurity among workers everywhere. While these changes were evident across the board, the worst affected were less educated workers, and particularly the younger ones among them, as well as women, especially single mothers. As is now generally recognised, today's younger generation in the advanced countries is at real risk of ending up poorer than their parents, and in any case already faces much more insecure working conditions.

This material reality is actually quite accurately reflected in popular perceptions. A survey conducted in 2015 of British, French and US citizens used in the McKinsey report confirmed this. Approximately 40% of those surveyed felt that their economic positions had deteriorated. Interestingly it was also such people, as well as those who did not expect the situation to improve for the next generation, who felt most negatively about both trade and migration. More than half of this negative group agreed with the statement, 'The influx of foreign goods and services is leading to domestic job losses,' compared with 29% of those who were categorised in advancing or neutral income groups. They were also twice as likely as those in advancing or neutral income groups to agree with the statement, 'Legal immigrants are ruining the culture and cohesiveness in our society.' The survey also found that those whose incomes were not improving and who were not hopeful about the future were more likely in France to support political parties such as Front National and in Britain to support Brexit.

One major driver of stagnant worker incomes has been the combination of labour market developments and public policies that have resulted in declining wage shares of national income. The report notes that from 1970 to 2014—with the brief exception of a spike during the 1973–1974 oil crisis—the average wage share across the six countries studied in depth (US, UK, France, Italy, the Netherlands and Sweden) fell by 5 percentage points. In the most extreme case of the UK, it declined by 13 percentage points. These declines in wage shares occurred despite increases in labour productivity, as the productivity gains were either grabbed by employers or passed on in the form of lower prices to maintain external competitiveness.

Such declining wage shares are commonly seen to be the result of globalisation and technological changes that have led to changing patterns of demand for low-skill and medium-skill workers. But even here, it is evident that state policies and institutional relations in the labour market matter (for context see Wade, 2017). In Sweden, where 68% of workers are union members and the government has in place policies that enforce contracts that protect both wage rates and hours worked, the median household received a greater share of output that went to wages, and even got more of the gains from aggregate income growth than households in the top and bottom income deciles over the 2005–2014 period.

By contrast, countries that have encouraged the growth of part-time and temporary contracts experienced bigger declines in wage shares. Once again, this is especially adverse for the young. According to European Union official data, more than 40% of workers aged between 15 and 25 years in the 28 countries of the EU have such insecure and low-paying contracts, while the proportion is more than half for the 18 countries in the Eurozone, 58% in France and 65% in Spain. This is obviously a concern for the young people who have to experience this, but it is as much a source of unhappiness and anger for their parents who worry for the future of their children.

In the meantime, they can all observe the counterpart in terms of rising profit shares in many of these rich countries. Economic processes and government policies increasingly appear to favour plutocratic tendencies. In the US, for example, post-tax profits of firms in the period 2010–2014 reached more than 10.1% of GDP, a level last reached in 1929 just before the Great Depression. Ironically, in the US this favoured the political rise of one of the biggest beneficiaries of this process, Donald Trump who is himself emblematic of such plutocracy.

If economic policies do not change dramatically to favour more good quality employment and better labour market outcomes through co-ordinated fiscal expansions that lift growth in more inclusive ways, things are likely to get even worse. The report projects that even if the previous high-growth trajectory is resumed (an unlikely prospect) at least 30–40% of households would not get income gains over the next decade, especially if technological changes like more automation accelerate. And if the slow growth conditions of 2005–2012 persist, the proportion of households experiencing flat or falling incomes could go to as much as 70–80% by 2025.

Economic Tensions Within Europe

Even before the results of the UK referendum, the European Union faced a crisis of popular legitimacy, especially within some of the largest member countries. The Brexit result, especially in England and Wales, was certainly driven by the fear of more immigration, irresponsibly whipped up by xenophobic right-wing leaders who now appear uncertain themselves of what to do with the outcome. But it was as much a cry of pain and protest from working communities that have been damaged and hollowed out by three decades of neoliberal economic policies. And this is why the concerns of greater popular resonance across other countries in the EU—and the idea that this could simply be the first domino to fall—are absolutely valid. So the bloc as a whole now faces an existential crisis of an entirely different order, and its survival hinges on how its rulers choose to confront it (see Galbraith, 2016; Patomäki, 2017).

A little history is in order first. The formation of the union itself, from its genesis in the Treaty of Rome in 1957, was as much a result of geopolitical pressure from the US as it was of the grand visions of those who led it. The six founding countries (Belgium, France, Germany, Italy, Luxembourg and the Netherlands) built on the hope of the European Coal and Steel Community that was established in 1950, that greater economic relations would secure lasting peace and prosperity. Somewhat ironically, they were egged on by the US, which in the post Second World War period not only provided huge amounts of Marshall Plan aid to western Europe, but urged the reduction of trade barriers between them to encourage more intra-regional economic activity and provide an effective counter to eastern Europe during the Cold War.

Subsequent expansion of membership has brought the number of member countries in the EU to 28. The UK joined the EU in 1973, along with Ireland and Denmark, followed in the 1980s by Greece, Spain and Portugal, and then by Austria, Finland and Sweden in the 1990s and then some years after the fall of the Berlin Wall, a large intake of 12 central and eastern European countries in the 2000s, with the most recent member being Croatia in 2013 (for the UK, see Guldi, 2017). Over the years, expansion has been accompanied by the push for 'ever greater union': the Maastricht Treaty in 1993 that laid down the ground rules for economic engagement and strengthened the institutional structure of the European Commission and the European Parliament; the creation of the Single Market of free movement of goods, services and people starting from 1994; the Treaty of Amsterdam that devolved some powers from national governments to the European Parliament, including legislating on immigration, adopting civil and criminal laws, and enacting the common foreign and security policy; and even a common currency, the euro, shared by a subgroup of 19 members from 1 January 1999.

Some would say that it is remarkable that a continent with a fairly recent history of wars and extreme regional conflicts could have achieved such a combination of expansion and integration. There is no doubt that, from the start, this was a project of the political and corporate elite of Europe, and the 'voice of the people' was not really taken into account. Yet in many ways it was also a visionary, even romantic, project that could only go as far as it has gone because, even as it increasingly furthered the goals of globalised finance and large corporations, it still contained the (inadequately utilised) potential for ensuring some citizens' rights across the region.

However, as the EU bureaucracy expanded and as the rules—particularly the economic ones—became ever more rigid and inflexible, with the forceful imposition of fiscal austerity measures in countries with deficits and even in countries where there was no real need to do so, the Commission itself and the entire process came to be seen as distant, deaf to people's concerns and impervious to genuine pleas for help, and lacking in a degree of empathy. Germany, the undisputed leader of the bloc, epitomised this sense of rigid adherence to (often nonsensical and contradictory) rules. The lack of consistency in creating a monetary union without a genuine banking union or any solidarity with fiscal federalism has created years of economic depression in some countries and deflationary pressures across the Eurozone and most of the EU. Nowhere has this been more evident than in the tragic case of the Greek economy, but this is also true of other countries in the periphery that have been forced into austerity measures with little to show in terms of benefit for more than five years now.

So in the expanding but unfinished project that is the European Union, corporate elites have basically achieved their goals and won—as indeed they have been winning in pretty much every region of the world over the past three decades. The implicit project of aiding finance and other large private capital and dismantling the welfare state in these countries has moved ahead.

The result has been not only economic stagnation and continued increases in inequality, but a breakdown of communities and a pervading sense of hopelessness among people across the region, who feel they are no longer able to control their own destiny. Low and receding employment prospects, precarious work contracts, flat or falling real wages, increasing insecurity in material life, reduced access or lower quality of essential public services such as health and education, less social protection, and a general sense of economic decline have become pervasive features, even though these are by and large still prosperous societies (see Morgan, 2017; Pettifor, 2017). All these are indeed not common only to Europe, but are felt in many other parts of the world as a result of economic policies favouring the rich and large capital, and suppressing the rights and aspirations of ordinary people on the grounds that 'there is no alternative'.

In this context, the EU decision to accept (relatively few, around a million) refugee migrants from war-torn regions of West Asia—mostly tragic victims of instability in the region resulting from wars entered into by the governments of the US and the EU themselves—was in some ways the final straw. In some countries like the UK, there was already resentment at the entry of EU citizens from eastern Europe, who were seen to be driving up house rents and lowering wages. But the possibility of particularly Muslim immigration that was cynically used by the Leave campaign in Britain is also a major element of the public response in many other countries like France and even Germany, where other people, rather than corporate capital, are seen as the threat.

Concerns about migration have been widely portrayed as the dominant concern that propelled the slight majority vote that turned the result in favour of leaving the European Union in England and Wales in particular. But that would be too simplistic an interpretation, because obviously such concerns are in turn reflective of other changes in material and social conditions that have left people feeling disempowered and alienated from the system (see Hobolt, 2016). Several commentators have pointed out how such feelings of despair, helplessness and anger have been exploited by unscrupulous politicians with a more explicitly xenophobic and 'anti-Europe' agenda (see Kagarlitsky, 2017; Worth, 2017). Decades of neoliberal economic policies that have led to the hollowing out of communities in depressed parts of the country and the lack of any attractive employment opportunities for the youth were wrongly attributed only to the EU, generating resentment that was exacerbated by EU policies of open borders that allowed more migrants.

This is not just a failure in terms of managing perceptions; it reflects a more fundamental economic failure of the European Union. And it is this failure that should worry the leadership of the EU, if they do not want the popular disaffection now openly expressed in Britain to translate into equally or perhaps even more devastating responses in other countries, that could even cause a disintegration of the union. This is all the more serious because the UK is not among the worst performers even among the large economies in the EU, and causes for popular unhappiness could be even stronger in other countries.

So the tragedy is that growing alienation of many people who have become the victims of financial globalisation has also left them unable to pick on their real enemy. Instead, the tendency has been to pick on others, who are equally or even more the victims, but can be isolated and made into scapegoats because of some apparent differences, particularly recent migrants fleeing either enormous physical threats or economic hardship. The vote in England and Wales both indicates and further strengthens an increasingly unpleasant right-wing surge across Europe, in which 'nationalism' is little more than a fig leaf for open or suppressed racism and intolerance to ethnic/cultural differences.

What Next for the EU?

For several years now, it has been evident that the EU as an economic project has been more or less a failure. This may stem from the very design of the economic integration (flawed, for example, in the enforcement of monetary integration without banking union or a fiscal federation that would have helped deal with internal imbalances) as well as from the template of neoliberal economic policies that it has effectively forced its members to pursue.

This has been especially evident in the adoption of austerity policies across the member countries, remarkably even among those that do not have large current account or fiscal deficits. As a result, growth in the EU has been sclerotic at best since 2004, and even the so-called 'recovery' after 2012 is barely noticeable, with the Eurozone performing even worse than the wider group of 28 countries (Figure 1).

What may be more significant is that even this lacklustre performance has been highly differentiated, with Germany emerging as the clear winner from the formation of the Eurozone. Figure 2 indicates how the other four large economies in the EU have fared in terms of per capita income (in current euros) relative to Germany. Interestingly, the UK performed the best relatively, even though its gap with Germany increased until recently. France, Italy and Spain all experienced deteriorating per capita incomes relative to Germany from 2009 onwards. This, combined with overt and covert fears of German domination, probably added to the barely concealed resentment that is now being expressed in both right-wing and left-wing movements across Europe.

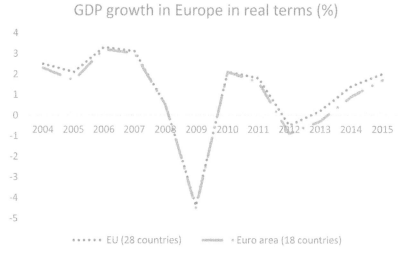

Figure 1. GDP growth in Europe in real terms (%).
Source for all figures: www.europa.eu statistical database.

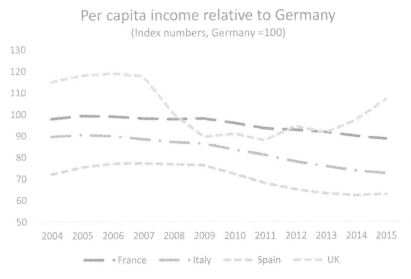

Figure 2. Per capita income relative to Germany (Index numbers, Germany = 100).

The misguided emphasis on neoliberal policies and fiscal austerity packages has also contributed to the persistence of relatively high rates of open unemployment, which are higher than they were more than a decade ago for EU-28, the Eurozone countries and the big five other than Germany (Figure 3). Open unemployment rates are now higher than they were even in 2010 in France, Italy and Spain—although ironically, they actually fell in the UK, where the rate is now closer to the German rate.

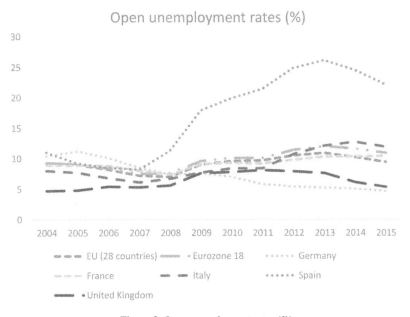

Figure 3. Open unemployment rates (%).

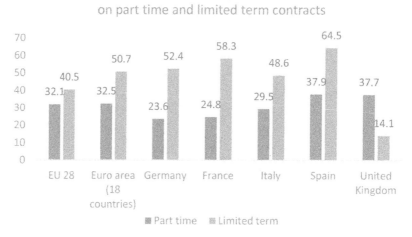

Figure 4. Percent of workers aged 15–24 years on part time and limited term contracts.

But even for those who manage to find employment—and particularly for the young amongst them—work contracts are increasingly insecure and short term (Figure 4). 'Precarity' is the dominant feature of work contracts for the young in these countries—and once again, conditions in the other large countries (even Germany) are much worse in this respect than in the UK! (The two categories in Figure 4 are not exclusive: it is possible even for part-time work to be on a limited term contract.) Even older workers find themselves at the receiving end of the new flexibility of labour markets, for example, in the infamous 'zero hours' work contracts in which employers are not required to offer workers any minimum working hours, but workers are forced to be available or 'on call' even when they are not actually working, and then get paid only for the exact number of hours that they are called upon for.

Recent research in the UK (Citizens Advice, 2017) indicates that at least 14% of the workforce (around 4.5 million people) are in such insecure work—and the proportion among the young is obviously much higher. But Figure 4 points to a more frightening fact: that such insecure work contracts are even more widespread in the other big European nations. It is worth noting that these proportions have increased substantially since 2004 in all countries. It is a mistake to think that having to deal with such work insecurity is a problem only for those like the youth who have to suffer it: it is also a problem—and therefore a source of unhappiness and anger—for their families, including parents who worry for the future of their children.

So if economic insecurity, and related despair and rage, were major factors in the vote against the European Union in Britain, then these economic pressures seem to exist in even greater magnitude in other major European countries. The implications of this should not be underestimated. All these countries, including Germany, are witnessing the increasing strength of Eurosceptic forces. The union would not survive a similar poll result in any one of them, or even in some of the smaller countries where calls for such a referendum are gaining strength. And ignoring democratic expression at this point in time in Europe is fraught with risk. There is already a significant movement against immigration and against the EU, driven again by anger, despair and frustration at economic trends, that is growing across different member countries. If a clear result in this referendum is blatantly denied (despite the best intentions of those working to have a second referendum) or leads to a delayed and watered down response without Britain actually leaving the EU, this will fuel an even greater right-wing response and further strengthen this movement. Then the right-wing surge has the potential to become a veritable tsunami across Europe.

To come out of this severe existential crisis, the EU needs to change several things, most of all its underlying approach to economic policies. Instead, it has hardened its positions on deficits in Spain and Portugal and banking problems in Italy. In the current context, this almost seems like the EU leadership has a death wish. The immediate response appears to be a closing of ranks and circling of the wagons, with strict terms applied to the UK as punishment and also deterrence to other would-be leavers. But stronger political union with much greater federal powers no longer seems to be on the table. Instead, there are also likely to be calls for greater flexibility, with respect to both economic policies and migration. Donald Tusk, the Polish President of the European Council, has already warned that ordinary European citizens do not share the enthusiasm of some of their leaders for 'a utopia of Europe without nation states, a utopia of Europe without conflicting interests and ambitions, a utopia of Europe imposing its own values on the external world, a utopia of Euro-Asian unity'. It is likely that there is much less political appetite for greater integration, for example, in a banking union, and this will make other forms of economic union even less effective, especially in countries experiencing continued economic difficulties and consequent social unrest.

So which way will the European Union go now? The European Union as it exists today is unstable and probably unsustainable. But it will be tragic indeed if it collapses under the weight of its own contradictions only to yield to the petty and xenophobic forms of national neoliberalism that are currently the most forceful alternative to neoliberal economic integration.

What Europe and the world require are more internationalist alternatives based on popular sovereignty, solidarity, the improvement of workers' conditions and the rights of citizens. Some of the voices calling for alternative policies based on less fiscal austerity and more economic and social solidarity are becoming louder—but they still need much more political traction if they are to make a difference. There are incipient progressive movements like Diem25, but such movements need to expand and be embraced by many more people across the continent, if the EU is to be saved from itself. Only a more progressive and flexible union based on the solidarity of peoples can show the way forward; the current more rigid format may be too brittle to survive.

Disclosure Statement

No potential conflict of interest was reported by the author.

References

Citizens Advice. (2017). *How can job security exist in the modern world of work?* Retrieved April 23, 2017, from https://www.citizensadvice.org.uk/about-us/policy/policy-research-topics/work-policy-research-surveys-and-consultation-responses/work-policy-research/how-can-job-security-exist-in-the-modern-world-of-work/

Fullbrook, E., & Morgan, J. (Eds.). (2017). *Trumponomics: Causes and consequences*. London: WEA Books.

Galbraith, J. (2012). *Inequality and instability: A study of the world economy just before the crisis*. Oxford: Oxford University Press.

Galbraith, J. (2016). *Welcome to the poison chalice: The destruction of Greece and the future of Europe*. New Haven: Yale University Press.

Ghosh, J. (2017). Trumponomics and the developing world. *Real World Economics Review*, *79*, 29–34. Reprinted in Fullbrook and Morgan 2017.

Guldi, J. (2017). The case for utopia: History and the possible meanings of Brexit a hundred years on. *Globalizations*, *14*(1), 150–156.

Hobolt, S. (2016). The Brexit vote: A divided nation, a divided continent. *Journal of European Public Policy*, *23*(9), 1259–1277.

Kagarlitsky, B. (2017). Brexit and the future of the left. *Globalizations*, *14*(1), 110–117.

McKinsey Global Institute. (2016, July). *Poorer Than Their Parents? Flat or falling incomes in advanced economies.* Retrieved April 23, 2017, from http://www.mckinsey.com/global-themes/employment-and-growth/poorer-than-their-parents-a-new-perspective-on-income-inequality

Morgan, J. (2017). Brexit: Be careful what you wish for? *Globalizations*, *14*(1), 118–126.

Patomäki, H. (2017). Will the EU disintegrate? What does the likely possibility of disintegration tell about the future of the world? *Globalizations*, *14*(1), 168–177.

Pettifor, A. (2017). Brexit and its consequences. *Globalizations*, *14*(1), 127–132.

Piketty, T. (2014). *Capital in the twenty first century.* Cambridge, MA: Harvard University Press.

Stockhammer, E. (2013) Why have wage shares fallen? A panel analysis of the determinants of functional income distribution. *ILO Conditions of Work and Employment No 35*, Geneva.

Wade, R. (2017). Is Trump wrong on trade? *Real World Economics Review*, *79*, 43–63. Reprinted in Fullbrook and Morgan 2017.

Worth, O. (2017). Reviving Hayek's dream. *Globalizations*, *14*(1), 104–109.

In the Yugoslav Mirror: The EU Disintegration Crisis

JOACHIM BECKER

ABSTRACT *The Yugoslav and the present EU integration crisis display several parallels. In both cases, the integration models have proved to be unable to attenuate the uneven development patterns, and the state has been characterised by strong confederal elements. Deep economic crisis strengthened in both cases the centrifugal tendencies. The political discourse became increasingly dominated by the question 'who exploits whom?'. While central authorities pursued policies of neo-liberal structural adjustment eroding its legitimacy among the popular classes, the republican authorities in Yugoslavia, respectively, the national governments in the EU tried to shift the burden of the crises to the others and strengthened their role during the crisis management. With the deepening of the crisis, constitutional reform became an issue in Yugoslavia. In the Yugoslav case, the various proposals proved to be irreconcilable. In the EU, a debate on its future shape has begun as well. This issue is highly controversial. In the EU, a key problem is the relationship between euro zone and non-euro zone states. Such an institutional divide did not exist in Yugoslavia. It is significant that the leading state of the non-euro zone group, the UK, is the first state to exit the EU. A key question is whether the EU has already passed the critical point where a deep reform is still possible.*

'Europe like former Yugoslavia'. This was the headline of an interview with the Slovenian economist Jože Mencinger in the Serbian weekly *Vreme* in 2011. In the interview, Mencinger who had been a key politician in Slovenia during the Yugoslav disintegration process compared the debates in crisis Yugoslavia in the 1980s and the EU today. He observed strong parallels regarding rifts between the most developed parts and the poorer regions and the ensuing mutual recriminations in both cases (Radić, 2011). Mencinger is not the only intellectual in former Yugoslavia who sees parallels between the disintegration of Yugoslavia and the present centrifugal tendencies in the EU. Following the Brexit decision in the British referendum in June 2016 and the subsequent initiation of the exit process in March 2017, the disintegration of the EU has been set in motion. Though the two cases differ in regard to the socio-economic and political order—'self-management' socialism in the transition towards capitalism in Yugoslavia, capitalism in the EU—they show some striking structural parallels in other regards: the very uneven patterns of development and the political mixture of federal and confederal elements. In both cases, a 'great crisis' decisively strengthened the disintegrative tendencies. This makes a comparison between the two cases worthwhile.

In the analysis, structural features and elements of the political-economic 'conjuncture' will be distinguished. 'Great crises' are particularly important junctures since actors develop new strategies in such situations. Political and economic strategies have a spatial dimension. Under specific circumstances, actors might aim at changing the territorial order (Becker, 2002, p. 264). In both, Yugoslavia in the 1980s and the early 1990s and in the EU today, actors at the republican/national level have aimed either to transform the existing set-up of the multi-national state in conflicting ways or to split directly away from the state. In this way, they wanted to change the 'strategic selectivity' (Jessop, 2002, p. 40) of the state structures in order to promote their interests. The 'strategic selectivity' of the state defines the differential access to and control over state capacities. In principle, the territorial strategies might be developed from above, that is, forces within the dominant bloc, or rather from below, that is, the lower social classes. Forces of the dominant bloc might try to integrate forces of the dominated classes in an alliance cutting through class lines in their territorial project (Becker, 2002, p. 242). This article explores the alliances behind 'YU-federal'/EU-wide territorial projects and those favouring 'national' solutions.

The Disintegration of Yugoslavia

When the Communist partisan emerged victorious from the Second World War, they were confronted with a very difficult economic heritage. The country was devastated by the German occupation and the war. The country was very unevenly developed and in a peripheral position within the European division of labour. The development project of the League of Communists aimed at overcoming these two features. It launched an ambitious industrialisation project and put particular emphasis on developing the poorest regions of the country where a kind of semi-subsistence agriculture predominated. A special fund for building infrastructure and industries in the less industrially developed regions of Yugoslavia was created. Phases of centralisation and decentralisation of economic decision-making alternated (cf. Samary, 1988). In 1965, a major decentralisation with the strengthening of decision-making of the 'social enterprises' and subsequently the republics was commenced (e.g. Kirn, 2014, p. 213). The decentralisation led to an increasing economic divergence and widening of per capita income differences between the richest republics and poorest regions. The gap between the per capita Social Product of the poorest region—Kosovo—and the richest republic—Slovenia—widened from 1:4 to around 1:7 between 1952 and the late 1980s (in the prices of 1972; Borak, 2002 p. 214, tab. 214). Enhanced powers of the directors of 'social enterprises' and the technocratic strata were the second effect of decentralisation (cf. Kirn, 2014, p. 244).

At the political level, decentralising tendencies culminated in the passing of a new Constitution in 1974. The constitution redefined the distribution of powers between the Federal government and the Republics (and autonomous regions). It instituted a mixture of federal and confederal elements, but moved decisively closer to 'confederal political institutions' (Kirn, 2014, p. 198). As in other state socialist states, the Yugloslav state had dual government and

Communist Party structures. Strategic decisions were taken by superior organs of the Party (cf. Becker, 2009, p. 35). In the early 1970s, the composition of the cadre structure of the party also started to change. The older generation of partisans was increasingly supplanted by younger, often better educated cadres. 'These young Party leaders owed their power and prestige mostly to the environment in which they originated, that is, to their republics of origin' (Centrih, 2014, p. 15). This facilitated the transformation of the League of Communists in a way parallel to the government structures: 'The LCY had in fact become a veritable federation of seven separate Leagues of Communists (the republican branches plus the communist organization in the army, each with its own establishment, leaders and particular interests' (Centrih, 2014, p. 16).

Thus, by the time a significant crisis hit the country in the 1980s, the country was characterised by strong patterns of uneven development plus a strong proliferation of decentralised, republican structures of both party and government state structures. This crisis had its roots in the attempt to bridge the chronic current account deficit and to modernise the economy through capital goods imports, which incurred external debt in the 1970s. The government reacted by applying several austerity programmes in the 1980s—partially backed and controlled by the International Monetary Fund (IMF) (cf. Borak, 2002, p. 143; Djeković, 1989, p. 31; Weissenbacher, 2003, p. 154). The consequences were stagnation and temporary declines in GDP, high inflation, massive real income losses, increasing poverty, and rising unemployment. The impact of the crisis hit different parts of Yugoslavia unevenly. As Djeković (1989, p. 25) pointed out, unemployment in Kosovo reached about 30%, whereas Slovenia still enjoyed almost full employment with an unemployment rate of 1.9% in the mid-1980s.

The deteriorating social situation produced a series of strikes of workers that were 'short, atomised and ever more unsuccessful' as Unkovski-Korica (2015, p. 40) observes; and 'family, neighbourhood and friendship networks became to replace workplace loyalties' (p. 40). The party leaders in the republics tried to capture malcontent workers by promising protection along national lines (cf. Woodward, 2002, p. 79). The republic leaderships tried their very best to shield their own republic as much as possible from the impact of the crisis. Economic policy-making increasingly fragmented, whereas nationalist rhetoric strengthened. The rhetoric had economic undertones: 'Who exploits whom?' was the denominator of acrimonious debates on economic relations and fiscal transfers between the republics (cf. Madžar, 1996).

In the late 1980s, the problems came to a head. As the crisis exacerbated, the new federal government of Ante Marković signed a new agreement with the IMF and passed a package of tough austerity measures and structural neo-liberal transformative reforms. The IMF came out in favour of strengthening the economic policy-making powers of the federal government (Weissenbacher, 2003, p. 168). This was counterproductive, since the undertaking met the resistance of the republics. An extremely controversial debate on constitutional changes for re-ordering the (economic decision-making) powers between the federation and the republics ensued (cf. Borak, 2002, p. 171).

Marković was in a very weak position. The main support pillar of his government was an external one—the IMF. The Marković government did not have sufficient backing within the central party apparatus and federal state institutions had been massively weakened over the previous 15 years. Whereas the anti-inflation bias of the programme was popular, the social consequences were not. His government got support from the newly formed Udruženje za jugoslovensku demokratsku inicijativu (UJDI) that had been founded by left and left-liberal intellectuals who tried to promote a democratic Yugoslav alternative. This initiative came out in support of Marković's economic programme (Spaskovska, 2015, p. 42). In view of the deteriorating economic situation and the inability of the programme to deal with the development impasse in Yugoslavia, this support hardly enhanced the popularity of the UJDI. It remained fairly isolated. However, peace and human rights activists emerged out of the UJDI.

The republican leaderships had different and conflicting conceptions. Slovenia and Croatia favoured a loose confederation with sweeping powers, including the economic sphere, for the republics (cf. Borak, 2002, p. 187). Free from the burden of the periphery, they wanted more leeway for decision-making. Serbia was economically more orientated towards the other republics and argued for a federal solution—but with a much stronger role for Serbia. And the republics systematically took measures and passed legislation that undermined the decisions and decision-making powers of the federal government (cf. Borak, 2002, p. 180). The leading forces in the republics—party leadership, technocracy, and directors of state enterprises—shared an interest in securing territorial control of 'property rights' and, thus, leverage over the privatisation process (cf. Samary, 2008, p. 175). They managed to get many workers onto their side with promises of 'national' protection.

The party was the first of the pillars of the state to collapse (Centrih, 2014, p. 5). With the disintegration of the party on its 14th extraordinary congress in January 1990, the strategic decision-making centre of the state withered away. The governmental structures of the state followed suit. The premature German recognition of the independence of Slovenia and Croatia fuelled the disintegration process (cf. Weissenbacher, 2005, Section VIII).

Slovenia's subsequent political and socio-economic trajectory differed from the rest of the successor states to a significant extent. Due to its economic specialisation and closer links to Western Europe, Slovenia was economically more advantageously positioned than the rest. In Slovenia, trade unions were able to influence the transformation through strong labour action (Bembić, 2015, p. 163). A social compromise based on neo-corporatist institution ensued. With entry into the EU and the election of a right-wing government in 2004, financialisation and the strong impact of the global crisis, this compromise has been significantly eroded (Becker, 2016, pp. 56, 62). In the case of others, capitalist transformation brought about politically well-contacted local capital groups and, thus oligarchic structures. The conflictive form of disintegration, wars and, in the case of Serbia and Montenegro, international sanctions favoured particularly opaque forms of privatisation (cf. Becker, 2015, p. 422). With the increased orientation towards pre-accession and, partial accession talks, transnational firms were able to get a foothold in strategic sectors, like banking. Apart from Slovenia, the Yugoslav successor states have suffered from lasting de-industrialisation. Their growth has been highly dependent on foreign capital inflows. Unemployment is structurally very high. In successor states like Serbia, Montenegro, and Bosnia-Herzegovina, real GDP had at the beginning of the 2008 global crisis not yet recovered to the 1989 level (cf. Myant & Drahokoupil, 2011, tab. A2.). In Bosnia-Herzegovina and Macedonia with their forms of institutionalised ethnic power-sharing arrangements, disintegration tendencies similar to the Yugoslav case have been reproduced.

Disintegrative Tendencies in the EU

The European Economic Community (EEC) was founded in 1957 both as consequence of the World Wars and as a child of the Cold War. Economic cooperation and integration was perceived as a way to prevent the renewal of new conflicts within Western Europe. West European integration was intended to cement unity vis-à-vis the state socialist camp. From the very beginning, this European integration project combined intergovernmental and supranational institutions. Though the role of parliamentary institutions has been increased over time, a clear bias in favour of the executive branches of the state—the European Commission and the various Councils of Ministers—has remained in place. The role of technocracies with little or no democratic accountability like the European Central Bank has been increasing over time. This institutional design has shielded the EU decision-making centres from public pressures from below (cf. Müller, 2012, p. 40; Vauchez, 2014). Thus, the 'strategic selectivity' of the EU is biased against the popular classes and in favour of Europeanised business.

In the ambiguous blend between confederal and federal/supranational elements, there are parallels between Yugoslavia and the EU. However, the Federal elements were stronger in Yugoslavia and its state structures were more uniform. With the growing heterogeneity of member states through successive enlargements, integration into the EU state project has become differentiated. The most fundamental differentiation concerns money. Most, but not all EU members are members of the euro zone. The euro zone has emerged as an institutional core of the EU. It had been conceived as such by key German politicians. Wolfgang Schäuble and Karl Lamers underlined in their famous 1994 paper that currency union ought to be the 'hard core of the Political Union' (CDU/CSU-Fraktion im Deutschen Bundestag, 1994, p. 6). At that time, they argued in favour of a small and homogeneous core—even excluding Italy (CDU/CSU-Fraktion im Deutschen Bundestag, 1994, p. 5). From controversies over the shape of the currency union, a much broader euro zone emerged in the end. Since the 1990s, a debate on 'core Europe' and its geographical shape has haunted the EU. This type of internal differentiation did not exist in Yugoslavia. However, there was a recurrent debate on the role of Serbia—whether it played a dominant role or should play such a role—in the Yugoslav federation.

The 'strategic selectivity' of the EU has favoured its increasingly neo-liberal orientation from the 1980s onwards. Projects like the Single Market and the euro zone have deepened uneven development patterns because they removed protective mechanisms from the peripheral economies without creating sufficient compensatory mechanisms (like regional industrial policies). Compared with Yugoslavia, uneven development had been much less of an issue at the founding of the EEC. At that time, the periphery of the EEC of six consisted only of Southern Italy and was, thus, relatively small. Through the successive enlargements, first in the 1980s in the South and then later from 2004 to 2013 in the East, the EEC and later EU incorporated vast peripheries. Trade liberalisation—either through incorporation in the EEC in the case of Southern Europe or through the pre-accession trade agreements in the case of Eastern Europe—often led to de-industrialisation or stunted at least temporarily industrial development. Overvalued exchange rates and incorporation into the euro zone tended to aggravate negative effects on productive sectors. Though the EEC created funds for regional development, their activities have been geared mainly to infrastructure. The EU never has engaged in regional industrial policies (Becker & Weissenbacher, 2014, p. 17). Thus, the EU has been less energetic and systematic in its efforts to attenuate uneven development than Yugoslavia.

Central Eastern European countries and Ireland were the only exceptions to the rule. Here, processes of dependent industrialisation took place. They rely almost exclusively on foreign capital which is attracted by relatively cheap labour and very low corporate taxation. The Central Eastern European economies have turned into suppliers for German export industries (Becker, 2016, p. 52). Already in the years before the global crisis, the divergence of development patterns in the EU and euro zone grew. On the one hand, core countries around Germany relied on an export-oriented model. They showed an increase of the current account and exported capital, inter alia to the EU peripheries. On the other hand in Southern Europe, surplus liquidity in the core countries and euro zone membership implied access to cheap credit. Credit expansion facilitated consumption and real estate booms. The productive sectors tended to be neglected. Soaring current account deficits and external debts were the consequences. In Italy and France, current account deficits were not particularly high, but manufacturing has suffered from significant decline (Álvarez Peralta, Luengo Escalonilla, & Uxó González, 2013, p. 89; Becker, Jäger, & Weissenbacher, 2015, p. 86). The debt-driven tendency towards GDP per capita convergence was deceiving because the productive structures in the periphery tended to decline. And the divergence in GDP per capita is enormous: 1:14 between Bulgaria, the poorest member state, and Luxemburg, the richest one. The gap is still an enormous 1:7.6 between Bulgaria and the EU country with the second highest GDP per capita, that is, Denmark (own calculation based on 2015 Eurostat data).

The rift between the institutional core of the euro zone and the rest and between the economic core and periphery proved to be structural starting points for disintegrative tendencies, which were set in motion in the wake of the global crisis. The EU economies were hit unevenly by the global crisis. The highly financialised EU economies, both in the West (UK, Ireland, Luxemburg, Denmark, and Sweden) and the East (Latvia) were early hit by the crisis. They recorded a fall of the GDP already in 2008. In the UK, the 2009 recession was more or less in line with the EU average. The UK mobilised early on particularly large funds in order to re-stabilise the banking sector (Panetta et al., 2009, p. 13, tab. 1.2). This had obviously quite negative repercussions for the budget, the UK governments applied strict austerity measures. The Irish economy was massively hit by the banking and real estate crisis, but also by the decline of exports. The models of dependent financialisation in Eastern and Southern Europe were severely affected by the drying up of capital inflows. The higher the pre-crisis current account deficit, the worse the crisis. In Eastern Europe, a high degree of informal euroisation of the credit system proved to be fatal. The East European economies were hit early on already in autumn 2008, whereas euro zone membership proved a temporary shelter for the Southern European EU countries. However, they faced increasing interest rates and refinancing problems from 2010 onward. Northwest European countries like Germany and the Netherlands were affected both by the financial fallout of the crisis and declining exports. The German fall of exports affected in turn the suppliers in Austria and Central Eastern Europe. Germany and its immediate industrial periphery in the East recovered relatively early from the crisis (cf. Becker et al., 2015, p. 88).

Like the republics in crisis-ridden Yugoslavia, the EU member states tried to reduce the impact of the crisis in their own countries and to shift negative consequences to other countries. However, their ability to do so proved to be uneven. The creditor countries, particularly the German government, saw their influence in the EU strengthened (cf. Cafruny, 2015). The strategic decisions of EU crisis management were taken by the governments of the member states (Lenaerts, 2015, p. 139). And those decisions implied that the brunt of the costs was to be borne socially by lower middle strata, workers, pensions, and unemployed and spatially by the peripheral countries in Eastern and Southern Europe.

Joint IMF/EU Structural Adjustment Programmes implying massive austerity in order to bring imports and current account deficits down were first applied from autumn 2008 onwards in East European member states. From 2010 onwards, it was the turn of South European euro zone member states. Due to particularly significant vulnerabilities like the enormous current account deficit, Greece was the first country that saw itself obliged to apply for conditioned financial support. And Greece was to be the case that brought the politically disintegrative tendencies in the euro zone into the open. The governments and the media in the core countries, like Germany, depicted the emergency credits for Greece as a rescue operation for the Greek state. However, the banks of the core countries were at the beginning highly exposed in Southern

Europe and had, thus, a vital interest that the IMF and the EU would provide refinancing for Greece and other South European debtor states (Cafruny, 2015, p. 64). This side of the coin tended to be neglected in the German, Austrian, etc. public and media debates. Instead, negative stereotypes about 'lazy Greeks' came to abound in the media (cf. Chilas & Wolf, 2016, 123 f.). Anti-EU sentiments increased (cf. Cafruny, 2015, p. 65). Vast sectors of the Greek society have suffered severely from the impact of the austerity policies. The German-inspired policies were massively resented—and this was mirrored in media reporting. The ensuing controversies have brought up similar topics and stereotypes as the Yugoslav debate, 'who exploits whom?'

To the dismay of liberal-conservative governments at the EU core, austerity policies wore down the traditional Greek parties PASOK and Nea Dimokratia. In the wake of strong social protests, the left-orientated Syriza became stronger at each parliamentary election. In early 2015, Syriza was able to form a coalition government with a small nationalist formation based on an anti-austerity mandate. The Syriza government hoped to find allies in the euro group for attenuating austerity. Its calculation was that the euro zone member states were willing to make concessions in order to keep the euro zone together (cf. Varoufakis, 2015, p. 10, 20ff., 50ff.). This proved to be an erroneous assessment of the position of key member states, particularly the German government. The German Minister of Finance, Wolfgang Schäuble, confronted the Syriza government with an alternative: accept the austerity programme of the Troika or exit the euro zone. This position that reflects rather the view of the national conservative wing of the CDU/CSU is coherent with his 'core Europe' concept of the 1990s. Thus, Schäuble put the expulsion of economically peripheral euro zone members from the institutional euro zone core towards an institutionally more peripheral position onto the political agenda.

Under extreme pressure from the rest of the euro zone and the ECB, the Greek government first organised a referendum on austerity to strengthen its democratic mandate. Since it had not prepared concrete measures for an alternative (i.e. immediately realisable steps towards leaving the euro zone), it eventually submitted to external pressures.

Though Greece was not expelled in 2015, the issue of peripheral euro zone states exiting the euro zone involuntarily or voluntarily is not off the agenda. There are significant right-wing currents favouring 'core Europe' concepts. And the Greek example has had an impact on left debates as well. On the left, the Greek precedent has strengthened those currents that argue that preparing at least an emergency exit from the euro zone should be an essential feature of alternative strategies (cf. e.g. Lapavitsas, Flassbeck, Durand, Etiévant, & Lordon, 2016). For them, some exiting the euro zone is a strategic option in order to gain policy spaces both for more egalitarian policies and for rebuilding productive structures. For others, leaving the euro zone is rather an emergency exit in order to be able to break with austerity and regain policy spaces. One of the lessons from the Greek experience is how essential the role of the central bank in providing liquidity to the banking sector is. In order to be able to refinance banks, it might be necessary to return to a national bank in order to withstand the external pressures on the liquidity front.

With Brexit, the disintegration issue has become even more explicit. The UK has a unique position in the European division of labour. On the one hand, the financial centre in London, a heritage of the bygone Empire, plays a key role in international financial markets, providing the British economy with features typical of a core economy. On the other hand, the British economy has suffered from profound de-industrialisation. This has translated into structural current account deficits. This is rather a feature of a peripheral economy. The financial interests have played a predominant role in British economic policy-making. The UK has always been in a special position within the EU. This was reflected in some specific concessions to Britain. Due to the importance of the City of London, the UK governments have decided to stay outside the euro zone. However, the euro zone has gradually evolved into the institutional core of the EU. This trend has been strengthened in the wake of the global crisis. This has implied an institutional marginalisation of the UK though the German government had sought in recent years to build a 'free trade'-axis with London. The deepened political integration around the euro zone was met with hostility by a significant subset of British Conservatives. The global crisis revealed the structural fault lines of the euro zone. As a consequence, entering the euro zone has become even less attractive for British financial interests and the Tories (MacShane, 2016, pp. 184, 193). An increasing EU-scepticism in British business circles could be observed over the last years—and this tendency has been strengthened by the crisis. 'Some British company chairmen and CEOs appear to want common rules for everyone else in Europe, but a régime of exception for the City and other British firms', observed MacShane (2016, p. 142). This radicalised partially into the demand for leaving the EU in order to be able to compete more aggressively by lowering standards. To the right of the Conservatives, the openly anti-EU UKIP got stronger. It was partially able to tap the generalised discontent of the popular classes in the de-industrialised English and Welsh regions—though their malaise was mainly due to Thatcherite and New Labour policies of the national governments.

In order to shore up the position of the Conservative Party, David Cameron launched the proposal to hold a referendum on EU membership—expecting that the 'Remain' option would win (cf. Jessop, 2017, p. 134). This proved, however, to be a miscalculation. The main slogan of the Brexit camp—'Take back control'—found strong societal resonance and was able to unite temporarily a very heterogeneous referendum alliance. The slogan took up the transfer of powers from the national parliament to EU institutions. Parliamentarism is very deeply rooted in the political tradition of the UK and has positive connotations. The Brexit campaign could refer to this. The slogan also insinuated socio-economic protection. The British right was able to deflect the anger regarding Thatcherite de-industrialisation and social degradation to migrants (cf. Patomäki, 2017, p. 169). This part of the campaign was addressed primarily to workers and lower middle-class strata. It has some resemblance with the promises of protection by the Yugoslav republics in the crisis of the 1980s. For sections of the bourgeoisie and the upper middle strata, 'taking back control' implied regaining control on trade and related policies. This is in line with the reasoning of the leaderships of the Yugoslav republic in seeking their own way out of the crisis. In comparison to the 'Leave' campaign, the 'Remain'-campaign of the Tories remained pale. The left was equally divided and was not able step out of the shadow of the right (cf. Watkins, 2016, 17ff.).

The 52:48 vote in favour of leaving the EU went against the grain of the majority current in the British ruling class. The 'Yes' was strongest among the professional and managerial classes. It predominated in London, a few Northern cities as well as Northern Ireland and Scotland. The 'No' found particularly strong backing among workers and in the towns of de-industrialised areas in England 'with GDP per capita less than half inner London levels, and now hardest hit by cutbacks in services and benefits' (Watkins, 2016, p. 23). In late Yugoslavia, likewise pro-Yugoslav tendencies tended to be relatively strongest in some of the urban centres. And exclusionary nationalism took particularly strong roots in crisis-stricken rural areas and small towns—with very significant regional variations. Thus, there are some parallels in the socio-economic and spatial dividing lines between pro-YU/pro-EU and 'nationalist' camps in Yugoslavia and the UK. In both cases, the pro-supranational forces were not able to link their pro-federal respectively pro-EU perspective with any promising and realistic socio-economic vision for the popular classes. Though there is a debate on which event—the disintegration of the League of Communists in January 1990 or the declarations of independence by Slovenia and Croatia—proved to be the watershed in the disintegration of Yugoslavia (cf. e.g. Vllasi, 2016, p. 23), there can be no doubt that decisions of exiting federal structures were particularly crucial caesura in a multifaceted process. The UK Brexit decision is a similar turning point for the EU. As Watkins (2016, p. 5) points out, '(i)t also represents a signal defeat for the EU, a reversal of the Union's sixty-year run of expansion and integration'.

As a reaction to the Brexit decision, the European Commission initiated a debate on the 'Future of Europe'. In its 'White Paper on the Future of Europe', the Commission outlined several options. The options range from deepened integration for all on the same lines to differentiated integration and to focussing on the Single Market and Free Trade Agreements (European Commission, 2017, 15ff.). None of the scenarios question the neo-liberal approach to integration. Though a series of reflection papers is planned, none of them will discuss finance or industry. The prevailing economic policy approach is not to be discussed. Thus, a key reason for the increasing alienation, particularly of the popular classes, is not to be addressed (cf. Bayer, 2017, p. 8).

In the first response to the White Paper, the governments of Germany, France, Italy, and Spain came out in favour of a deepened integration of the 'willing'. This is a version of the 'core Europe' concept. It would widen the institutional divide in the EU. Šimečka (2017, p. 9), an attentive observer from Central Eastern Europe, did not fail to read between the lines which regions are to be outside the core: Central East and South East European countries. For him, this is an acknowledgement that, for Western governments, 'enlargement did not work'. The socio-economic rifts between Western core and Western periphery are, however, deep as well. Responses to the integration crisis and Brexit show multiple conflict lines and disintegrative logics.

Conclusion

In both, Yugoslavia of the 1980s and today's EU, entrenched patterns of uneven development and hybrid forms of statehood combining federal/supranational and confederal elements set the structural stage for disintegrative tendencies, which were finally unleashed by deep economic crises. In the EU, the differentiated degrees of integration, in particular the divide between countries inside and outside the euro zone, has proved to be a source of disintegrative tendencies that did not exist in Yugoslavia. The Yugoslavian governments had been more energetic in dealing with uneven development patterns than the EU though their success has been limited. In both cases, the crisis and crisis management have triggered acrimonious debates on 'who exploits whom' pitching core and periphery against each other.

In both, Yugoslavia in the 1980s and the EU today, the initiatives for separating from the supranational set-up or at least loosening the ties have been taken by parts of the dominant block in the republics/member states. Thus, these initiatives have originated primarily from the richer parts of Yugoslavia and the EU. These forces wanted leeway in charting their own way out of the crisis, and, usually wanted to get rid of the 'burden' of the periphery. In the wake of the crisis, the role of the republics was enhanced in Yugoslavia, and the role of the dominant nation-states has been strengthened in the EU.

In both cases, the central institutions lost legitimacy through neo-liberal austerity and structural adjustment policies, particularly among the popular classes. The Yugoslav case shows that, for left-orientated forces defending democratised federalism, a strong identification with austerity policies of the central authorities is the way to self-marginalisation. This is a lesson that the left in Europe should learn from Yugoslavia.

Both in Yugoslavia and in the UK, nationalist forces have successfully mobilised vast segments of the working class for their nationalist cause by promising protection. This enabled them to build multi-class alliances.

In both cases, the disintegration crisis has fed debates on constitutional and institutional reform. In Yugoslavia, institutional quarrels, constitutional debates, and real disintegration processes went hand in hand. In the EU, the stage of open disintegration has been reached with the British decision to leave the Union. The Brexit decision is a watershed for the EU. Negotiations on the modalities of Britain's exit from EU and a limited debate on the further course of the European integration project will be unfolding in a parallel way. Both the European Commission and the main member states are not willing to engage in a debate on the neo-liberal approach to integration or on the 'democratic deficit'. Beyond that, there are serious disagreements among the member states on the further course of integration. A strong left initiative for a thorough democratisation and change of economic direction of the EU does not exist. A move towards fundamental changes of the basic EU treaties would most likely end in disintegration because the disintegrative tendencies are already so strong. Like Yugoslavia in the late 1980s, the EU seems to have passed already a critical point in the disintegration process.

It is not yet clear how far the disintegration of the EU will go and which political forces will finally shape it. It is not irrelevant whether the disintegration process will be shaped primarily by a competition-driven political right or whether left-wing forces would be able to insert a social and cooperative agenda into it. For the left, the minimum target should be that cooperation and coordination policies would still be possible even after (partial) political disintegration.

Disclosure Statement

No potential conflict of interest was reported by the author.

References

Álvarez Peralta, I., Luengo Escalonilla, F., & Uxó González, J. (2013). *Fracturas y crisis en Europa*. Buenos Aires: Eudeba/Madrid: Clave Intelectual.

Bayer, K. (2017, March 16). Gut gemeint ist meist nicht gut. *Wiener Zeitung*, p. 8.

Becker, J. (2002). *Akkumulation, Regulation, Territorium. Zur kritischen Rekonstruktion der französischen Regulationstheorie*. Marburg: Metropolis.

Becker, J. (2009). Anatomie der Sozialismen. Wirtschaft, Staat und Gesellschaft. In J. Becker, & R. Weissenbacher (Eds.), *Sozialismen. Entwicklungsmodelle von Lenin bis Nyerere* (pp. 13–56). Vienna: Promedia, Südwind.

Becker, J. (2015). Oligarchie – eine Form bürgerlicher Herrschaft. Das Beispiel osteuropäischer semi-peripherer Kapitalismus. *Prokla, 45*(3), 409–431.

Becker, J. (2016). Europe's other periphery. *New Left Review, 99*, 39–64.

Becker, J., Jäger, J., & Weissenbacher, R. (2015). Uneven and dependent development in Europe. The crisis and its implications. In J. Jäger & E. Springler (Eds.), *Asymmetric crisis in Europe and possible futures. Critical political economy and post-Keynesian perspectives* (pp. 81–97). London: Routledge.

Becker, J., & Weissenbacher, R. (2014). Berlin consensus and disintegration. Monetary regime and uneven development in the EU. In W. Dymarski, M. Frangakis, & J. Leaman (Eds.), *The deepening crisis of the European Union: The case for radical change. Analyses and proposals from the EuroMemo group* (pp. 15–32). Poznań: Poznań University of Economics Press.

Bembić, B. (2015). Odnosi snaga u slovenskoj tranziciji i organizacije radničke klase. *3k: kapital, klasa, kritika, 2*(2), 161–191.

Borak, N. (2002). *Ekonomski vidiki delovanja in razpada Jugoslavije*. Ljubljana: Znanstveno in publicistično središče.

Cafruny, A. (2015). The European crisis and the rise of German power. In J. Jäger & S. Springler (Eds.), *Asymmetric crisis in Europe and possible futures. Critical political economy and post-Keynesian perspectives* (pp. 61–77). London: Routledge.

CDU/CSU-Fraktion im Deutschen Bundestag. (1994). *Überlegungen zur europäischen Politik.* 1.9.1994. Retrieved October 21, 2016, from www.cducsu.de/SchaeubleLamers.94.pdf

Centrih, L. (2014). *The road to collapse: The demise of the League of Communists of Yugoslavia.* Research Paper Series of Rosa Luxemburg Stiftung Southeast Europe No. 2. Belgrade: Rosa Luxemburg Stiftung Southeast Europe.

Chilas, N., & Wolf, W. (2016). *Griechische Tragödie. Rebellion, Kapitulation, Ausverkauf.* Vienna: Promedia.

Djeković, L. (1989). Privredna kriza i privredna reforma u Jugoslaviji. In M. Korošić (Ed.), *Quo vadis, Jugoslavijo?* (pp. 23–40). Zagreb: Naprijed.

European Commission. (2017). *White paper on the future of Europe. Reflections and scenarios for the EU27 by 2015.* Brussels: Author.

Jessop, B. (2002). *The future of the capitalist state.* Cambridge: Polity.

Jessop, B. (2017). The organic crisis of the British state: Putting Brexit in its place. *Globalizations, 14*(1), 133–141.

Kirn, G. (2014). *Partizanski prelomi in protislovja tržnega socializma v Jugoslaviji.* Ljubljana: Sophia.

Lapavitsas, C., Flassbeck, H., Durand, C., Etiévant, G., & Lordon, F. (2016). *Euro, plan B. Sortir de la crise en Grèce, en France et en Europe.* Vulaines-sur-Seine: Éditions du croquant.

Lenaerts, K. (2015). Demoicratie, constitutioneel pluralisme en het Hoof van Justitie van de Europese Unie. In L. Middelaar & Ph. Van Parijs (Eds.), *Na de Storm. Hoe we de democratie in Europa kunnen redden* (pp. 129–144). Tielt: Lannoo.

MacShane, D. (2016). *Brexit. How Britain left Europe.* (Fully revised ed.). London: I.B. Tauris.

Madžar, L. (1996). Who exploited whom? In N. Popov (Ed.), *The road to war in Serbia. Trauma and catharsis* (pp. 160–188). Budapest: CEU Press.

Müller, J.-W. (2012). Beyond Militant Democracy? *New Left Review, 73,* 39–47.

Myant, M., & Drahokoupil, J. (2011). *Transition economies: Political economy in Russia, Eastern Europe, and Central Asia.* Hoboken: John Wiley & Sons.

Panetta, F., Faeh, T., Grande, G., Ho, C., King, M., Levy, A., . . . Zaghini, A. (2009). *An assessment of the financial sector rescue programmes* (BIS Papers, No. 48).

Patomäki, H. (2017). Will the EU disintegrate? What does the likely possibility of disintegration tell about the future of the world? *Globalizations, 14*(1), 168–177.

Radić, D. (2011, November 10). Intervju – Jože Mencinger, slovenački ekonomista: Evropa kao bivša Jugoslavija. *Vreme,* No. 1086. www.vreme.com/cms/view.php?id = 1018992&print = yes, retrieved: 20/12/2011

Samary, C. (1988). *Le marché contre l'autogestion: l'expérience yougoslave.* Paris: La Brèche.

Samary, C. (2008). *Yougoslavie de la décomposition aux enjeux européens.* Paris: Éditions du Cygne.

Šimečka, M. (2017, March 27). Rím a čitanie medzi riadkami. *Denník N,* p. 9.

Spaskovska, L. (2015). Horizonti otpora, nade i poraza: Jugoslovenski supranacionalizam i antinacionalizam. In B. Bilić, & V. Janković (Eds.), *Opiranje zlu. (Post)jugoslavenski antiratni angažman* (pp. 29–54). Zagreb: Jesenki i Turk.

Unkovski-Korica, V. (2015). Self-management, development and debt: The rise and fall of the 'Yugoslav Experiment'. In S. Horvat & I. Štiks (Eds.), *Welcome to the desert of post-socialism. Radical politics after Yugoslavia* (pp. 21–43). London: Verso.

Varoufakis, Y. (2015). *Notre printemps d'Athènes.* Paris: Éditions les liens qui libèrent.

Vauchez, A. (2014). *Démocratiser l'Europe.* Paris: Seuil.

Vllasi, A. (2016). *Kosovo. Početak raspada.* Sarajevo: Sahinpašić.

Watkins, S. (2016). Casting off? *New Left Review, 100,* 5–31.

Weissenbacher, R. (2003). Der IWF und die Dialektik der marktwirtschaftlichen Ideologie in Jugoslawien. In J. Becker, R. Heinz, K. Imhof, K. Küblböck, & W. Manzenreiter (Eds.), *Geld Macht Krise. Finanzmärkte und neoliberale Herrschaft* (pp. 149–172). Vienna: Promedia, Südwind.

Weissenbacher, R. (2005). *Jugoslawien. Politische Ökonomie einer Desintegration.* Vienna: Promedia.

Woodward, S. (2002). The political economy of ethno-nationalism in Yugoslavia. In L. Panitch & C. Leys (Eds.), *Socialist register 2003. Fighting identities. Race, religion and ethno-nationalism* (pp. 73–92). London: Merlin.

Index

www.ingramcontent.com/pod-product-compliance
Ingram Content Group UK Ltd.
Pitfield, Milton Keynes, MK11 3LW, UK
UKHW010021280225
455677UK00023B/734